Creative
Storytelling

Creative
Storytelling

§

Building Community
Changing Lives

Jack Zipes

ROUTLEDGE
New York and London

Published in 1995 by

Routledge
29 West 35 Street
New York, NY 10001

Published in Great Britain in 1995 by

Routledge
11 New Fetter Lane
London EC4P 4EE

The author gratefully wishes to acknowledge permission to republish the following:

"And The the Prince Knelt Down and Tried to Put the Glass Slipper on Cinderella's Foot," from If I Were in Charge of the World and Other Worries, by Judith Viorst. Copyright © 1981 by Judith Viorst. Reprinted with permission of Atheneum Books for Young Readers, an imprint of Simon & Schuster Children's Publishing Division, and Lescher & Lescher, Ltd., and Scholastic Australia, Pty. Ltd.

"The First Donkey," from Histoires, by Jacques Prevert (Paris: Editions Gallimard, 1963), reprinted with permission from the estate of the author and Editions Gallimard.

"The Tortoise and the Hare," from Tales of an Ashanti Father, by Peggy Appiah. Copyright © 1967 by Peggy Appiah. Reprinted by permission of Beacon Press, Scholastic Publications, Ltd., and David Higham Associates, Ltd.

Library of Congress Cataloging-in-Publication Data

Zipes, Jack David
    Creative storytelling : building community, changing lives / by Jack Zipes.
        p.   cm.
    Includes bibliographical references (p.) and index.
    ISBN 0–415–91271–7. — ISBN 0–415–91272–5 (pbk.)
    1. Storytelling. 2. Fiction genres. I. Title
LB1042.Z56   1995
372.64'2 — dc20
                                                  95–18349
                                                    CIP

To Herb Kohl

with admiration and respect for all his innovative projects

Contents

Acknowledgments

This book is the outcome of over twenty years of work with children, teachers, storytellers, actors, and educators, who formed a "community" of friends and collaborators and provided me with great support in all my endeavors. It would be impossible to list all the people who have helped me develop my ideas and methods, particularly the children, who repeatedly challenged and questioned me during my storytelling programs. Nevertheless, I do want to make specific mention and thank as many as possible of those people who have stimulated me in the different phases of my work. Without their input and mediation, I would not have attempted to write this book. Therefore, I want to express my gratitude to Joan Barr, Pat Bowen, Terry Caroccio, John Colligan, Kevin Crossley-Holland, Theda Detlor, Klaus Doderer, Mike Dunstan, Monika Edinger, Helen East, Grace Hallworth, Janinine Hawley-Girard, Ben Haggarty, Jane Hislam, Larry Johnson, Joan Jones, Herbert Kohl, Wolfgang Mieder, Alex Molnar, Anita Moss, Roni Natov, Judy Passmanick, Karen Prager, Betty Rosen, Harold Rosen, Patrick Ryan, Penninah Schramm, Sandy Sevre, Louisa Smith, Sandra Tolleson, Susan Weimer, Cristy West, Rick Wilson, Joe Winston, and Elaine Wynne. The final impulse to complete my work came from the members of the Society for Storytelling in Great Britain and the annual gathering in March 1994, where I benefited from a lively and remarkable exchange of ideas and stories. Throughout the production process I received superb editorial guidance from Adam Bohannon, Christine Cipriani, and Bill Germano. Of course, this book would not have been possible if it had not been for the encouragement of my wife, Carol Dines, and for the patient and often critical listening of my daughter, Hanna Zipes.

§

If not otherwise indicated, all the tales included in this book are my own. Some I have adapted from folk tales, and others I have translated and retold from German, French, or Italian sources. I also include several that I have conceived myself.

Prologue

Many years ago, there lived a king and queen who did not allow their subjects to learn to read and write. "The dumber they are," they said to themselves, "the easier they are to rule." So they posted signs all over their kingdom:

"Beware of the Big Bad Storyteller!"

You see, in those days, storytellers gave people ideas free of charge, and the king and queen knew that ideas lead people to think, and thinking people might have ideas of their own, and soon they might want to learn to read and write, or even put their ideas into action to govern themselves. So the king and queen were quick to spread nasty rumors about storytellers and claim that they twisted people's minds and shrunk their heads.

So fearful did the people become that it was easy for the king and queen to convince their subjects to give them their money for protection and to build a huge fortress out of straw, wood, and brick so that they would be protected from the ferocious storytellers. This fortress was so large that it could house all the people of the kingdom. So whenever a storyteller was seen on the horizon, the king would ring a bell from the tall tower as an alarm, and all his subjects would run from the streets and fields as fast as they could to save themselves from the big bad storyteller.

Since storytellers rarely go to places where they are not invited, they stopped visiting this kingdom. That is, until one day when a mighty good and curious storyteller became lost and found his way to this realm. When the king saw him coming with his telescope, he sounded the alarm, and the people were scared for their lives. They made a mad dash for the gigantic house, and when they were all inside, the king and queen locked the door tight, right in the face of the storyteller. When the storyteller knocked, the king asked, "Who's there?"

> "It's just me," said the storyteller. "Let me in."
> "Not by the hair of your chinny chin chin!" cried the queen, and
>   she commanded all her subjects to repeat.
> "Not by the hair of your chinny chin chin!"
> "Well then," said the storyteller,
> "I'll huff and I'll puff,
> And I'll blow your house in.
> Then I'll tell a tale
> To smash this jail.
> And when I'm through,
> Good-bye to you."

So the storyteller huffed and puffed a glorious tale that filled the people with wonderful ideas and excited their imaginations. When he was done, the house came tumbling down with a crash and a thud. So frightened were the king and queen that they fled the land, never to be seen again. On the other hand, the people were surprised to see that they were unhurt, and they realized that the storyteller was not as mean as he was supposed to be. To their delight he began telling them even more stories, which the people liked so much that they have passed them on to their children and their children's children up to this very day.

And this, my friend, is why we are just as wise as we are today.

Introduction

Storytelling in Schools

If the culture of the community is to enter the culture of the school, its stories must come too and, more profoundly perhaps, its oral story-telling traditions must become an acknowledged form of making meaning.

—Harold Rosen, *Narratology and the Teacher*

About twenty years ago, I founded a small children's theater in Milwaukee with a group of young actors, and occasionally we went into schools and conducted workshops based on scenes from our plays. Using techniques from Viola Spolin's *Improvisation for the Theater*, we were able to transform a classroom into a stage, and on this stage the children created their own stories and skits and displayed talents they did not know they possessed. In turn, their imagination ignited mine, and I thought to myself that, if I had the time one day, I would like to work more closely with children in schools to see how improvisational skits might enable them to develop their creative talents and perhaps complement their formal schooling.

In 1978, a few years after my children's theater had disbanded, I finally had this opportunity. In the meantime, I had discovered a book entitled *Grammatica della fantasia* (*Grammar of the Imagination*) by Gianni Rodari, a remarkable Italian storyteller and journalist who had conceived and used innovative techniques for storytelling in Italy.[1] After reading this work and contemplating the different possibilities for using Rodari's methods in the States, I decided to adapt some of his ideas, combine them with creative dramatics, and conduct a storytelling experiment in Milwaukee. The goal of my storytelling was to see how children would react to the radical transformation of classical fairy tales, and whether I could stimulate them to think up stories as alternatives to the traditional messages the tales conveyed. Fortunately, in an open school on 38th Street I found a courageous teacher of seven- and eight-year-olds who was willing to participate in this experiment, and for six months I held my storytelling sessions in a classroom setting and watched the children transform it into a world of their own for two hours once a week. From that time on, thanks to their enthusiasm and receptive spirit, I have told tales in schools as often as I can and have tried to work with teachers and librarians to use storytelling in their classes to complement their standard curriculum.

During the past twenty years, I have refined and changed my methods and ideas, and I have worked in many different settings, such as youth centers, libraries, universities, and summer institutes. I have also dealt with different age groups, including adults, and have traveled to England, France, Italy, and Germany, where I either told stories with children and adults or worked with storytellers. At various times I took notes about my experiences and recorded them in journals to help me improve my methods and understand the problems I had been confronting but could not solve. I never intended to publish these notes because of their personal nature, but I did share them with students and friends who were interested in storytelling, and they encouraged me to publish them in some form or other.

This book is a result of their encouragement, and it is a book that I have written with some hesitation and trepidation, for I am not fond of manuals and self-help books. They have always seemed to me to pretend to offer the ultimate solution to a problem or the definitive way to cure a malady. Therefore, I have written this book as an anti-manual, not to instruct but to *share* my experiences with the hope that readers may be encouraged to experiment with my methods and ideas, which are not really "mine" because I have borrowed them from many different critics, storytellers, teachers, and children over the years.

I have also written this book to oppose and deal with two (of many) dangers I perceive to be threatening children in schools. The first danger is a trend toward rigid standardization of curricula in the name of cultural literacy, and toward increased national and state testing determined by officials outside the schools who are basically interested in achievement for achievement's sake. Here the threat is an instrumentalization of the imagination of children, who are expected to comply with controls that are basically set up to protect society from "misfits" and that have very little to do with the needs of the children. The children are perceived as "underachievers" in competition with the Japanese and Europeans, and in order to maintain "our" rank as "number one" in the world, we must improve the children's test scores and their literacy. No thought, however, is given to what values the children are to learn in competition, nor what they are supposed to consume to make them "culturally" literate.[2] As Michael Apple has pointed out in his important book *Offical Knowledge: Democratic Education in a Conservative Age,*

> A "common culture" can never be an extension to everyone of what a minority mean and believe. Rather, and crucially, it requires not the stipulation and incorporation within textbooks of lists and concepts that make us all "culturally literate," *but the creation of the conditions necessary for all people to participate in the creation and recreation of meanings and values.* It requires a democratic process in which all people—not simply those who see themselves as the intellectual guardians of the "Western tradition"—can be involved in the deliberation of what is important. It should go without saying that this necessitates the removal of the very real material obstacles (unequal power, wealth, time for reflection) that stand in the way of such participation.[3]

The second danger is the commercialization of storytelling. That is, during the past fifteen years, there has been a renascence of storytelling throughout the United States and Europe,[4] and many storytellers have made their storytelling sessions into performance-for-profit gigs or tried to transform storytelling into a cult with mystical and religious overtones. In both instances the storytellers turn themselves into stars and initiates of a secret sect, as if only they possess the secret of a good story. This negative development should not detract from the positive aspects of the work of gifted storytellers who have demonstrated the value of storytelling to the general public and have tried to share their craft with children and adults. Without their inspired efforts, storytelling in schools and in other public places like libraries and youth centers would not have the exciting potential to create democratic communities.

Yet the efforts of these artists must be seen in the contexts of a struggle over education and storytelling and the current threat to children, who are often treated as potential consumers of products that have the stamp of approval from self-appointed legislators of culture. The preachers of cultural literacy, like E. D. Hirsch, William Bennett, and their associates, and the commercial and cult storytellers are related here and collaborate through the manner in which they undermine the autonomy of teachers and children, who are regarded as passive recipients of cultural goods that are deemed (from above) appropriate for their work and development. In contrast, I believe that teachers and children must set their own standards in response to community needs, and that storytelling can be one way to create and strengthen a sense of community that is severely lacking in America and Europe. But I am not speaking of storytelling in a traditional sense; I am speaking of storytelling as animation and self-discovery, storytelling that uses models, ethical principles, canons of literature, and social standards to *play* with the prescribed models, principles, canons, and standards to see if they are worthy of the children's respect and useful in the community.

The process of learning how to tell a story is a process of empowerment. We all want to narrate our lives, but very few of us have been given the techniques and insights that can help us form plots to reach our goals. We need to learn strategies of narration when we are very young in order to grasp that we can become our own narrators, the storytellers of our lives; and as Gianni Rodari has suggested, there are certain "grammatical rules" of the imagination that all children must learn before they can successfully play with them and create their own original lives, for we are all constantly trying to act out or realize the fictional lives that we imagine for ourselves. We try to put the dreams of our lives into effect.

In my own work I have found that the crucial age for children is between six and ten, the period during which they are learning how to read, write, draw, sing, and calculate. It is a period when their minds are being formed, and they are developing a social and political consciousness. As Penelope Leach has stated in her book *Children First*:

> Whether the focus is on children's feelings, understandings or thoughts, their judgments, beliefs or reasoning, the beginning of middle childhood promises a new maturity and a new desire to learn that is recognized in every culture. All over the world, it is at about seven years of age that children become increasingly aware of a wider society surrounding the family. They want to acquire its knowledge and skills; they need to learn its history; they strive to understand its concerns and aspirations. And because children are, above all, social animals, they do all that learning within a context of social value systems and come to behave as others in their social group behave.[5]

Many other psychologists and educators, like Jean Piaget and Arthur

Applebee,[6] have also focused on this age group because a major shift in the children's operational thought occurs at this time, and they are very susceptible to learning new modes of conceiving and playing. Therefore, most of my remarks will focus on this age group, but I hope to make it apparent that my ideas will have relevance for other age groups, including preschoolers and adults. I do not want to imply that the period between six and ten is the only phase in our formation during which storytelling can have a significant impact; I simply want to signal that these years of middle childhood are crucial for giving children a sense of story and an ability to play with story as they may later play with their lives: in a joyful and responsible way.

Though I have not worked with infants, I have witnessed my own daughter, who began hearing stories when she was about a year old, develop an extraordinary knack for storytelling because she has confidence in herself—the confidence to recognize narrative structure, genres, and conventions and to challenge them with her own daring ideas and conceptions. I am not certain what will happen to her "talents" as a storyteller, and a storyteller in a school does not and cannot have a recipe for the perfect formation of children. But I do believe that storytellers can intervene with teachers in schools to instill confidence in children so that they can readily acquire the instruments and skills they will need to determine their destinies.

The Importance of Storytelling for Schools

Schools are always in a state of transition or crisis. In every city or country in which I have worked, the demands placed on schools and teachers are enormous because the public perceives that "they" are failing our children. In response, school administrators and teachers, who are under great stress, sometimes react defensively to parents and governments who provide little support and few initiatives to improve the conditions under which teachers labor—and they often labor with great frustration instead of having time to experiment with innovative teaching methods. There is much talk about "saving our children and schools," but little evidence to show that people care enough to pay and to force governments to alter their priorities, which are geared toward making children into successful consumers and competitors in a "free" world dictated by market conditions. If there is a failing in Western society, the blame must be placed *not* on schools and teachers but on our attitudes toward schools and teachers and on a socioeconomic system that tends to make children into "consumers" of education who are expected to cultivate consumer attitudes based on spectacle, competition, and success. Consequently, if storytelling is to be introduced into schools, it must be in cooperation with teachers and librarians, and it must be done in a manner that helps teachers, librarians, and children to question the values of our society and the contradictions—why they are where they are—and to change the conditions in the school and community. Storytelling that is not *engaged* in the everyday struggles of the teachers and children is just another form of commercial amusement, and a school could save more money by installing more TV sets and computers in classrooms to divert the children than by hiring a storyteller who simply wants to perform or talk about the "gift of story."

If storytellers are to be effective on behalf of children in schools—and if teachers and librarians are to use storytelling themselves—it is important to try to instill a sense of community, self-reflecting and self-critical community, in the children to demonstrate how the ordinary can become extraordinary. The storyteller is in many respects like the big "bad" wolf, a rabble-rouser whose stories are meant to incite, *not* to destroy, to provoke thought and curiosity; to point a way toward creating a network within a community that brings people together around the concerns they may have for the future of their children.

Schools are an ideal setting for this "subversive" type of storytelling, and such storytelling is ideal for schools, if schools want to create a sense of community and show that they can be other than the institutions of correction, discipline, and distraction that they tend to be.

In America, the busing of children to schools from different places in a city or area has led to the diminishment of neighborhood input and to the alienation of the children in the schools. In many respects, school is an alien world. The children in a school come from different neighborhoods and backgrounds, and the school building itself is different from the structures that the children call home. The rules and requirements are not of the children's making, and they do not get to choose their teachers. Moreover, even in their neighborhoods, if they have any, the children do not know whom to trust or what communal cooperation means. It is often the school that has the function of providing a sense of identity or community to compensate for the lack of community that the children bring with them. Paradoxically, the alien world of the school is supposed to provide a home for the children for the better part of the week, but teachers often shy away from creating such a home or community because everyone—children and teachers alike—wants to leave the school building as fast as they can when the day comes to an end. The stress of the day tears away the possibility for creating community at school. And yet, everyone knows that if school provided a real sense of community, the work of teachers and children would be more effective and pleasurable.

Teachers—and clearly I include principals and librarians as teachers—do not need storytellers to build their own school communities. They do not need storytellers to help them solve the numerous problems that they confront every day. However, storytellers can play a key role in developing a sense of community among children within the classroom and school and among the teachers. Moreover, storytellers can improve and strengthen the literacy of the children, and by this I do not mean that the storyteller can turn children into "better" readers or "get them" to read, but that the story-teller can animate them so they feel a *desire* to read, write, act, and draw, so they want to express themselves critically and imaginatively with tech-niques they may learn from the storyteller and teacher.

Paradoxically, it is from the storyteller, who comes from the outside into the school—that is, it is from the alien, who comes from some unknown place—that the inside can be made known, that children can learn who they are and what their school is. They can sense what they want to conceive and realize. It is the alien figure, the mysterious stranger, who can bring the children together to learn skills through play and who can use story in such a way that they gain insights about themselves. However, the storyteller's work is incomplete without close cooperation with the teacher and, if possible, the administration and outside community.

Storytellers are not just performers. They may perform, but they are first and foremost listeners and animators. They listen to tales before telling or performing them. They listen to phenomena, experiences, and conditions, and they observe. Then they share experiences and animate people to learn something from the shared moment of the telling. In schools, their tales will have no real effect, no impact, no meaning, unless the teachers first share their own experiences with the storytellers and find ways to make the storytelling part of the class program or curriculum. Ultimately, teachers themselves can become storytellers, as Betty Rosen has admirably shown in her book *And None of It Was Nonsense: The Power of Storytelling in School*, based on her experiences as a teacher in London during the

1980s. Other helpful books, such as Bob Barton and David Booth's *Stories in the Classroom*, Margaret Read MacDonald's *The Storyteller's Start-Up Book*, Edie Garvie's *Story as Vehicle: Teaching English to Young Children*, and Patsy Cooper's *When Stories Come to School*, also illustrate how teachers can make use of different methods of storytelling in their classes. In fact, Kieran Egan argues in his book *Teaching as Storytelling* that one can model practically any kind of curriculum on storytelling to make teaching more exciting and commensurate with children's needs. He says, "A model for teaching that draws on the power of story ... will ensure that we set up a conflict or sense of dramatic tension at the beginning of our lessons and units. Thus we create some expectation that we will satisfy at the end."[7] Indeed, I believe that it is clear to anyone who has had experience with the use of storytelling in schools that it can bring teachers and children closer together by focusing on issues and conflicts, thereby forming a bond of understanding that benefits the entire class.

In this book I concentrate on storytellers from the outside who can have a special function in schools and communities because, unlike teachers, they have more time to cultivate very important skills and complement the work that teachers do. Not every teacher wants to become a "storytelling" teacher, and the opportunity to collaborate with a proficient and committed storyteller from the outside can be an invigorating experience for a teacher.

At present, however, storytelling has not been fully explored or developed by schools in the United States or Europe. There is a certain fear that storytellers may interfere with the school curriculum, and a belief that schools can do without them. Anyway, aren't there story hours led by librarians or mass-media experts? Aren't children read to and taught to memorize stories? Aren't they taught to perform and recite their stories? Yes, but is this all that storytelling in schools should do? Is this what storytelling is about?

The Need for Long-Range Programs

Even when storytellers from the outside are invited to schools, libraries, youth centers, and bookstores, it is generally on a one-time basis as entertainers, and if they delight the crowd and perform well, they might be invited back to earn a bit more money. Of course, there is nothing wrong in having children watch a storyteller perform one time, for some children may be encouraged to develop an interest in stories and may thus become more curious about storytelling. But is such storytelling much different from watching a stand-up comic on TV or attending a play one time? A performance is just what it is, a performance, no matter how much the storyteller may care for children or love his or her art.

In my opinion, if storytelling is to become an integral part of the school, it should not be done on a one-time basis. A storyteller should visit and work with a teacher over a prolonged period of weeks or months, preferably for a two-hour session once a week for three months. Depending on what the teacher and children need and desire, and what the storyteller has to offer, it is possible to set up various types of programs that will help children learn about different genres such as the fairy tale, legend, myth, fable, proverb, poem, and even science fiction, and will help them give expression to these genres through their own storytelling, writing, drawing, acting, and even dancing with music. Throughout the three-month period, the teacher can continue to work between sessions with the material that has been presented. The teacher and the children will ultimately replace the storyteller by becoming their own storytellers—the true goal of the wise storyteller, who wants his or her story to touch children and to be passed on. Otherwise, why tell stories?

But to return to the relationship between teacher and storyteller: it is crucial. The storyteller is not in the classroom to give the teacher a much-needed break. The teacher is a participant in the storytelling sessions and a guide for the storyteller. Before the storyteller enters a classroom, the teacher and the storyteller should meet to discuss the needs of the class, the teacher's program, and the repertoire and skills of the storyteller. Without being rigid, the two should agree upon a tentative program that they will review once a week after each session. This need not be done in formal meetings, but the storyteller should receive feedback from the teacher, and the storyteller should make the teacher aware of the problems and difficulties that he/she may be having. Moreover, there are all sorts of follow-up games and exercises that the teacher and storyteller can develop together.

Once a good working relationship is established between the teacher and the storyteller, the two can explore other possible relationships for the storytelling sessions. For instance, in Milwaukee, Gainesville, and Minneapolis I asked for the assistance of older children and parents, who helped the children in the home classroom with their writing and drawing. Such cooperation was important because it created a larger sense of community and established links between older and younger children. Here, too, the older children gained a sense of responsibility as mentors; they shared their knowledge with their younger friends and learned something about storytelling as they helped in the class. In some instances, teachers from other classes participated as well.

For the most part, the schools in which I worked were hospitable and open to my projects and experiments. On the other hand, some were resistant, and many teachers have told me that it is difficult to incorporate storytelling or a storytelling program into their curriculum. Though it is difficult to generalize, my impression is that most schools could use a storyteller to provide a change of pace and a refreshing creative force from the outside. Schools need to transform themselves constantly into cultural domains where work becomes play, and play, work. The classrooms and buildings can become like theaters with moveable sets and seats, theaters in which the actors and audiences exchange roles and become conscious of how they can alter the dramas of their lives. But more schools must seek out the opportunity to work with storytellers, and storyellers must initiate more programs.

I do not believe it is too idealistic to ask schools to open their doors to storytellers and to the possibility of introducing innovative programs for their students at all levels. I have seen it work, and, of course, I have experienced setbacks. But never have I thought that a session was a failure or not worth the effort, nor do I believe that the children felt that way. What I have seen in schools, however, is death. Death in the form of discouraged faces, helpless grimaces, fear of something new, and intimidation. I have also seen frustrated teachers who are overworked and exploited. I have seen crowded classrooms, boredom, and wild behavior. However, whenever I have begun a storytelling session, I have seen curiosity, hope, and the possibility for change, and I have seen that whatever the eventual response to a session may be, the storytelling has made an incision. The storyteller intervenes, and in the best of scenarios, the storyteller subverts. The children cannot carry on their normal routine exactly as they have done before, nor can the teacher. They must adjust in some way, must reflect consciously or unconsciously, especially if the storyteller has been sensitive to their needs and has actually animated them to ponder who they are and where they are.

The very first encounter with the children can be the most important. In Gainesville, before I began my program, I met with the two teachers who had invited me, discussed my plans with them, and made some alterations after our discussions. Then I went to each class, introduced myself, and told the children something about my life and work. Afterward, the children introduced themselves and told me about their interests and hobbies. A week later I began the storytelling sessions. These meetings, I believe, put the children at ease with me, and I, too, felt more comfortable when I returned to the school.

However, it is not necessary to meet with the children in advance before starting a storytelling program. It is much more important to make contact with the teacher and work through some tentative guidelines. There is a certain "shock" or "surprise" when a storyteller enters a classroom for the first time without a formal introduction. The curiosity of the children is aroused. They want to know the stranger. They can be startled and challenged by the new person and may hope that he or she will break their everyday routine.

Transforming the Classroom

When I enter a classroom for the first time, I normally say a few words about myself, and, depending on the size of the class, I ask the children to tell me their names and something about themselves. Generally, the class is too large to do this. So after I introduce myself, I ask the children to clear a large space by moving the tables and chairs off to one side. If they are unmovable, then I ask the teacher to reserve a room where there is enough space for acting. However, I prefer to work in a home classroom because it is a familiar place for the children, a place that I want to change with their help to make the familiar unfamiliar. Storytelling and creative dramatics have a distancing effect that enables the children to step back from themselves, to step out of themselves, and to become someone new.

Once a space has been cleared, I sit on the ground with the children in a circle so I can see all of their faces. Since they are smaller than I am, I want to come down to their physical level as much as possible. I dislike standing before children, unless we are all standing and unless I have to move during the course of the story. Once we are together, I generally begin by telling a story that involves their participation so that they remain alert and feel part of the process. When I finish the participation

story, I tell two or three tales that deal with the same topic but that contradict each other or reveal different perspectives. Though the children may
comment on the stories and want some explanation, I do not always solicit
their reactions. Of course, I answer their questions, but I do not interpret
the stories for them, even though they may be puzzled by the contradictions and the differences in the stories. It is not my purpose to check and
see if they have understood the logic of the story on some rational level.
Instead, they will play with the plot, and through their play, they will
develop their cognitive skills.

After the children have listened to the stories, I ask them whether they
want to act the stories out. The answer is always a resounding "yes," particularly in the six-to-ten age group, where there are few inhibitions.
Sometimes I introduce limbering-up exercises to get the adrenalin flowing
and to teach them some basic techniques of movement. Aside from Viola
Spolin's *Improvisation for the Theater* and *Theater Games for the Classroom*,
other useful books concerned with creative dramatics in the classroom are
Vivian Paley's *You Can't Say, You Can't Play*, John McRae's *Using Drama in
the Classroom*, Herbert Kohl's *Making Theater: Developing Plays with Young
People*, and Patsy Cooper's *When Stories Come to School*. Dramatization of
stories can cause friction in the classroom, so it is important that the storyteller and teacher follow some basic rules, like rotating roles and stressing
how important it is to be a good audience while classmates are "performing" their plays. Patsy Cooper suggests:

> Establish terminology and basic rules using familiar terms: "The inside of
> our circle will be the stage for our play." "Authors" and "actors" and "act
> out" are some terms you may need to explain. You won't need to explain
> everything ahead of time, however, during the first couple of dramatizations,
> opportunities will arise to discuss "dialogue," "offstage," and other dramatic
> terms. It is very helpful to establish a No Touching rule for dramatization.
> This means just what it says. Young children don't always restrain them-
> selves when acting out aggressive behavior. The No Touching rule helps
> avoid this problem.[8]

For the most part, I trust the children to be the actors they are. I am not
there to train them to become actors, but I do give pointers and coach.
Since the classes are large, I divide the children into two or three groups
and assign roles on a volunteer and rotating basis as best I can (always with
the teacher's help). One child is always the narrator/director, whose task it
is to keep the story moving, and I often create new roles with their sugges-

tions if there are not enough characters for each child. There may be some coaching during this first session on movement and terms, but in later sessions this will not be necessary. The groups that are not acting form the audience, and the actors "onstage" create their own props with objects found in the classroom.

After the groups take turns performing the different tales, I ask the children to reassemble the chairs and desks, and we distribute writing and drawing paper along with crayons and colored pencils. At this point I ask the children to write and illustrate their favorite scene from the stories that I told. Or, depending on their age, I ask them to write their own version of one of the stories, to change it as much as possible, and to illustrate it. Aside from the emphasis that I place on creative dramatics, I always include drawing in my sessions. The reason for this is that many children may have some difficulty expressing themselves with words but have none whatsoever with visual expression. As Edward de Bono explains in *Children Solve Problems*,

> Young children are not always very good at expressing their ideas in words and it would be a pity if their ideas were to be restricted by insisting that they use words. Again, words can sometimes be difficult to understand and interpreting the meaning behind them may become a matter of guesswork. Drawings, however, are clear and relatively unambiguous. To make a drawing you have to commit yourself to a definite idea: you cannot say "the bricks are put in a position more quickly than usual" in a drawing because you have to show exactly how this is done. There are more advantages. With a drawing the whole idea is visible all at once and you can work at it with addition, alteration, modification, change, etc.[9]

Along with drawing illustrations, there are numerous games that a storyteller can introduce in any session. For instance, there is the "What If?" game, acrostics, cards, sharing tales, etc., and in the ensuing chapters, I shall demonstrate how I work some of these games into my sessions. Here it is useful to have helpers, whether two or three older children, parents, or other teachers. The children will ask for help with spelling, ideas, etc. Some will have a difficult time getting started and will need prompting. However, I never force a child to participate, and I place no emphasis on correct spelling and grammar. Since the children work at different speeds, I am not interested in a finished product. Those children who finish ahead of the others are encouraged to draw another scene or write a bit more. After a certain time has passed, however, I ask for volunteers to read their stories and to show their pictures, even if they do not consider them finished. Again, numerous spin-offs from a particular session can lead to research and investigation, especially on the part of older children who might work on a community project or gather family stories. In some cases, older children can be animated to collect the legends and stories of a community or region and design books or produce plays based on their collective work.

The type of storytelling session that I have briefly described generally takes one-and-a-half to two hours. In consultation with the teacher, I will probably have covered topics and issues that will enable her or him to continue to work with the children on other days. The animation, if effective, should free the children to read and write and draw in any way they desire and can. It may also help stimulate their vocal expression and cooperation, both of which they learn through improvisation and creative dramatics. It is up to the teacher to follow through on what he or she perceives valuable for the curriculum and program in the class.

This storytelling session is a flexible frame that can be varied in many different ways, as I shall show. It offers a frame to begin long-term work with the teacher and children, provided that a storyteller can work over a period of time with a class. If there are no funds for more than one session with a class, the session still provides a model that I believe teachers can draw on for their own storytelling with children.

Funding for Storytelling Programs

Here is perhaps the best place to talk about funding and its importance for both storytellers and schools. In most of the states in which I have worked—Wisconsin, Florida, New York, North Carolina, and Minnesota—funds are available to invite storytellers and other artists for residencies in the schools. To be sure, these funds are meager, and it is important that boards of education and teachers demand more money for storytellers and other artists so that their work can be sustained over a period of time and so that they can earn a livelihood. Most professional storytellers are dedicated to their craft and do not make huge profits from their work. Some will, however, be tempted to become stand-up comics and entertaining performers who seek high fees outside of schools or charge high fees for theatrical performances in schools, if they do not see any way to earn an adequate living through cooperation with schools and communities. To be frank, if they are to be encouraged to play a more responsible role in communities and schools, their work must be honored and concretely reimbursed with decent fees, not to mention the work of the teachers. Moreover, it is important that storytellers develop long-term relationships with schools so that there is some continuity to their work. As Penelope Leach and other critics of education have pointed out, there are not enough teachers in schools; they are underpaid; and we expect them to take on all sorts of tasks from coach to tour guide, from disciplinarian to therapist. To top it all off, they do not receive the respect they deserve. If they were provided more assistance and relieved of some of their roles, as in the case of storytelling, they would certainly not burn out as fast as they do, and they might become more effective in teaching the skills they know best.

In Minnesota, there is an excellent program called Compas, which serves as an example of how outside organizations can help schools expand their horizons. Compas was established by the State Arts Board and has established a network system to place poets, musicians, painters, story-tellers, and dramatists in one-week residencies in schools throughout the state. These artists share their experiences in workshops organized by Compas, and they are carefully selected for their unique talents, which have been put to use by schools in diverse ways. However, in my opinion, the residencies are too short and exhausting. The resident artist must meet with three or four different classes, and the pace is too intense for the artist. Nor is there any guarantee of continuity for the school. I believe that artists can be more effective if they accept two- to three-month resi-dencies in a limited number of classrooms rather than work the entire day in several classrooms for only one week. This way, there is more continuity in their work for the children, the teachers, and themselves. While at the school, the artist can hold workshops with other teachers so that his or her methods can be tested in other classes.

I mention the Compas program not to criticize it but to suggest that there are already fine storytelling programs throughout the United States, Great Britain, and Europe that can be revamped to serve communities in a more efficacious way. To a certain extent, I am arguing that the story-teller resume his or her traditional role as a *member* of a community, not an outside performer who comes to entertain, divert, and then leave. Schools must seek to adopt their storytellers so that the knowledgeable storyteller knows them, knows their problems, and knows how to provide counsel.

Storytelling projects that originate in schools can lead children to become better acquainted with their families and communities. For instance, in one class for older children I created an oral history project in which the students used tape recorders to gather stories from their parents and relatives in order to learn more about their family history. Then I asked them to take one outstanding event and fictionalize it by exaggerating the incidents to see how legends and sagas develop and are spread, and to trace how "heroines" and "heroes" are born. In another instance, older students were asked to form a research team and to collect all possible information about a controversial event in their city's history. After several weeks of gathering books, documents, reports, articles, etc., they pieced together a story that they thought was the "true" story of this controversy. Finally, they were asked to dramatize the story and present it to the entire school. The controversial event was presented and discussed by the other students and covered in the papers, and it worked itself back into the community by word of mouth in a different form.

In yet another instance, a friend of mine, Mike Dunstan, who works in schools and youth centers in England, won the confidence of teenagers by telling stories that he had collected in playgrounds, schools, and pubs, stories that related directly to their lives and were filled with remarkable folklore. The students were so enthused by his stories that, with his help, they formed storyteller clubs with newsletters at various schools and centers. Their stories were a mixture of literature, folklore, and contemporary events and made them more attentive to what they were reading and experiencing in their local communities.

I mention these three examples because it is obvious that none of them could really have been developed in the space of a week. Nor could a teacher easily initiate these events by herself or himself. Storytellers need time to become part of a community and time to cultivate a sense for their craft among young people, who all have the potential to become storytellers in their own right.

Learning and Challenging the Classics through Storytelling

In the following chapters, I outline a program that can span a period of three months at a school or can be varied as storytellers and teachers see fit. The purpose of this program is to introduce literary genres to children in an active "hands-on" manner so that their writing, reading, acting, and drawing skills are animated. Once they are in touch with their skills, they will feel confident using them to find their own voices. In particular, I want to familiarize them with the genres of the fairy tale, fable, legend, myth, fantasy, and science fiction so that they learn to make distinctions, think about subtle categories, and apply abstract thinking in imaginative and concrete ways. As Kieran Egan has maintained,

> Young children have the conceptual tools to learn the most profound things about our past; as a struggle for freedom against arbitrary violence, for security against fear, for knowledge against ignorance, and so on. *They do not learn those concepts; they already have them when they arrive at school. They use those concepts to learn about the world and experience.*[10]

In most of the sessions of my program, which aims to further the conceptual and cognitive skills of children, I begin with the telling or reading of a classical tale, often a tale written by the Brothers Grimm, Hans Christian Andersen, or Charles Perrault. It is important, I believe, for the children to hear or read a classical tale that they are "supposed" to know, according to society's standard-bearers, even though I personally may find the tale sexist, racist, or abusive to children in some way. In order for children to be able to innovate and use the characters, motifs, and narrative strategies of the tales, they must gain a sense of what a classical model is and be able to distinguish the differences between genres. They must know what "proper" order is, the rules of the game, so that they can play with the order and the rules. They must recognize that people thought differently in the past and set great stock in establishing a certain tradition and way of life. At the same time, they must also become aware that they do not have to adjust themselves to this tradition, just as they do not have to adjust themselves to their own environment if they cannot live harmoniously with it. Here is where storytelling is connected to what Herbert Kohl calls "creative maladjustment." He states:

> When it is impossible to remain in harmony with one's environment without giving up deeply held moral values, creative maladjusment becomes a sane alternative to giving up altogether. Creative maladjustment consists of breaking social patterns that are morally reprehensible, taking conscious control of one's place in the environment, and readjusting the world one lives in based on personal integrity and honesty—that is, it consists of learning to survive with minimal moral and personal compromise in a thoroughly compromised world and of not being afraid of planned and willed conflict, if necessary. It also means searching for ways of not being alone in a society

where the mythology of individualism negates integrity and leads to isolation and self-mutilation.[11]

To a certain extent, storytelling with classical models can provide both "healthy" adjustment and creative maladjustment because it relies on a questioning attitude toward the canonization of art and literature but also encourages respect for tradition, which furthers the personal integrity and honesty of children. Since the value of a classical tale can best be established through comparison, I try to introduce two or three related versions as alternatives to the traditional tale to see how the children "adjust" themselves to the different tales. As Bob Barton and David Booth point out,

> It can be an exciting adventure for children to meet literary versions of a story they think they know. Suddenly, their preconceptions are jolted, and they move into an altered state, caught in a web of changing perception, noticing every minute difference. The story brain is engaged. When children experience two or more stories that are related in some way, their understanding of each is altered and enriched by the other as they make connections between their expanding lives and the stories. Often one story prepares the reader for another one, facilitating the understanding of the subsequent story. And, of course, each new story sheds light on past story experiences, creating a changing view of the stories in the child's story repertoire.[12]

Though I shall be dealing with different genres in this book, it will be obvious that my work is grounded in the fairy tale and that I favor the genres of fantasy. The reason for this emphasis stems from my belief that these genres are what children hear and imbibe through television, movies, and video games well before they can read, write, or think for themselves. Even more important, I believe that there is something subversive and utopian in these genres that can enable young people to develop their critical faculties. To play with authority, to play with strict models of "classical" literature, and to explore and question them will give children a sense of power, autonomy, and self-certainty. That is, if the substance and forms of the classical structures do not hold up to their questioning, the children will realize that the substance and forms may no longer be productive and fertile, and that it may be time to create new devices, strategies, and structures to deal with particular topics and issues that interest them.

So that there will be no misunderstanding: my program is not intended to dismiss the classics, to remove them from schools, or to negate their qualities. Like all "good" literature, the classics are significant because they reveal a great deal about their times and continue to reveal something about ourselves. At their very best, classical models have something indelible about them because they touch upon our deep yearning for a better world. On the other hand, they often contain anachronistic ideas and forms that need to be recognized and discussed if we are to create a literature more commensurate with our own times. Placed in a storytelling context, which also includes the great tradition of folklore and popular culture, the classics are appropriated and illuminated in a communal sense, and the community is the school, where the play with texts can reinforce the confidence of the children and their sense of community and can ultimately enable them to become their own storytellers.

Setting the Scene
with
Fairy Tales

The Initial Encounter

Little Red Riding Hood

I begin all my of programs with *Little Red Riding Hood*, for it is the most popular tale in the world and raises numerous issues and questions for children and adults which demand our immediate attention. Indeed, I would argue that it is popular today because the conflict at the center of this story is still pertinent and unresolved: Charles Perrault's "ancient" tale of 1697 is a story about rape in which the girl bears the responsibility for her own murder and the violent death of her grandmother.

Let us recall Perrault's 1697 literary version, the first model for many similar tales to come (including *Little Red Cap*, written much later, in 1812, by the Brothers Grimm).

Little Red Riding Hood

Once upon a time there was a little girl who lived in a village. She was the prettiest girl for miles around. Her mother doted on her, and her grandmother even more. This good woman made her a little red hood which suited her so well that she was called Little Red Riding Hood wherever she went.

One day, after Little Red Riding Hood's mother had baked some biscuits, she said to Little Red Riding Hood, "Go see how your grand-mother's feeling. I've heard that she's sick. You can take her some bis-cuits and this small pot of butter."

Little Red Riding Hood departed at once to visit her grandmoth-er, who lived in another village. In passing through the forest she met Old Neighbor Wolf, who had a great desire to eat her. But he did not dare because of some woodcutters who were in the forest. He asked her where she was going, and the poor child, who did not know that it was dangerous to stop and listen to a wolf, said to him, "I'm going to see my grandmother, and I'm bringing her some bis-cuits with a small pot of butter from my mother."

"Does she live far from here?" the wolf asked.

"Oh, yes!" Little Red Riding Hood said. "You've got to go by the mill, which you can see right over there. Her cottage is the first one in the village."

"Well, then," said the wolf, "I'll go and see her, too. You take that path there, and I'll take this path here, and we'll see who'll get there first."

The wolf took the shorter path and ran as fast as he could while the little girl took the longer one. Along the way she amused her-self by gathering nuts, running after butterflies, and making bou-quets of small flowers. It did not take the wolf very long to arrive at the grandmother's house, and he knocked:

"Toc, toc."

"Who's there?"

"It's your granddaughter, Little Red Riding Hood," the wolf said, disguising his voice. "I've brought you some biscuits and a little pot of butter from my mother."

The good grandmother, who was in her bed because she was not feeling well, cried out to him, "Pull the bobbin, and the latch will fall."

The wolf pulled the bobbin, and the door opened. He pounced on the good woman and devoured her quicker than a wink, for it had been more than three days since he had last eaten. After that he closed the door and lay down in the grandmother's bed to wait for Little Red Riding Hood, who after awhile came knocking at the door.

"Toc, toc."

"Who's there?"

When she heard the gruff voice of the wolf, Little Red Riding

Hood was scared at first, but she thought her grandmother had a cold and responded, "It's your granddaughter, Little Red Riding Hood. I've brought you some biscuits and a little pot of butter that my mother's sent for you."

The wolf softened his voice and cried out to her, "Pull the bobbin, and the latch will fall."

Little Red Riding Hood pulled the bobbin, and the door opened.

Upon seeing her enter, the wolf hid himself under the bed covers and said to her, "Put the biscuits and the pot of butter on the bin and come lie down beside me."

Little Red Riding Hood undressed and went to get into bed, where she was quite astonished to see the way her grandmother was dressed in her nightgown, and she said to her,

"What big arms you have, Grandmother!"

"The better to hug you with, my child."

"What big legs you have, Grandmother!"

"The better to run with, my child."

"What big ears you have, Grandmother!"

"The better to hear you with, my child."

"What big eyes you have, Grandmother!"

"The better to see you with, my child."

"What big teeth you have, Grandmother!"

"The better to eat you with."

And upon saying these words, the wicked wolf pounced on Little Red Riding Hood and ate her up.

Moral

One sees here that young children,
Especially pretty girls,
Polite, well-taught, and pure as pearls,
Should stay on guard against all sorts of men.
For if one fails to stay alert, it won't be strange
To see one eaten by a wolf enraged.
I say a wolf since not all types are wild,
Or can be said to be the same in kind.
Some are winning and have sharp minds.
Some are loud or smooth or mild.
Others appear just kind and unriled.

They follow young ladies wherever they go,
Right into the halls of their very own homes.
Alas for those who've refused the truth:
The sweetest tongue has the sharpest tooth.

We tend to forget that Perrault implied that a young girl, who was irresponsible and naive if not stupid, was responsible for a wolf's behavior and consequently caused her own rape. Nor is it well known that he had dramatically changed an oral folk tale that had probably been circulating in the South of France before and during his lifetime. According to the French folklorist Paul Delarue, who composed a composite tale based on oral sources,[1] the tale was probably told as follows:

The Story of Grandmother

There was a woman who had made some bread. She said to her daughter:

"Go carry this hot loaf and bottle of milk to your granny."

So the little girl departed. At the crossway she met *bzou*, the werewolf, who said to her:

"Where are you going?"

"I'm taking this hot loaf and a bottle of milk to my granny."

"What path are you taking," said the werewolf, "the path of needles or the path of pins?"

"The path of needles," the little girl said.

"All right, then I'll take the path of pins."

The little girl entertained herself by gathering needles. Meanwhile the werewolf arrived at the grandmother's house, killed her, and put some of her meat in the cupboard and a bottle of her blood on the shelf. The little girl arrived and knocked at the door.

"Push the door," said the werewolf, "It's barred by a piece of wet straw."

"Good day, Granny. I've brought you a hot loaf of bread and a bottle of milk."

"Put it in the cupboard, my child. Take some of the meat which is inside and the bottle of wine on the shelf."

After she had eaten, there was a little cat which said: "Phooey! . . . A slut is she who eats the flesh and drinks the blood of her granny."

"Undress yourself, my child," the werewolf said, "and come lie down beside me."

"Where should I put my apron?"

"Throw it into the fire, my child, you won't be needing it anymore."

And each time she asked where she should put all her other clothes, the bodice, the dress, the petticoat, and the long stockings, the wolf responded:

"Throw them into the fire, my child, you won't be needing them anymore."

When she laid herself down in the bed, the little girl said:

"Oh, Granny, how hairy you are!"

"The better to keep myself warm, my child!"

"Oh, Granny, what big nails you have!"

"The better to scratch me with, my child!"

"Oh, Granny, what big shoulders you have!"

"The better to carry the firewood, my child!"

"Oh, Granny, what big ears you have!"

"The better to hear you with, my child!"

"Oh, Granny, what big nostrils you have!"

"The better to snuff my tobacco with, my child!"

"Oh, Granny, what a big mouth you have!"

"The better to eat you with, my child!"

"Oh, Granny, I've got to go badly. Let me go outside."

"Do it in bed, my child!"

"Oh, no, Granny, I want to go outside."

"All right, but make it quick."

The werewolf attached a woolen rope to her foot and let her go outside.

When the little girl was outside, she tied the end of the rope to a plum tree in the courtyard. The werewolf became impatient and said: "Are you making a load out there? Are you making a load?"

When he realized that nobody was answering him, he jumped out of bed and saw that the little girl had escaped. He followed her but arrived at her house just at the moment she entered.[2]

If we compare the two tales, we can see that Perrault changed a young, unnamed peasant girl, who is brave and uses her intelligence to outsmart a predatory male, into a spoiled bourgeois girl who, he believed, deserved to be punished for her naive coquetry with a wolf. Dead at the end, "her" tale was to serve as a warning to women, young and old, to mind their ways and curb their adventurous spirits. In contrast, the folk tale, which can be linked to sewing communities in southern France and northern Italy, tells about the initiation of a girl who chooses needles over pins because she is ready to become a seamstress and to replace her grandmother. She returns from her difficult voyage in one piece, unscathed, without the help of a male, whom the Brothers Grimm added in their 1812 version because they believed that a woman could not fend for herself but had to be saved from her mistakes by a type of gamekeeper/policeman. In any event, there is no escaping the fact: the original folk tale celebrates the manner in which a clever and brave young girl comes into her own.

As we can see, *Little Red Riding Hood*, which now has thousands of oral and literary versions in numerous languages, is a tale that has a unique history in the West and that captures our imagination because it is filled with unresolved problems that still create tension in our lives today. I like to use the tale in my initial storytelling session because:

1. It is a mixed genre: it contains elements of the warning tale, initiation tale, fairy tale, and fable.
2. It is a metaphorically erotic tale that focuses on relations between the sexes and gender roles.
3. As an erotic tale, it poses the question of violence and sexism in the Perrault and Grimm versions.
4. It is a short, finely sculpted tale that demonstrates key functions of narrative strategy: the necessary departure from home, the encounter with a villain pretending to be friendly in the woods, the arrival at what seems to be a safe destination, the comic interlude in bed, the sudden fall in fortune of the protagonist, and finally, in the Grimms' version, the happy end through rescue by a male hero.
5. It is a shocking tale, especially when I tell the story in the Perrault version, for every child expects and wants the girl to be saved from the wolf. Yet in many respects, Perrault's tale is more honest, even if "sexist," about what happens to girls when they do not learn to fend for themselves. It reveals a great deal about how men imagine who is to

blame when a girl is violated: the finger always points at the girl, a victim of her own failings.

But before I begin telling the Perrault version of *Little Red Riding Hood*, I sit down on the floor with the children and I ask them, "Does anyone know the story of Little Red Riding Hood?" Of course many hands shoot into the air, and I ask one of the children to tell me the story. It will undoubtedly be one that is a mixture of the Grimm and Perrault tales, one that often has the grandmother and Little Red Riding Hood escaping the wolf because the contemporary sanitized versions do not want to offend parents, who are against wolves swallowing grannies and little girls. When I ask whether this is the "true" version, the other children will correct and contradict it. What is interesting here is that very few children really do know the "classical" Perrault and Grimm stories, and finally, I ask them whether they would like to hear the first literary version of *Little Red Riding Hood*. Curious, they respond in the affirmative.

Once I tell them the Perrault version, they sit there, stunned and in disbelief. After a brief moment of silence, they start asking some questions, most of them wondering why the hunter did not arrive on time, why granny did not hide in a closet, why Little Red Riding Hood did not run around the room and yell for help. They are incredulous, and yet, they begrudgingly accept the tale as "the way it was written down and told at one time."

At this point, I ask them whether they would like to hear a totally different and new version of *Little Red Riding Hood* called *Polly Riding Hood and the Stupid Wolf* by Catherine Storr.[3] This tale is a perfect counterpart to the Perrault and Grimm stories. It concerns a dumb wolf who has just finished reading *Little Red Riding Hood* and approaches Polly, who lives in London, to tell her all about this wonderful story in which the wolf captures and eats a little girl. (Obviously the wolf prefers the Perrault version to the Grimms' tale.) Polly tells him that she has read another story in which the girl escapes. The wolf is upset, but Polly is not concerned and rushes off on her way to visit her grandmother for tea. The wolf chases after her but is thwarted because he does not have the correct change for the bus. Two weeks later, the wolf tries again, but this time Polly is driving with her parents to visit her grandmother. The wolf stops the car and babbles to the parents that he wants to eat Polly. Horrified, the parents almost run him over. Finally, after another two weeks, the wolf finds the correct change for the bus and goes to the grandmother's house early. But when he arrives, the grandmother will not let him enter because she wants to protect the wolf, who claims he is Polly. The grandmother mocks the wolf by saying that someone else is inside, that and it must be the wolf, and that if this is the case, she wants to protect her Polly, i.e., the wolf masquerading as Polly. Once again the stupid wolf is foiled. Polly sticks her head out of the window and explains that she had decided to visit her grandmother for an early tea instead of supper, and that if she is indeed the wolf, he had better scoot. Totally frustrated, the wolf asks Polly why he can never seem to capture her when he follows the story exactly as it is written in the book. Her last words to him are, "Because this is not a fairy story, and I'm not Little Red Riding Hood. I am Polly and I can always escape from you."

If I have time, I like to introduce a second version of *Little Red Riding Hood* entitled *The Little Wolf* by Sue Porter. In this story, a cute wolf cub is asked by his mother to take some cupcakes to his grandmother, who lives on the other side of the woods. The little wolf is afraid that there may be giants in the woods, and he is afraid to go. Nevertheless, he gathers his courage and bravely goes off into the woods. However, as he skips along, he suddenly hears a noise and becomes scared. So he begins to run, and he hears the footsteps of a giant behind him. He runs through a thicket and hears the branches break behind him. He runs over a thin wooden bridge and hears the roof collapse under the weight of the giant. Finally, as he desperately tries to avoid the giant, he falls into a hole, and the giant's hand reaches down to pick him up. Then the giant smiles and says, "You dropped a cupcake as you began skipping, and I only wanted to return it to you." The wolf breathes a sigh of relief and then invites the giant to have tea and cupcakes at his grandmother's house. As they are leaving the forest, the little wolf says something like, "I'm not afraid of giants anymore, but I am afraid of witches. Do you think that there are any witches in the woods?" The giant replies, "Don't be silly. There are no witches in the woods." But in the last illustration of the book, we see a witch in the distance picking up something that the giant has dropped.

Since I want the two contrasting versions to Perrault's *Little Red Riding Hood* to have an emotional impact, I do not wait for questions or encourage discussion after telling them. Instead, I ask the children whether they would like to act out these stories as well as the Perrault version. At this point I work with the teacher to form two or three groups, and the children act out the stories through improvisation. Here I use five basic principles in setting up the improvisation:

1. I encourage each child to take a role, but I do not force anyone to play a part.
2. I help set a playing space and ensure that each child begins to learn how to block a play though simple demonstrations of movement and the creation of place.
3. During the first session, I coach the narrator/director of the play, who tells the story as the actors enact it in their own way. In later sessions, I shall do less coaching unless I am there to develop a full-scale play. My purpose is to prompt the children to help each other.
4. I focus on the process: inventing lines, creating characters, exploring space, transforming the room.
5. The audience is as important as the play. I encourage the children who are watching to give their support to the actors and to pay close attention to what they are doing.

When they are finished, I ask them to sit down at their desks with pencils, crayons, and drawing materials, and depending on their age, I use one of the following activities or games to have them comment on the stories through their art.

1. If the children are very young and are just learning how to read and write, I ask them to choose their favorite scene, write about it, and illustrate it. Since they may have difficulty writing, I tell them that two or three lines are sufficient, and that I or the teacher will help them if they run into problems. In addition, I let them know that they can combine the stories and make up new scenes or characters, but that I would like them to write something about their inventions.
2. Another possibility is to ask the children to find ten words that begin with r, such as:

   rodent, reptile, road, rain, referee, rake, ram, rope.

   Then they are to name ten different colors, such as:

   violet, yellow, blue, brown, black, orange, green.

   Next, they are to name ten animals:

   bear, panther, monkey, rabbit, cat, lion, elephant, donkey.

   After I write these lists on the board, I ask the children to take a word from each list to form a story title using big or little, such as:

"The Little Violet Rodent and the Bear"

or

"The Big Green Referee and the Lion."

Once they have a title, I ask them to write a short story about the rodent and the bear or the referee and the lion. It can be very short, and the children are also asked to illustrate the story.

3. Instead of beginning with a writing exercise, I ask the children to draw a picture first:

"How do you think Little Red Riding Hood and the Wolf could get along with one another? Show how you would stop the wolf from attacking either the grandmother or Little Red Riding Hood."

After they draw their picture, I ask them to put a title on it, or to write a few lines about it.

4. If the children already know the basics of writing, I play the "What If" game with them. For instance, I ask them to make up their own stories by asking questions like, "What if Little Red Riding Hood was a boy named Little Blue Runner?" "What if the wolf was an Owl?" "What if Little Red Riding Hood met another girl in the woods carrying a basket?" "What if Little Red Riding Hood knew magic and could change the wolf into a tree?" After making a few suggestions, I ask them for ideas, and their ideas are generally extraordinary and unpredictable. For instance, Red Riding Hood has been transformed into a disco dancer, a ballerina, and a well-known movie star. She has met mice, tigers, dragons, and aliens. She has had help from the Ninja Turtles and Superman, or she has saved herself because she knew karate. What is important here is that the children are familiar enough with the plot and structure of the original story to feel that they can play with it and alter it with their own ideas. Not all the results are to my liking, for there is often a great deal of violence in the stories and illustrations. However, I address the question of violence in later sessions, and the teacher can do follow-up sessions in which she or he discusses violence, the cause of the violence in the tale, and whether it is possible to write a nonviolent version of *Little Red Riding Hood*.

5. Depending on the situation, I may also come with my own version and use it to stimulate their writing and drawing. For instance, I have told the following tale with good results.

One day, right in the middle of lunch, the phone rang, and Little Red Riding Hood picked up the receiver and heard an excited voice at the other end.

"Little Red Riding Hood! Little Red Riding Hood! It's me!"

"Grandma, what's wrong?"

"You've got to come quick. The wolf's caught in a trap!"

"I'll be right there!"

Little Red Riding Hood hung up the receiver and rushed back to the kitchen table.

"Who was that, dear?" her mother asked.

"Grandma. I've got to go help her."

"Not until you finish your sandwich."

"Mom!"

"I mean it."

"I'll eat it on the way. Grandma really needs me."

"Oh, all right. But be back by dinner time."

Little Red Riding Hood grabbed the sandwich from her plate and dashed out of the house. She knew her way through the forest and took a shortcut to her grandmother's house. As she was running through some trees, she saw a hunter in the distance. "Oh, no!" she said to herself, increasing her speed. "I'd better hurry!" She jumped over a bush, ran through a thicket, skipped over a log, and tore through a fence that surrounded her grandmother's house. When she arrived at the door, she didn't even bother to knock but burst right into the living room.

"Grandma, Grandma, where are you?"

"A new world record!" her grandmother cried out, as she clicked her stop watch. "You made it in fourteen minutes and 3.2 seconds!"

Her grandmother was dressed in army fatigues and ready to go.

"I saw a hunter along the way," Little Red Riding Hood said.

"Well, we've no time to lose," said her grandmother, and she grabbed Little Red Riding Hood's hand and dragged her out the back door. They ran as fast as they could until they came to a group of blackberry bushes.

"He's in there," said Grandmother as she stopped and pointed. "I was gathering blackberries to make you a blackberry tart when I heard him."

Just then, Little Red Riding Hood heard a whimper. She pushed back the leaves and glanced down at the ground. There he was— the wolf! Caught in a trap. Whining. Blood streaming from his paw, which was clamped in the jaw of a steel trap.

"Those lousy hunters!" Little Red Riding Hood cried. "Wolfie wouldn't hurt a flea. He's the last wolf in the forest!"

As she said that, she heard the shot of a rifle not too far from where she stood.

At this point, I stop my story, and I ask the children to finish the tale any way they want and to illustrate it. If they have questions, I answer without providing hints about how I might end the tale. The apparent changes in this version lead the children to think about guns, nature, and animals, and there can be follow-ups by the teacher that deal with all these subjects.

Aside from these writing/drawing games, I would like to suggest that there are stories other than Catherine Storr's *Little Polly Riding Hood and the Stupid Wolf* that the storyteller or teacher can use as a counterpart to the Perrault and Grimm versions. For instance, one could choose:

Chiang Mi's *Gold Flower and the Bear*, a Chinese version, in which a young girl saves her brother and thwarts a bear, who has invaded their house.

Michael Emberley's *Ruby*, in which a tiny streetwise mouse tricks a slick, predatory white cat, who is eventually overcome by a dog named Mrs. Mastiff.

Gianni Rodari's *Little Green Riding Hood*, in which a grandfather keeps mixing up the characters to tease his grandchildren and to send them on their way so he can read his newspaper.

Philippe Dumas's *Little Aqua Riding Hood*, in which Little Red Riding Hood's granddaughter sets a wolf free from a Paris zoo and points him toward her grandmother's apartment. She intends to save her grandmother and then become famous by killing the wolf. However, the wolf knows what will happen to him if he goes to the grandmother's apartment, so he runs off to Siberia to enjoy the freedom of the wilderness.

Max von der Grün's *Little Red Cap*, in which a young girl is picked on at school because she has a red cap with a star on it. There are touches of anti-Semitism or racism in this tale. Until the girl learns to conform, and does away with the hat, the people and children of the town ostracize her and her family.

All of these tales[4]—and there are hundreds more—can be employed to question the classical Perrault and Grimm versions of *Little Red Riding Hood* and to address issues of violence, sexuality, animal rights, ageism, etc. They can all be dramatized, and it is often through improvisation of a tale that children gain a concrete sense of movement and plot.

The storytelling session with *Little Red Riding Hood* can also be effective with high school and university students. I have often visited classes that were discussing the nature of different genres such as the fairy tale, myth, and legend, and I have told the Perrault version followed by the folk tale about the peasant girl who outsmarts a werewolf. Then I quickly summarize the Grimm version. After the students are familiar with all three versions, I ask them to point out the differences in characters, motifs, settings, articles, plots, etc. Once the differences are clear, I talk about the distinction between the oral tradition of tales and the literary, and why it is important to know something about the historical background of a fairy tale: that is, in order to grasp why there have been so many transformations between the oral and literary traditions. In some classes I have used this discussion as a springboard for a research assignment. The students are to choose any well-known fairy tale they wish from the collections of Perrault, the Grimms, and Andersen, and they are given a few weeks to find five or more distinctly different versions of the same tale. In addition, they are to analyze and discuss the differences with the purpose of trying to explain why the authors make various changes. Since the illustrations are also significant, I often encourage students to examine these as well. In some instances, I ask them to write their own versions of *Little Red Riding Hood*, and after they read or tell them in class, we discuss how and why they developed their tales as they did.

Well over a hundred scholarly studies and books have been written about *Little Red Riding Hood*, for it is a shocking tale on many different levels, especially when children grasp that the tale is about violence and about who bears the responsibility for violence. And what better way to begin a storytelling session than with a shock? From this point on, the children as listeners are on edge each time the storyteller enters their room. They don't know what to expect, either from the storyteller or from themselves.

§ 2 §
Mixing It Up with Salad Games and Acrostics

The Frog King and Cinderella

I n my first session, I do not talk about the structure of a fairy tale or the elements that make a good story. For the most part, the children begin to narrate their lives and to learn spontaneously what a story can mean for their lives through writing, drawing, and acting. It is the active process that counts. At the same time, throughout my storytelling sessions I introduce terms, notions, concepts, techniques, and generic distinctions that will enable the children to become more conscious of choices that they can make when they tell their own stories.

In each session after the first, I set a frame to my work that will become familiar and obvious to the children. I always begin with one or two classical versions of a tale type, which I read from a book or recite without the text. If I read from a book, it is because many teachers have told me that children *need* to see an adult using a book in this manner. A reader serves as a model for young children, who are normally more apt to watch television than to sit down and read a book, much less read it aloud to hear the music of the words. In addition, I can show how a story can be wonderfully illustrated. Here, slides can be useful as complements or supplements to the reading. If I recite—and I recite most of the time—it is because I want to maintain eye contact with my listeners, who can sometimes be restless. I feel I can be more effective this way in conveying the message of the tale. Like most storytellers, I *never* memorize a tale word for word. Rather, I retain key phrases and components of a tale, practice different modes of telling at home, and keep making changes until I feel that the story is my own. It is important to stress this last point. No matter who the "original" author may be, I must develop an attachment to a tale, otherwise it is not worth telling. In the case of tales that I use as classical models, such as *Little Red Riding Hood*, I am telling them for a purpose and want to make them effective, even though I may not agree with their message. As long as I counter the "traditional" story with a tale that I find more ideologically suitable, I feel comfortable telling the traditional tale. When I finally tell the tale, I vary it in reaction to the audience so that it is constantly new. After I tell the classical version, I recite one or two "subversive" tales to challenge the so-called definitive text. Here the children sense the purpose of my animation. They are stirred up, but I do not impose my views on them. Telling a counter version to a classical tale is enough provocation.

Right after this, I ask the children to act out the stories, and I follow the improvisations with a writing/drawing game. While they write and draw, I walk around, help, give compliments, and make suggestions. If there is time, I ask the children to volunteer to share their stories with the class. The stories and drawings are kept in folders, and sometimes I take them with me, but I always return them when I return to the class.

This frame is almost like a story itself with a beginning and an end, and it allows the children to sense an order or scheme, to anticipate, and to work within that frame. But let me stress that this frame is not made out of iron; it is flexible, and I myself break out of the frame when the children least expect it, just as they do on their own. The frame is important as a frame of reference, and it also represents the transformation of the classroom into a different sphere, a world in which we collaborate and agree to play for a certain amount of time.

Given that the children have seen, in my session with *Little Red Riding Hood*, how order can be reordered through various games and their own retellings, I want to demonstrate more clearly in my second session how reconfiguration of traditional stories can come about. Here I suggest using two classical tales like *The Frog King* or *Cinderella*. Either one will do, or both if there is time.

These two tales are important because they are much more typical of the traditional magical fairy tale or wonder tale than *Little Red Riding Hood* is.

They exemplify what the French call the *conte de fée* and the Germans, the *Zaubermärchen*. Each one concerns a damsel in distress. The young "heroines," obviously ready for marriage, are humiliated, degraded, and besmirched. Their major virtue is patience and, to a certain extent, opportunism. They must wait for the opportune time to make themselves available to a man. Without a man, they are nothing. Only when they find their prince, who comes from outside to rescue them, can their lives assume meaning, and the meaning is marriage and departure for another realm.

Both *The Frog King* and *Cinderella* have strong sexist overtones to our day and age, for their female protagonist is essentially passive. The princess does throw the frog against the wall, but it is more out of frustration than anything else, and anyway, in most versions of this tale, she must kiss a beast or promise to marry it before she can realize her happiness. Indeed, *The Frog King* and *Beauty and the Beast* are related, each belonging to the folktale tradition of the beast/bridegroom cycle. *Cinderella*, too, belongs to an old oral tradition that involves the reincarnation of the mother as a tree or bird, who guides her daughter through her initiation. In other words, both *The Frog King* and *Cinderella* are rich in sunken meanings from ancient tribes and societies, and they contain concealed traces of mysterious rites that shine forth and appeal to children in different ways. Given the abundance of inexplicable symbols and their profound layers of meaning, there is no "correct" way to interpret a fairy tale. Nevertheless, the classical fairy tales have become fixed in Western society in ways that often belie their own richness and the actual possibilities for girls and boys to realize their potential. This "freezing" of a tale often happens in ways that reinforce negative gender roles and an ideological thinking that stabilizes the hierarchy of a class and race.

This tendency toward the "freezing" preservation of conservative strands in the classical fairy tales makes the telling of counter-versions all the more important. We must remember that our ideas of what we think a fairy tale should be emanate from the nineteenth century and were developed by writers like the Brothers Grimm and Hans Christian Andersen within a patriarchal framework. Therefore, the codes of the classical fairy tales are not universal. They were not always told and written down the way the Grimms, Andersen, Bechstein, or even Walt Disney imagine they were. They are specific to a male, middle-class ideology that has set the frame for their inscription. This male hegemony is clear in *The Frog King*, in which the frog and the father "collaborate" to blackmail and humiliate the princess until she is ready to do what they want. Therefore, after reading the Grimms' version *The Frog King*, I often introduce a version like the following.

Mathilde and the Frog

There was once a princess who was homely and lonely. Not only was she homely and lonely, but she was seven feet tall and was so good at basketball that nobody would play with her, not even the players on The Royal Five, the king's team, which had won the realm's championship three years in a row. Mathilde was just too tall and too good. She could dribble with each hand, dribble between her legs, dunk, and run like a gazelle. She was too good to be true, and even her father had to agree that it was unfair for her to play on any team. Indeed, he was somewhat ashamed of her. Mathilde was like a freak.

So Mathilde would often go off by herself to the private basketball court that her father built for her next to a gigantic swimming pool. And it was there that she practiced for hours and invented games all by herself. One time, however, the ball got away from her and bounced into the middle of the pool. Now, there was only one thing that Mathilde feared, and that was water. Her parents had made her take so many baths when she had been a baby—four times a day— that she had grown to dislike water and had never learned how to swim. Nor could she wade into the water, because this was a gigantic pool twenty or thirty feet deep all around.

Mathilde felt like crying. It was her favorite basketball, a gold colored one, and she felt lost without it. Tears started flowing down her cheeks when all of a sudden, a head popped out of the water, green and ghastly. It was a frog.

"Don't cry, Mathilde! I'll fetch your ball," the frog croaked.

Surprised, Mathilde looked at the large frog. She was about to say "Yes, please do" when she remembered that, if she did, she would have to give him something, and maybe even kiss him so that he could become a prince. So she yelled, "No, thanks!"

"What do you mean, no, thanks?" the frog responded.

"Exactly what I mean," Mathilde said, and she turned and ran back to the castle.

When she arrived, she rushed to take a shower and was just in time for dinner. As she took her place at the table, her mother asked, "Did you take a bath?"

"Yes, mother," she said.

"Are you sure?" her father checked.

"Quite sure," Mathilde said.

Then the king looked and smiled at Mathilde's six brothers, who looked like tiny toddlers sitting next to her, but they were really just your average height for boys ranging in age from eighteen to thirty. Since they were all princes, none of them worked. None of them studied. None of them wanted to marry, for they liked the luxury and comfort of their father's castle and liked to be waited upon. Their only displeasure in life was Mathilde. "Why does she have to be so homely and lonely?" they always asked. "If only some one would take her away and marry her."

That was the way the king and queen thought, too. They had hoped to have a seventh son, so when Mathilde arrived they were disappointed, and they became even more disappointed when she grew to seven feet by the time she was sixteen, and they asked themselves, "why does she have to be so homely and lonely?"

"Time to eat," the king said as he rang a little bell to call for the servants. But just then there was a loud knock at the door. The king asked one of the servants to see who was knocking, and when the servant opened the door, in popped a humongous green frog with water dripping down his back. In his mouth he was carrying the large gold basketball, and he spit it out so that it rolled to the table.

The king stood up and said in an angry voice, "Just who do you think you are?"

"I'm a frog. Can't you tell?"

"He's right, dear," the queen said. "He is a frog."

"I'm not blind," the king said.

"And I'm not just a frog," the nasty creature said. "I'm the frog! I'm the frog with whom your daughter made a bargain. She promised that she'd be my friend and kiss me if I fetched her basketball from the pool."

"I did no such thing!" Mathilde protested.

"You certainly did," the frog maintained.

"He's lying," Mathilde replied.

"Are you sure?" the king intervened, remembering that he had a role to play and had to take the side of the frog if everything was going to turn out right.

"I'm sure," Mathilde said. "He's nothing but a ghastly frog!"

"Mathilde, that's no way to treat our guest," the queen scolded her.

"Now I want you to keep your part of the bargain," the king said. "You take Mr. Frog upstairs to your room and be nice to him. And if he asks for a kiss, you know what to do!"

Mathilde stood up, all seven feet of her, and she glared at the frog, and she glared at her mother and father.

"I guess there's nothing left for me to do," Mathilde said.

"Wonderful," the king said.

"Be nice to him," the queen said.

But Mathilde did not pick up the frog. She strode toward the open door and whistled through her fingers. All at once a coach pulled up to the door, and Mathilde stepped inside.

"Where are you going?" her parents yelled.

"You can't leave me like this!" the frog cried out.

"Let my parents kiss you, or one of my brothers," she responded as she stuck her head out of the window. And suddenly, as the coach took off, she smiled and was no longer homely or lonely. She seemed miraculously transformed. Now, to tell you the truth, I am not sure how this happened, but if you follow her trail you may be able to find the answer.

Many other versions can be used in this instance, such as Janosch's *The Frog Prince* or Jon Scieszka's *The Frog Prince Continued*. One of the best is Babette Cole's *Princess Smarty Pants*, in which a feisty princess who does not want to marry kisses an annoying prince and turns him into a frog. Aside from counter-versions of *The Frog Prince*, I also work with counter-versions of *Beauty and the Beast* and *Hans My Hedgehog*. The fundamental question that I attempt to explore with the children is why a young girl/woman is always expected to sacrifice her life for her father or a beast. Domination always appears to be sweetened when the beast turns into a prince. But is the prince really much different from the beast? Will the girl's life really be changed through sacrifice often portrayed as compassion?

Some of the same questions can be posed in the case of *Cinderella*, but the conflict is much different. Here is a case of riches to rags to riches, and the heroine proves her worth by being industrious and patient. That is, her worth is determined by domestic virtuosity. This is clear in either the Perrault or the Grimm classical versions, which serve as my models. After telling one of these, I sometimes recite Judith Viorst's brief poem, " . . . And then the Prince Knelt Down and Tried to the Put the Glass Slipper on Cinderella's Foot," if I decide to work with poetry.

> I really didn't notice that he had a funny nose.
> And he certainly looked better all dressed up in fancy clothes.
> He's not nearly as attractive as he seemed the other night.
> So I think I'll just pretend that this glass slipper feels too tight.

If I tell a prose counter version, then I often retell Tanith Lee's *Princess Dahli*, which is about a poor princess invited to spend some time at the castle of some rich relatives, who exploit her. Despite being mistreated, she cleverly turns everything to her advantage, and she brazenly attends a rich prince's ball without being invited. There she meets the rich prince's poor cousin, who has experienced many of the same things that she has. In the end, they realize that they are suited for each other, and they go off together. As in the case of *The Frog Prince*, there are other fine revisions of *Cinderella* like Robert Munsch's *The Paper Bag Princess*, Jane Yolen's *The Moon Ribbon*, Babette Cole's *Prince Cinders*, Bernice Myers' *Sidney Rella and the Glass Sneaker*, and Russell Shorto's *Cinderella and Cinderella's Stepsister*, that can be incorporated into a storytelling session. In addition, Neil Philip has collected an interesting variety of "Cinderella" folk tales from different countries and historical periods in *The Cinderella Cycle*, which can be put to good use. Another fascinating version is the *Indian Cinderella* in Cyrus Macmillan's adaptation, which I have slightly changed.

The Indian Cinderella

On the shores of a wide bay on the Atlantic coast there dwelt in olden days a great Indian warrior. It was said that he had done many wonderful deeds. But that is something no man knows, for he had a very wonderful and strange power: he could make himself invisible and thus could mingle unseen with his enemies and listen to their plots. He was known among the people as Strong Wind, the Invisible and lived with his sister in a tent near the sea, where his sister helped him greatly in his work. Many maidens would have been glad to marry him, and they sought him because of his mighty deeds. Yet, it was known that Strong Wind would only marry the first maiden who could see him as he came home at night. Many made the trial, but it was a long time before one succeeded.

Strong Wind used a clever trick to test the truthfulness of all who sought to win him. Each evening at sunset, his sister walked on the beach with any girl who wished to pass the test. His sister could always see him, but no one else could. And as he came home from work in the twilight and as his sister saw him drawing near, she would ask the girl who sought him, "Do you see him?" And each girl would falsely answer, "Yes." And his sister would ask, "What is he using to draw his sled?" And each girl would answer, "The hide of a moose," or "A pole," or "A great cord." And then his sister would know that they all had lied, for their answers were mere guesses. And many tried and lied and failed, for Strong Wind would not marry any who were untruthful.

Now, there lived in the village a great chief who had three daughters. Their mother had died some time ago, and he had raised them by himself. One of his daughters was much younger than the others. She was very beautiful and gentle and well beloved by all, and for that reason her older sisters were very jealous of her charms and treated her very cruelly. They clothed her in rags and cut off her long black hair so that she would look ugly; they burned her face with coals from the fire so that she might be scarred and disfigured. Then they lied to their father, telling him that she had done these things herself. But the young girl was patient and kept her gentle heart and went gladly about her work.

Like other girls, the chief's two eldest daughters tried to win Strong Wind. One evening at sunset, they walked on the shore with Strong Wind's sister and waited for his coming. Soon he came home from his day's work, drawing his sled. And his sister asked, as usual, "Do you see him?" And each one, lying, answered, "Yes." And she asked, "What has he used to make his shoulder strap?" And each guessed, "Rawhide." Then they entered the tent where they hoped to see Strong Wind eating his supper, and when he took off his coat and his moccasins, they could see nothing but these garments; for Strong Wind knew that they had lied, and he had kept himself from their sight. Dismayed, they went home and sobbed.

One day the chief's youngest daughter made up her mind to see Strong Wind despite her rags and her burnt face. She patched her clothes with bits of birch bark from the trees, put on the few little ornaments she possessed, and went forth to see the Invisible One just as all the other girls of the village had done before. Her sisters laughed at her and called her a fool. And as she passed along the road, all the people laughed at her because of her tattered frock and her burnt face, but she silently went her way.

Strong Wind's sister received the maiden kindly, and at twilight she took her to the beach. When Strong Wind came home drawing his sled, his sister asked, "Do you see him?" And the girl answered, "No," and his sister was astounded because she spoke the truth. And again she asked, "Do you see him now?" And the girl answered, "Yes, and he is very wonderful." And she asked, "What is he using to draw his sled?" And the girl answered, "The Rainbow," and she was very afraid. Then the sister asked again, further, "What has he used to make his bowstring?" And the girl answered, "The Milky Way."

Then Strong Wind's sister realized that, because the girl had spoken the truth from the very beginning, her brother had made himself visible to her. So she said, "There is no doubt that you have seen him." And she took her home and bathed her, and all the scars disappeared from her face and body. Moreover, her hair grew long and black again like the raven's wing, and the sister gave her fine clothes to wear and many rich ornaments. Then she told her to take the wife's seat in the tent. Soon Strong Wind entered and sat beside her and called her his bride. The very next day she became his wife, and from then on she helped him accomplish great deeds.

Of course, the girl's two elder sisters were very cross, and they were very curious to learn what had happened to their sister. But Strong Wind, who knew of their cruelty, decided to punish them. Using his great power, he changed them both into aspen trees and rooted them in the earth. And ever since that day, the leaves of the aspen have trembled. Indeed, they shiver in fear of the approach of Strong Wind, no matter how softly he comes, for they are still very much aware of his great power and anger, which they roused with their lies and their cruelty to their sister long ago.

After I introduce the appropriate material for either *The Frog King* or *Cinderella* and do some playacting, I focus during the writing-and-drawing segment on a salad game or acrostics. For instance, in the salad game, which always involves mixing fairy-tale motifs, I ask the children to name the characters, places, and things that they think are most important, and I write all this on the board. Then I ask them to suggest some characters, places, and things that come to their mind out of the blue, and I add several to the list on the board. In the end, I may come up with a list like this:

princess	golden ball	frog	palace	king
food	servants	bed	kiss	motorcycle
policeman	forest	peach	gun	Mickey Mouse

In the case of *Cinderella*, I may have a list like this:

father	daughter	stepmother	Cinderella	stepsisters
kitchen	ball	doves	oak tree	pumpkin
mice	dance	prince	glass slipper	rock music
airplane	singing contest	dwarf	Cadillac	banker

Once the lists are compiled, I ask the children to use all the elements on the list in their own story, and I encourage them to mix the elements in any manner they desire. I make sure to mention that they can also add characters and objects. However, they must make sure that every word on the list is included in their story. The purpose of this game is to stimulate the children to play with the elements of a story and rearrange them so that they break out of the traditional mode and discover how the children can appropriate a classical story as their own.

Here are some examples written by students, eleven to twelve years old, at a Gainesville middle school. As will be evident from their stories, the lists from which they worked varied a great deal. Another one of the salad games that I play with the children involves the mixing of three or four different fairy tales like *Little Red Riding Hood*, *Cinderella*, *Snow White*, and *The Frog King*, from which the children are prompted to include as many of the characters in their mix as possible. These short tales were written and illustrated within a time span of ten to fifteen minutes in class.

The Frog King

Once upon a time a very fat princess with bad breath was playing with her golden ball beside a pond that led to a skyscraper of a well. She was not very smart, but that wasn't her fault. She had been put under a spell by King Midas.

—*Bryan Cruce*

A Fairy Tale

Once upon a time Snow White and the dwarfs went to this disco. But Cinderella got very mad because Little Red Riding Hood and Snow White had a better-looking dress then she did. So Cinderella started tearing off their dresses with her man-eating claws. Prince Charming came and stopped Cinderella from ripping their dresses apart. Then the king said, "Are you ladies all right?"

—*Tiffany Green*

A Fairy Tale Mix

Once upon a time there was a witch named Cinderella, and one day she got mad at the king and turned him into a grandma. The grandma got killed by a hunter who was really a wolf in disguise. And when Little Red Riding Hood told the king, the king said, "Hoora." And then he went and told his wife Snow White. And Snow White said, "Oh, that's too bad." And then she left and went to her secret lovers the seven dwarfs, and there she found out that she was going to have seven kids. And then she passed out and fell on a frog, and the frog's guts went all over her dress.

—*Randy Hill*

Fairy Tale Mix

Once upon a time there was a princess, and her name was Lady Diana. She had a deer that played the saxophone. One day she told the deer to go out and get her some sushi because she was having sushi and potatoes for supper. But her two stepsisters were so evil, and they made her eat pumpkins and mice for dinner. But one day her stepmother came along and told those two stepsisters to stop.

—*Alicia Myers*

Tale of the Queen

One day there was a young princess named Snow White. She was a beautiful princess, and she loved dwarfs. Snow White had a sister named Cinderella. Cinderella was always put to work, and she was always doing everybody else's chores. Cinderella had two small friends. One was Red Riding Hood. That was her name because she always wore a red hood, for her mother had woven it for her when she was younger.

Cinderella's other friend was Rumpelstiltskin. He was about twelve inches tall, and he granted wishes. Snow White's stepmother was an ugly mean witch. She acted as a snobby queen but wasn't.

One day the stepmother decided to kill Cinderella. She was going to send a hunter out to kill her and whoever she was around. Rumpelstiltskin found out somehow and told Cinderella. Cinderella wept for days. Rumpelstiltskin, feeling sorry for her, granted her two wishes. Cinderella thought for a moment. Weepingly, she asked that her stepmother become a loving kind person and not be a witch. Next, she asked that her mother not kill her.

The next day Rumpelstiltskin went to a miller's house and asked him to do something to keep Cinderella from being killed. He said he'd have a wolf to fetch the hunter and devour him. The wolf did it, and Rumpelstiltskin granted the man two wishes. The first was that his grandmother be healed of polio. The second was that he become a prince and be rich and to buy a castle.

It all became so, and afterwards Cinderella found out what the miller had done, and she went to him and thanked him very much. He then saw how beautiful she was and asked her to be his bride. She said yes, and they got married in the town palace. Cinderella had finally become queen. They lived happily ever after and loved one another forever, as far as we know.

—*Tonya Look*

The Surprise Birthday Party

One day Red Riding Hood's grandmother threw her a surprise birthday party. She invited the Big Bad Wolf, Prince Vespar, Queen of Sheba, Cinderella, Snow White and her dwarfs, and she invited

Rumpelstiltskin. Well, when the witch and her friend the miller heard they weren't invited, they got ticked. The witch and the miller went to the witch's castle and thought about what they could do to get back at them. They decided to play a prank on them. What could they do as a prank? They decided something.

They rode their skateboards to the castle and hid. When the cake arrived, they took the wax cake they brought and switched it with the real cake. After the miller and the witch finished the cake, they went inside and hid in the dining room. After they ate, they cut the cake. The witch and the miller had to cover their mouths to keep from laughing. Everyone ate the cake. Then everyone started throwing up. "Euueeh!" everyone exclaimed.

"That was grody," said Cinderella.

"Wha-wa-what happened?" said Red.

"I don't know her!" grandmother said.

And everyone had a fabulous time.

—*Scott Trucano*

In addition to the salad games, I often use acrostics to free the children from the sequential plot of the classical version and to show them how free association can form the basis of poetry. Since there is generally some bias against poetry, one of my aims is to reveal to the children that poetry can be exciting and that their images are poetic. I talk about metaphors and comparisons. I tell them to listen to the beat of their words and to write down whatever comes to their minds. To give them an example, I generally present an acrostic poem of my own on the board like:

Crying
I heard a babe
Nestling
Down in the darkness of
Eternity
Reaching
Endlessly
Longing
Lovingly
And I wept with joy.

I ask the students some questions before they begin to write: What does the name evoke? What feelings? What notions? What does each letter mean? See if you can picture something. See if you can write an image.

Here again are some examples from Gainesville:

Cinderella

Christmas Eve with merry singing,
In the jail of Pembroke City,
Nine bells bouncing and ringing
Down the halls of heaven.
Even though this sounds so stupid,
Running away won't help you.
Everyone knows you'll get shot by cupid,
Lots and lots of arrows,
Love will always get you,
Always sleeping.

—Carl Merry

Snow White

Snow White was in the woods one day
Needling all her clothes away.
Over on the other side
With her was the blind man's guide.
William was his name,
Hockey was his game.
It made him want to scratch and bite, I was
Telling him not to fight, but he insisted
Everyone watch him fight for a girl named Snow White.

—Theresa Brannon

White Snake

When I was young I got
Hit playing football.
It hurt very bad and
Tears came to my
Eyes, and when the coach asked me if I was
all right, I just
Shrugged my shoulders, and he said do I
Need to call the doctor about your
Ache in your
Knee. I said, no, because the pain is about to End

—Jay Klein

Snow White

Snow White was walking one day,
No one saw her walking so happy and gay.
Out of the bushes came a snake.
Wow! he said my name is Jake.

What do you want, she said.
How about a kiss on the head?
I'll think about it, Jake.
Tell me, how long will it take?
Ever and ever, just as long as I can take.

—Alicia Myers

Sleeping Beauty

Snoring
Loudly
Except when
Eating
Playing
Ickey poohey music
Nicely
Giggling

Being crazy,
Examining
An
Undergarment
Telling about a
Yellow gown she desires in a store window.

—Kim Pearson

Snow White

Soft skin
Not having pimples
Owning a dress
Wearing it nicely

With a wicked stepmother
Having her killed
In the forest
Taking out her heart
Ending, happily ever after.

—Jacqueline Shelton

Some of the examples contain rhymes. However, I do not talk about rhyme when I discuss poetry. The emphasis is more on free association and image, and I advise the children to listen to the music and beat of their own words. In other experiments with children, I have asked them to set the stories to skipping rhymes, playground chants, and other popular children's songs. In one case, I used substitutions in traditional nursery rhymes like *Jack and Jill* and got results as provocative as this version by Michael Sawyer, age seven:

> The prince and frog
> went in the pond
> to fetch a ball of gold.
> When frog returned
> he lost the ball
> For the prince took all the gold.

The songs and acrostic poems by the children are often stunning and revealing, and the use of acrostics and substitution rhymes along with the salad games enables the children to challenge classical versions and create their own pictures of tales in a spontaneous manner.

For older children, Monica Edinger, who teaches fourth grade at the Dalton School in New York City, developed a remarkable program based on *Cinderella* that consisted of a study cluster that lasted a few weeks. Here is an outline of her program.

1. Personal fairy-tale definitions.
    What is your definition of a fairy tale? Don't worry about trying to come up with the one "right" definition, because there isn't one! Just write down your personal idea of a fairy tale.
2. Memories of *Cinderella*.
    What is your version of *Cinderella*? We will do a retelling of the tale with everyone in the class contributing elements from their own personal version. Then we will discuss how each of us got these versions in our heads. Did your grandmother first tell you the tale? Did you read it in a book? Perhaps you got your idea from a movie. Let's find out.
3. Analyses of some *Cinderella* variants.
    You will be looking at many different versions. To keep track of all the

variants, please use the charts on the following pages. They will serve
as a record of all the different *Cinderellas* you study and help you as you
begin to create a description of what a *Cinderella* story really is.

Here are the categories that Edinger set up on work sheets:

Title	Author	Genre	Culture	Personal	Response

4. Now that we have studied many many different *Cinderella* variants, it is
    time for us to come up with elements or motifs that make up a *Cinderella* story. Clearly all the versions we have been studying have things
    in common. What are those things? We will make a class chart detailing our *Cinderella* motifs.

5. Read a non-*Cinderella* fairy tale. Compare this fairy tale to *Cinderella*.
    Think of the elements that make up a *Cinderella* story. How is the
    other tale similar or different from your favorite *Cinderella* variant?

6. Without looking back at your first definition, write your current definition of a fairy tale. When you are done (not before, please!), take a
    look at your first definition. We will have a class discussion on whether
    our ideas of fairy tales have changed from this study and, if they have,
    why.

7. Now it is your turn! You will create your own *Cinderella* variant! Select
    your own genre and style. It can be written, drawn, sung, videotaped,
    whatever you wish! Have fun!

Here are some results of the fun, by three fourth-graders.

A Weird Story of Cinderella

Once upon a time a long time a long time my mother, Cindy and I
lived in a house with everything one could want, except Cindy always
wanted more and more. She was so bad that my mother had to
punish her all the time so finally Cindy got so annoyed that she said
she enjoyed doing the housework, so my mother gave Cindy rags if
she wanted to do the housework. But she could have her good
clothes back whenever she wanted to.

Cindy dreamed that she could be a princess so she pretended to
be abused so the king would take pity on her and take her in and
later marry her to the prince.

And so the days went on. Until you know the big day arrived and my mother gave Cindy a dress and a pair of glass slippers so Cindy could go to the ball.

So Cindy went to the ball, danced with the prince but the prince wasn't interested in what she was telling him because she was telling him about her made up life. Cindy got so annoyed that she dug her heel into the prince's toe. At twelve Cindy flashed off, telling the prince to go look in another room to see if she was there. In the progress of running she lost a shoe.

Cindy came home the long way so when she came back everybody was asleep, and the door was locked, so Cindy decided to climb in by the window, but of course the alarm went off. Cindy landed on top of a chair which fell on top of her. What a commotion! My mother was frantic, thinking somebody had broken into our house. I had a pretty good idea it was Cindy (because she is always late!). I went to where I had heard the noise and found a tired and hurt Cindy sitting under a chair. I ran and told my mother it was only Cindy. My mother was relieved but punished Cindy for a week in her room. For once Cindy was too tired to argue and went to bed.

The next day Cindy climbed down the vines. Once down Cindy noticed a crowd of people talking. Cindy went over to them and asked what they were talking about. Somebody told her that it was because the prince was going to return a slipper and marry whoever it fits first. Cindy smiled to herself and waltzed off back to the window and up the vine. While she was still climbing up the wine I saw her but didn't say anything to my mother because I wanted to be a friend with Cindy. So instead I went to see what she was up to.

I peeked through her keyhole and saw her humming and dancing a waltz from the ball. A little while later Cindy and I heard a trumpet sound from outside our house. My mother took away the punishment so Cindy could go and try on the fabulous shoe. Cindy and I raced down the stairs. The prince himself was there (waiting for the maidens of the house!). Cindy went first but her foot was swollen so it didn't fit! My turn was next, it fit perfectly! So the prince and I lived happily every after. And Cindy wrote her version. The one everybody seems to know.

—Sarah Wertheimer

Cinderella goes to Camp!

There was once a little girl who lived with her father in a town in New Jersey. The girl's name was Ella, and she was seven. She loved her father very much, but her father was very sick. Her father died when he was forty-seven, when Ella had just turned eight. Ella went to live with her aunt and cousins in New York. Ella's cousins' names were Elizabeth and Rose. They were twins. They were nice to her when her father was around but they were mean to her now.

When Ella was nine, her aunt sent Ella and her cousins to sleep-away camp for the summer. Ella was in Elizabeth and Rose's bunk and she was really disappointed.

Ella had a lot of different night activities at camp, but she really liked night swim. So when swim came on Saturday Ella was really excited! So Ella went and she met a boy named Charlie and she liked him a lot, but so did her cousins unfortunately. Ella's cousins knew that Charlie liked Ella more than he liked them.

During the week Elizabeth and Rose forgot about Charlie and just went on with their week. But Elizabeth and Rose were getting more and more annoyed during the week because Ella was doing much better than them in every sport such as soccer, baseball, tennis, swimming, and archery. A whole week had gone by and Ella was having the most fun she had ever had, but Ella's cousins were miserable.

Finally it was Saturday the day it was night swim. Ella's cousins got into their bathing suits and got ready to go down to the lake. When everyone was ready to go, Ella's cousins locked her in the SMELLY bathroom, but, when they were walking to swim Ella's counselors asked Elizabeth and Rose where Ella was. They said "I don't know," but really they did.

So Ella's counselor went back to the bunk to look for Ella and found her in the bathroom holding her nose and throwing up from the smell of the bathroom. Ella was relieved to be let out of the bathroom, but her counselor said that she would have to be back from swim by 8:30 so she would have time to clean up the mess in the bathroom. Ella was really happy to see Charlie. But her cousins weren't happy to see Ella. But when Charlie saw Ella he was even happier!

Ella played in the pool with Charlie all night, and they were having so much fun. Charlie said to Ella, "What's your name?" Ella was about to tell him but when Ella looked at her watch, she saw it was 8:29 p.m. So she said goodbye to Charlie and ran as fast as she could. But when Ella was running, her Teva fell off. She was going to go back and get it but she saw that it was already 8:30, so she just kept running. Charlie ran to Ella's shoe, picked it up, looked at it for about a minute, and all of a sudden said, "Wait, but I don't even know your name!!"

Ella cleaned up the mess in the bathroom but when her cousins came back Ella just ignored them

The next day Charlie went all over camp looking for the girl whose foot fit the little Teva. Charlie had brought the Teva to ten girls' bunks and all of their feet were too big for the little Teva. Charlie FINALLY came to Ella's bunk and tried the Teva on every girl in the bunk but just as Charlie was about to leave, Ella busted down the door to the closet and went up to Charlie and asked if she could try on the Teva. But it was too late. Rose had already thrown the Teva out of the window. But Ella took the other Teva out of her pocket and put it on her foot.

So twelve years later Ella and Charlie got married and became directors of the camp. And they all lived happily ever after, except for the cousins. Who knows what happened to them!!

—*Erica Bromley*

Whether it be *Cinderella*, *The Frog King*, *Beauty and the Beast*, or *Hans My Hedgehog*, it is important to show the transformations of a fairy tale in the second session. It is through an emphasis on transformation and change that children realize how much they will change, and how important it is to gain a sense of their own narratives, to take charge of their own stories.

§ 3 §

Playing with Fortune

Rumpelstiltskin and Spinning Tales

By now the children have gained a sense of the structure of the classical tales and the different characters, motifs, and settings. Moreover, they have been sufficiently exposed to literature, television, and films so that the storyteller and teacher can always rely on their conscious and unconscious knowledge of the plots and conventions of fairy tales and adventure stories. Some of the best parodies and recreations of fairy tales have actually been produced for television. I am thinking here of "Fractured Fairy Tales" in the *Rocky and Bullwinkle* series and Jim Henson's Muppet productions of *The Frog Prince* and *Cinderella*, not to mention the remarkable skits like "Snow White" in the cartoon *Muppet Babies*. Of course, numerous fairy-tale films appear each year, and as Linda Dègh has demonstrated in her important book *American Folklore and the Mass Media*, most commercials on TV incorporate fairy-tale motifs and plots to induce people to purchase "magic" shampoos, drinks, cars, or jewelry that will change their lives. Aside from the commercials, the soap operas, talk shows, sitcoms, mysteries, and numerous other shows exploit folklore in all sorts of ways to enrich their plots and capture the attention of viewers. In other words, by the time children reach school age, they already have a referential system to which they allude and which they understand in some way, and to which the storyteller can also allude and can change in a creative way.

Of course, this referential system is loaded with different messages, and as Marsha Kinder has pointed out in her significant study *Playing with Power in Movies, Television, and Video Games*, the intertextuality of TV shows, movies, and video games reinforces consumer tendencies and patriarchal notions of gender and power. In this regard, the "playfulness" of many fairy-tale films and videos is deceptive because of the manner in which they are framed to induce children to perform as "transformative mutants," and as Kinder maintains, "television teaches viewers that commercial interactivity empowers precocious consumers by enabling them to assimilate the world as they buy into the system."[1]

This TV "manipulation" of fairy tales and fantasy stories necessitates a critical response and questioning attitude that, I believe, can be attained through storytelling. If children are going to learn to create their *own stories*, they must learn about the context in which they create. This means that they must learn to question and play with the classical fairy tales of the past and the commercial products of the present.

In this session, I like to begin with a series of *Rumpelstiltskin* versions—a classical tale that is very common in film and TV — because they raise questions dealing with parental abuse, the craft of spinning related to spin-ning tales, and the nature of helpers, who are sometimes kind and some-times blackmailers. I begin by telling the traditional *Rumpelstiltskin* version of the Brothers Grimm and stress the boasting of the father that causes his daughter's predicament. Then there is the king, who threatens her life and will only marry her because she can produce gold. Finally, there is the "demonic" creature Rumpelstiltskin, who is really not a helper but a black-mailer, who wants to take away the first born from the miller's daughter. By guessing his name at the end, the young queen seemingly banishes evil from her life. Certainly, she is rid of one of her abusers. This is one way to interpret the tale and to recite it.

But *Rumpelstiltskin* is also a tale about how the craft of spinning was taken from the hands of women and turned against them. For thousands of years, until the advent of technology in the eighteenth century, spinning was associated with women. Although there were also men who spun, it was basically a female craft, and women gathered together to spin yarn and wool for clothes, to make additional money for the family, and to talk and relate anecdotes and stories. Spinning was often done in special cottages, and in certain regions in Europe it was the place where young men came to court young women. Through spinning, a young woman could win a young man and determine her destiny. It all depended on how she wove the threads of her life. The work of spinning, though laborious, had its rewards if one knew how to spin well.

Looked at from this historical perspective, *Rumpelstiltskin* is also the tale of how spinning was taken out of the hands of young women by malicious creatures such as Rumpelstiltskin. The miller's daughter cannot spin for herself. By the end of the eighteenth and beginning of the nineteenth centuries, spinning had become mechanized and had been moved away from homes to factories where men took charge of mass spinning. That is, a domestic industry was on the verge of being transformed, and a craft that brought women together and gave them a sense of strength and community was being undermined. Therefore, the Grimm version of *Rumpelstiltskin* is a very revealing story because it depicts the fact that a young girl can no longer produce "gold" or make money through spinning. She is uprooted from her family due to her father's boasting and is then at the mercy of other men because she has lost the power to make money through spinning. She is saved only by chance, and she is married to a man who has threatened to kill her. What appears to be a happy ending is a life of compromise that was not really of her choosing.

To counter the "sanguine" ending of *Rumpelstiltskin*, I often tell the following tale by Rosemarie Künzler.[2]

Rumpelstiltskin

After the miller boasted that his daughter could spin straw into gold, the king led the girl into a room filled with straw and said: "If you don't spin this straw into gold by tomorrow morning, you must die."

Then he locked the door behind him. The poor miller's daughter was scared and began to cry. Suddenly a little man appeared and asked: "What will you give me if I spin the straw into gold for you?"

The girl gave him her necklace. The little man sat down at the spinning wheel and "whizz, whizz, whizz," three times the wheel went round, and soon the spool was full and had to be replaced. And so it went until morning. By then all the straw had been spun into gold.

When the king saw this, he was pleased. He immediately brought the miller's daughter to a larger room also filled with straw and ordered her again to spin the straw into gold by morning if she valued her life. And again the miller's daughter cried until the little man appeared. This time she gave him the ring from her finger. The little man began to make the wheel whizz, and by morning all the straw was spun into gold.

When the king saw the gold, he was overjoyed. But he was still not satisfied. He led the miller's daughter into an even larger room and said: "If you spin this straw into gold by tomorrow, you shall become my wife."

When the girl was alone, the little man appeared for the third time and asked: "What will you give me if I help you?"

But the miller's daughter had nothing to give away.

"Then promise to give me your first child when you become queen."

This demand jolted her and finally made her open her eyes.

"You're crazy!" the miller's daughter yelled. "I'll never marry this horrible king. I'd never give my child away."

"I'm not going to spin. I'll never spin again!" the little man screamed in rage. "I've spun in vain!"

The little man stamped with his right foot so ferociously that it went deep into the ground and jarred the door to the room open. Then the miller's daughter ran out into the great wide world and was saved.

In addition to this contemporary version, I also like to return to the Grimms and tell the children another older version called *The Three Spinners*, and since it is not well known, I include it here.

The Three Spinners

There was once a lazy maiden who did not want to spin, and no matter what her mother said, she refused to spin. Finally, her mother became so angry and impatient that she beat her, and the daughter began to cry loudly. Just then the queen happened to be driving by, and when she heard the crying, she ordered the carriage to stop, went into the house, and asked the mother why she was beating her daughter, for her screams could be heard out on the street. The woman was too ashamed to tell the queen that her daughter was lazy and said, "I can't get her to stop spinning. She does nothing but spin and spin, and I'm so poor that I can't provide the flax."

"Well," the queen replied, "there's nothing I like to hear more than the sound of spinning, and I'm never happier than when I hear the constant humming of the wheels. Let me take your daughter with me to my castle. I've got plenty of flax, and she can spin as much as she likes."

The mother was delighted to give her consent, and the queen took the maiden with her. After they reached the castle, she led the maiden upstairs to three rooms that were filled with the finest flax from floor to ceiling.

"Now, spin this flax for me," she said. "And if you finish all this, you shall have my oldest son for your husband. It doesn't matter to me that you're poor. You work hard and you never stop. That in itself is dowry enough."

The maiden was tremendously frightened, for she could not have spun flax even if she were to live three hundred years and sit there every day from morning until night. Therefore, when she was left alone, she began to weep and sat there for three days without lifting a finger. On the third day the queen came back to the room, and when she saw that nothing had been spun, she was puzzled. But the maiden made up an excuse and said that she had been so terribly upset about leaving her mother's house that she had been unable to begin working. The queen accepted this excuse, but upon leaving, she said, "Tomorrow you must begin your work for me."

When the maiden was alone again, she did not know what to do or where to turn. In her distress she went over to the window and saw three women coming in her direction: the first had a broad flat foot, the second had such a large lower lip that it hung down over her chin, and the third had an immense thumb. They stopped in front of her window, looked up, and asked the maiden what the matter was. She told them about her predicament, and they offered to help her.

"We'll spin your flax for you in no time at all," they said. "But only if you invite us to your wedding and are not ashamed of us. Moreover, you must call us your cousins, and let us eat at your table."

"With all my heart," she responded. "Just come in and get to work right away."

She let the three old women in and cleared a place for them in the first room where they could sit down and begin their spinning. One drew out the thread and began treading the treadle, the other wet the thread, and the third twisted it and struck the table with her finger. Whenever she struck it, a reel of yarn dropped to the ground, and it was always most delicately spun. The maiden concealed the three spinners from the queen, and every time the queen came, the maiden showed her such a large amount of spun yarn that there was no end to the queen's praise for her. When the first room was empty of flax, they moved on to the second and then the third until it too was cleared of flax. Now the three women took their leave and said to the maiden, "Don't forget what you've promised us. Your fortune will depend on it."

When the maiden showed the queen the empty rooms and the large piles of yarn, the queen arranged for the wedding, and the bridegroom was happy to get such a skillful and industrious wife and gave her tremendous praise.

"I have three cousins," said the maiden, "and since they've done so many good things for me, I'd like to remember them in my happiness by inviting them to the wedding. Please allow me to do this and let them sit at our table."

The queen and the bridegroom said, "Why, of course, we'll allow this."

When the wedding banquet was about to begin, the three women entered in bizarre costumes, and the bride said, "Welcome, dear cousins."

"Ahhh!" said the bridegroom. "How did you ever become related to such ghastly-looking creatures!"

Then he went over to the one with a broad flat foot and asked, "How did you get such a flat foot?"

"From treading," she answered. "From treading."

Next the bridegroom went to the second and asked, "How did you get such a drooping lip?"

"From licking," she answered. "From licking."

Then he asked the third one, "How did you get such an immense thumb?"

"From twisting thread," she answered. "From twisting thread."

Upon hearing this, the prince was alarmed and said, "Never ever

shall my beautiful wife touch a spinning wheel again."
Thus she was able to rid herself of the terrible task of spinning flax.

All three versions—and there are many more, especially in the *Tom-Tit-Tot* tradition in Great Britain—lend themselves to creative dramatics, and the children tend to focus dramatically on the banishment of the evil creature from the young girl's life so that she can have a better fortune or destiny. The tale can also raise other questions. For instance, Rumpelstiltskin is an intriguing figure because he is not simply a blackmailer; he is also a helper. As "helper," he is an ambivalent figure, for we are not sure why he wants the queen's first born. Is he lonely? Where did he get his magic powers? Why is he so small? Why are small characters often portrayed as evil or malicious? In one tale that I tell, I suggest that the queen, who has been mistreated by the king, proposes to Rumpelstiltskin that they go off together, provided that Rumpelstiltskin help look after her child. Since Rumpelstiltskin has strong paternal feelings and has always wanted to care for a baby, he accepts, and they go off together into the woods. But the questions about blackmail and help remain ambiguous even here.

It is not my purpose, however, to answer the questions or totally resolve the dilemma of either the miller's daughter or Rumpelstiltskin. Rather, I try to make the questions themselves clearer through my telling and through the dramatization of the tales with the children. Then, in the card games that I introduce after the improvisation of the different *Rumpelstiltskin* versions, the children learn about the narrative functions within the tale and how to mix and control these functions. The children can then tell their stories in a sequential order of their own and raise whatever questions they may have about the classical or contemporary versions. Here I want to introduce the two games that I use: one is a general explanation of the card game, and the other is more specifically related to *Rumpelstiltskin* and can serve as a model for working with particular tales.

In Vladimir Propp's formalist study *The Morphology of the Folktale*, he outlines how the narrative of the wonder tale is carried by thirty-seven functions given to various characters, creatures, and objects in the course of the story. A function for Propp is a basic and constant element of the plot, a requisite action by a character, that enables the story to proceed step by step to its conclusion. This conclusion is generally a happy resolution for the protagonist. Not every wonder story that involves magical helpers and miraculous transformations has all these functions, and some may even have more. Even if they have been omitted, or if the tale has been amplified, one can still see the basic scheme of the functions. Here is a short summary of the functions.

1. The protagonist is confronted with an interdiction or prohibition, that she or he has violated in some way. Generally speaking, there is a conflict or crisis within the family, and the end result is a departure and/or mission.
2. Departing or banished, the protagonist has either been given or assumes a task related to the interdiction, prohibition, or crisis. The task is *assigned*, and it is a *sign*. That is, the protagonist's character will be marked by the task that is his or her sign.
3. There is an encounter with: (a) a villain; (b) a mysterious individual or creature who gives the protagonist magical gifts; (c) three different animals or creatures who offer magical gifts to help the protagonist, who is in trouble. These gifts endow the protagonist with the power to change his or her situation.
4. The endowed protagonist is tested and moves on to battle and conquer the villain, hostile forces, or natural catastrophes.
5. There is a peripety or sudden fall in the protagonist's fortunes, which is only a temporary setback. A wonder or miracle is needed to reverse the wheel of fortune.
6. The protagonist makes use of endowed gifts (and this includes the magical agents and cunning) to achieve his or her goal. The result is: (a) three battles with the villain; (b) three impossible tasks that are nevertheless made possible to be fulfilled; or (c) the breaking of a magic spell.
7. The villain is punished or the hostile forces are vanquished. The protagonist proves he or himself to be a survivor.
8. The success of the protagonist usually leads to: (a) marriage; (b) the acquisition of money; (c) survival and wisdom; (d) any combination of the first three.

This narrative frame fits most wonder folk tales (*Zaubermärchen*) and literary fairy tales in some way, but instead of writing this summary on the blackboard, I write the following functions and motifs.

1.   birth
2.   the banished hero
3.   the troubled heroine
4.   the mean or helpless father
5.   the mean or helpless mother
6.   escape into the forest
7.   meeting with a giant
8.   meeting with a rabbit
9.   meeting with a bird
10. meeting with a fish
11. meeting with a witch
12. meeting with a wizard
13. the magic cape
14. the magic carpet
15. the magic sword
16. the magic horse
17. the magic lamp
18. the magic wand
19. the battle with the giant
20. the battle with the witch
21. the battle with the evil king
22. the battle with the evil queen
23. the kidnapping of the hero
24. the kidnapping of the heroine
25. the magic kingdom
26. the enchanted forest
27. the terrifying mountain
28. the rescue of the hero
29. the rescue of the heroine
30. survival
31. the marriage
32. the discovery of a great treasure
33. the sharing of the treasure
34. the voyage to a new country
35. the celebration party

After I write this list on the board, I discuss the different "functions" and motifs with the children, and I ask them if they want to add any more that I may have forgotten. Once we have a complete list, I distribute large, five-by-eight-inch cards to the children, and each one is assigned one of the functions on the board. The child is to print the function at the bottom of the card, as if it were a playing card, and to illustrate what the function means to him or her. I ask the children to use their imagination and to draw whatever comes into their heads. Once the children are finished drawing an illustration, the cards are collected and, depending on the number of children and the conditions in the classroom, we organize various writing games around the cards:

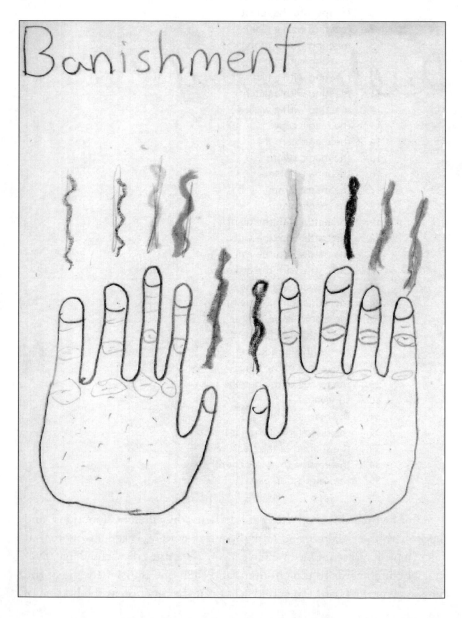

1. If there are approximately twenty-four children in the class, I divide them into four groups. Then I mix the cards and divide them into four groups. The cards are then placed on a table in front of the children without a specific chronological or thematic order. Each one of the children is free to compose a story based on the ordering of the five or six cards that are placed before him or her.

2. The class is divided into four groups. The cards are mixed. Each group has five or six cards, and they form a writing group. Together they are to decide how they want to order their cards to form a story. Then, on the basis of the ordering, they are to write a collective story. At the end of fifteen minutes, whether finished or not, they reveal their cards to the other groups and read their story.

3. I mix the cards before the class, and then I redistribute the cards to the children. On the basis of one card, each child is to tell a story that highlights the picture and topic of her or his card. They are encouraged to use the other functions that they see on the board, but they must begin their story with the card that they receive.

The general card game can be made more specific by taking the tale type of the day and listing the functions of the characters on the board with the help of the children. Here I ask them to describe the characters and their functions in the story, and in the case of *Rumpelstiltskin*, the result often turns out like this:

1. boasting father
2. powerful king
3. scared miller's daughter
4. castle
5. locked room
6. spinning wheel
7. crying helpless daughter
8. mysterious little creature
9. gift of necklace
10. gold
11. greedy king
12. gift of ring
13. the forced promise of the first child
14. marriage of miller's daughter and king

15. birth of baby
16. reappearance of mysterious figure
17. the messenger hunts for names
18. first day of name guessing
19. servants hunt for names
20. second day of name guessing
21. last messenger
22. the edge of the forest
23. little man dancing around a fire
24. the final day of name guessing
25. the destruction of the mysterious man
26. the saved queen and child

After writing the functions on the board, I distribute the cards and assign functions to each of the children. If there are more children than functions, I repeat the functions. Then they are asked to print their function and illustrate it. As in the general game, I collect the cards, mix them, and redistribute them either to groups or to the individual children, depending on the game we are playing.

Another card game can be played with *Rapunzel*, which is similar in some ways to *Rumpelstiltskin* because it deals with the abuse of a young child. In *Rapunzel*, a witch is successful in obtaining a baby girl, whom she locks up in a tower. When the girl becomes a young woman and disobeys the witch by letting her hair down to a prince, she is punished by banishment and the prince's eyes are poked out. Years later Rapunzel's tears miraculously restore the prince's sight, and they are happily reunited.

Of course, this story can be told in a much different way as I have shown by retelling an Italian tale, which I have taken from Thomas Crane's *Italian Popular Tales*:

Angiola

Once upon a time there were seven pregnant women, all good neighbors, who suddenly developed a great longing for some jujubes. Unfortunately, the jujubes grew in only one garden which was the largest in town and owned by a witch. Now, this witch had a nasty donkey that watched the garden, and informed the old witch whenever anyone tried to enter. The seven neighbors, however, had such a great yearning for the jujubes that they decided to bribe the donkey with some nice soft grass, rosy red apples, and mint juleps. While he devoured the delicious meal, they filled their aprons with jujubes and escaped before the witch appeared.

The neighbors did this several times until, at last, the witch noticed that someone had been in her garden, for many of the jujubes were gone. She questioned the donkey, but he pretended not to have noticed anything because he did not want to get into trouble for accepting the women's bribe. But the witch was suspicious and decided to hide in a hole right in the middle of the garden where she covered herself with leaves and branches, leaving only one of her long ears sticking out.

Once again the seven neighbors went into the garden and began picking the jujubes, when one of them noticed the witch's ear sticking out of the leaves. She thought it was a mushroom and tried to pick it. Then the screaming witch jumped out of the hole and ran after the women, all of whom escaped except one. The witch was going to eat her, but the poor woman begged hard for pardon and promised never to enter the garden again.

"Please," she said. "I'm still young, and as you can see, I'm pregnant. If you must kill me, then please wait until I give birth so that my child can have a future."

Finally, the witch forgave her on the condition that she would give up her child, yet unborn, whether boy or girl, when it was seven years old. In her distress, the woman promised to do as she said, and the witch let her go.

Some time later the woman had a beautiful little girl whom she named Angiola. When Angiola was six years old, her mother sent her to school to learn to sew and knit and read and write. On her way to school she had to pass the garden where the witch lived. One day, when she was almost seven, she saw the witch standing in front of her garden, and the woman called to Angiola and gave her some fine fruit.

"You see, dear Angiola," the witch said. "I'm your aunt. Tell your mother you have seen your aunt, who wants her to remember her promise."

Angiola went home and told her mother what had happened, and her mother was frightened. "Ah!" she said to herself. "The time has come when I must give up my Angiola!" Then she said to her daughter, "When your aunt asks you tomorrow for an answer, tell her you forgot your errand."

The next day Angiola did as she was told, and the witch replied, "Very well, but make sure that you tell your mother today that I expect her to keep her promise, and don't forget."

Several days passed. The witch was constantly on the watch for Angiola when she went to school, and kept asking for her mother's answer, but Angiola always responded that she had forgotten to ask her. One day, however, the witch became angry and said, "Since you're so forgetful, I must give you some token to remind you of your errand." Then she bit Angiola's little finger so hard that it began to bleed and left a mark. Angiola went home in tears and showed her mother the sore finger.

"Ah!" thought her mother. "There's nothing I can do. I must give my poor child to the witch or else she will eat us both in her anger."

The next morning, as Angiola was going to school, her mother had tears in her eyes said to her, "Tell your aunt to do with you as she thinks best."

Though sad, Angiola followed her mother's instructions, and the witch said, "Very good. Now come with me, for you are mine."

So, the witch took Angiola away with her to a tower outside the town that had no door and only one small window. It was there that Angiola began living with the witch who, much to Angiola's surprise, treated her very kindly, for she loved her as her own child. When the witch came home after her outings, she stood under the window and cried, "Angiola, dear Angiola, let down your hair and pull me up!"

Since Angiola had beautiful long black hair, she let it down and used it to pull the witch up into the tower. And she continued doing this many years until she grew to be a lovely young woman.

Now, one day a young prince who had been hunting in the forest chanced to come upon the spot where the tower was. He was astonished at finding a house without doors and wondered how people got in and out. So, he hid in some bushes to see if he could discover how people managed to enter and leave. Soon the witch returned home, stood under the window, and called, "Angiola, dear Angiola, let your hair down and pull me up."

Immediately the beautiful long hair fell down, and the witch climbed up the tower. The prince was pleased by what he saw, and he remained in hiding until the witch went away again. Then he went and stood under the window and called in a disguised voice, "Angiola, dear Angiola, let your hair down and pull me up."

Then Angiola let her hair down and pulled the prince up, for she believed it was the witch. When she saw him, she was frightened at first, but he spoke to her in a friendly manner and begged her to flee with him and become his wife.

"You have the kindest face I have ever seen. I myself am not particularly handsome, but I have a heart," he said, "and from the moment I saw you, my heart went out to you."

After listening to his sweet words, she finally consented and got ready for the journey to the prince's kingdom. In order to prevent the witch from knowing where she had gone, she gave all the chairs, tables, and cupboards in the house something to eat, for they were all living creatures and might betray her. However, the broom stood behind the door, so she did not notice it and gave it nothing to eat. Then she took three magic balls of yarn from the witch's room and showed the prince a secret opening in the tower, through which they fled. And they were followed by Muffy, a little dog, who loved Angiola so dearly that she could not bear to be without her.

Soon after they left, the witch came back and called, "Angiola, dear Angiola, let your hair down, and pull me up." But the hair did not appear, no matter how much the witch called, and since she did not know about the secret opening, she finally had to get a long ladder and climb in the window. When she could not find Angiola, she asked the tables, chairs, and cupboards, "Where has Angiola gone?"

"We don't know," they responded.

However, the broom called out from the corner, "Angiola has fled with the king's son who is going to marry her."

Then the witch grabbed hold of her magic broom and started in pursuit. Riding faster than the wind, she was about to catch them when Angiola threw down one of the magic balls of yarn, and a great mountain of soap sprang from the ground. When the witch tried to climb it, she slipped back, and the broom could no longer help her. Never one to give up, she used all her magic and kept trying until she at last succeeded in scaling the mountain, and she sped after the two young lovers. Just as the witch came close again, Angiola threw down the second ball of yarn and another great mountain arose, covered all over with large and small nails. Once more the witch had to struggle hard to cross it. When she did, she was almost exhausted, and her feet were bloody. But she kept going and soon caught up to Angiola and the prince. This time Angiola threw down the third ball, and a large river emerged from the ground. The witch tried to swim across it, but the river was deep and wild and kept increasing in size until she had to turn back. Then, in her anger, she yelled, "May your kind face be turned into the miserable face of a dog!"

The witch's curse was powerful, and within seconds, poor Angiola's face turned into the face of a dog.

The prince was dismayed by this and said, "How can I take you home to my parents? They would never allow me to marry a woman with a dog's face."

"You must leave me," she said, "leave me and forget me."

"Trust me," he said. "I'll never abandon you."

So he took her to a little cottage where she was to live until the magic spell was broken. He himself returned to his parents' castle, but whenever he went hunting, he visited Angiola and comforted her. Together they explored the forest and cultivated a garden filled with jujubes. Seven years went by, and she often wept bitterly over her misfortune until one day her little dog Muffy, who had followed her from the witch's tower said, "Do not weep, dear Angiola. I'll go to the witch and beg her to remove the spell."

Then the little dog started off, and when she arrived at the witch's house, she sprang onto her lap and looked at her with sorrowful but tender eyes.

"Are you here again, you traitor?" cried the witch, pushing the dog away. "You left me to follow the ungrateful Angiola. You're two of a kind!"

But the little dog kept licking her and wagging its tail until she grew friendly again and let it stay on her lap.

"Mother," said the little dog, "Angiola sends you her regards. She is very sad, for she cannot go to the palace with a dog's face, nor can she marry the prince."

"That serves her right," said the witch. "Why did she deceive me? She can keep her dog's face now!"

But little Muffy kept begging and told the witch that Angiola was tormented and had been sufficiently punished. Finally, the little creature convinced the witch, who gave her a flask of water and said, "Take this flask to her. Tell her to wash her face with the water and use every drop, and she'll become the dear Angiola that we once all loved."

The dog thanked her, ran off with the flask, and brought it safely to Angiola. As soon as Angiola washed her face in the water, her dog-features disappeared, and her face became kind again, more kind than it had been before. The prince, full of joy, took her to the palace, and the king and queen were so pleased by her kind and gentle appearance that they welcomed her. Soon after, there was a splendid wedding.

As for the little dog, she was appointed royal messenger and was the first to tell the witch when Angiola had twins. So happy was the witch about this event that she flew to the castle and became the first witch ever to transform herself into a fairy godmother, and it was this good woman who protected Angiola and her twins for the rest of their lives.

This version reveals how all the roles in a story can be transformed, especially the role of the witch, and the focus is also shifted away from abuse to compassion. Nevertheless, the card game should be based on the traditional *Rapunzel* tale because the changes of the functions should depend on the children. They are to play with the following functions:

1. Pregnant mother
2. Nurturing father
3. Forbidden garden
4. Theft of lettuce
5. Angry witch
6. Delivery of baby to witch
7. Rapunzel grows to be beautiful by thirteen
8. Rapunzel locked in tower without doors in forest
9. Rapunzel's long hair as ladder for witch
10. Rapunzel sings
11. Prince discovers the tower and Rapunzel
12. Prince climbs tower
13. Prince proposes to Rapunzel
14. Witch discovers Prince's visits

15.   Witch cuts Rapunzel's hair
16.   Witch banishes Rapunzel to desolate land
17.   Witch tricks prince
18.   Prince jumps off tower
19.   Prince loses sight
20.   Prince wanders
21.   Rapunzel lives in desolate spot with twins
22.   Prince recognizes Rapunzel's voice
23.   Rapunzel recognizes prince
24.   Rapunzel's tears restore sight to prince
25.   Return to prince's kingdom

No matter what tale is used by the storyteller, the card games enable the children to learn about motifs, characters, topoi, and other components of a story without seeming to be a grammatical lesson. The focus on one element helps them realize how dependent one function is on another and what the relationship is between the functions. Their drawings of different functions may also make them aware of how they depend on the work of the other children in the class. The very act of drawing a scene leads the child to concentrate on the specifics of a function and where it fits into the story.

When I form groups to write a group story, the intention is obviously to bring about cooperation and the sharing of experiences. However, there is always a danger that one or two children in a group will take over and dictate or try to dictate the new story. There are already groups of friends who will try to stick together. I try not to interfere in the group dynamics, unless there is a major argument. Here is where cooperation with the teacher is very important, for he or she can help arrange the groups so that they are balanced and friction is kept to a minimum. If a group has trouble getting started, I will work with the children and suggest ideas, as will the teacher, who can later incorporate some of the concepts and terms related to the functions into lessons of composition. The children can also be encouraged to produce a set of their own cards at home based on their favorite story. It is not necessary to use cards all the time, but children like to collect sports cards, movie star cards, postcards, etc., and they swap the cards. If they can produce their own cards with their favorite fairy-tale heroes, they can also swap these cards and write stories about the cards they exchange. This game is similar to the salad game, except here the children produce two or three cards at home, come back to school the next day, and then swap with the other students. Each child must use the characters from his or her cards in a story.

Stories evoke images in our minds. They stir us. Particular scenes reoccur and seem to play a role in our lives. Children will latch onto a particular story early in their lives, try to make it their own story for a certain period, and perhaps keep coming back to it. Cards are one way to help them record their images, sort them out, arrange, and rearrange, just as they will keep trying to do for the remainder of their lives.

§ 4 §

In Celebration of Peace

Soldiers, Strong Men, and Knights

Until the third session, most of the classical fairy tales that I tell focus on young women as passive objects of male desire. The male heroes all arrive toward the end of the story to save the girl, and their function is clearly that of savior or rescuer. In most traditional fairy tales, the males are the adventurers, the wanderers, and the fighters. They represent either the active movers of the plot, or the "executioners" of the plot who arrive at the end to make everything right. That is, they finish everything cleanly, often with the cut of a blade. They will stop at nothing to become powerful, rich, and famous, and they like to win a young woman as reward for their diligence, perseverance, and ability to kill dragons, witches, dangerous opponents, and competitors. This is not to say that all classical fairy and folk tales depict the valiant male hero in this way, as Angela Carter has shown in her important collection *The Old Wives' Fairy Tale Book* and Ethel Johnston Phelps in her two significant anthologies, *Tatterhood and Other Tales* and *The Maid of the North*, but an overwhelming number of fairy tales celebrate the raw power of men, the notion that might makes right in the interests of patriarchy.

There are also a number of interesting tales about soldiers or knights who loyally serve a king and are discharged at the end of their service without being rewarded in an appropriate manner. They risk their lives for their country and leaders, only to learn that they have been exploited and abandoned by their kings. Often these soldiers seek revenge or some sort of just compensation. In reality, as we know, the common soldier rarely sees dreams of justice fulfilled. Historically, common soldiers have always been exploited and treated like dirt. War is hell for the majority of soldiers, no matter who is right or wrong. They always lose in the end as they serve their leaders, desk-bound administrators, and businessmen. However, in many of these fairy tales about war and battles, the common soldiers have their dreams come true. Undoubtedly, the tales are the result of deep disappointment and wish-fulfillment. At the same time, there are also stories about the glory of war and struggle. And here we must always ask, Whose perspective was it? What will be our perspective?

Fairy tales celebrate all kinds of heroism. Ultimately, they celebrate the capacity of people from all walks of life to survive disaster and change their lives so that they can become masters or mistresses of their destiny. This is the utopian *gestus* of most fairy tales, but we often overlook how many of the traditional fairy tales stimulate violent action and legitimize aggressive behavior. We overlook the fact that war and battle are common in fairy tales, as if they were natural and could never go away. Commonly, to be a man, a real man, the fairy-tale hero must prove that he can compete and win the battle, that he can be number one, that he can triumph, and that he can kill if required.

But does the male have to kill? Does the male have to take part in wars and battles? Does the male have to compete against his brothers or against friends to become the new king? These are some of the questions that I raise in my fourth session of storytelling, taking into consideration the sensibilities of the young boys, who all want to be successful and are willing to fight at the drop of a hat to prove that they are not girls, that they are not afraid of anything or anybody. After all, they have "wonderful" role models like Rambo, Rocky, Hulk Hogan, Mr. T, Robocop, the Ninja Turtles, the Power Rangers, and even the second-grader in *Home Alone,* who is as brutal as they come.

But I do not want to raise the issue of violence and brutality in this session as much as I want to point toward peace by telling different fairy tales that deal with war, conflict, valor, and manliness. For this purpose I often use two classical fairy tales as a starting point: *The King of the Golden Mountain* and *The Blue Light.* In *The King of the Golden Mountain* a young man, the son of a merchant, shows through various tests how valiant he is and becomes king of the golden mountain. However, his kingdom is stolen from him by an unfaithful wife, and after he struggles to regain it, he has his magic sword chop off the heads of all his subjects who were disloyal to him, including his wife. In *The Blue Light*, which Hans Christian Andersen used as the model for *The Tinderbox*—and it is possible to use Andersen's tale here as well—a discharged soldier steals a magical light from a witch, and this light brings forth a black dwarf who, like a genie, can perform anything he wishes. Eventually, the soldier uses the dwarf, who beats everyone in sight, to help him take revenge on the king who discharged him. Both tales are rich in meaning and focus on the motifs of justice and revenge. My concern is that both tales imply that the highest goal in life for a male is to become an all-powerful king, and that violent means justify their ends.

To make my point even clearer, I sometimes tell the following tale, which I have composed from various motifs in other heroic tales.

The Iron Knight

Hundreds of years ago, when many kings sent their knights on holy crusades, there was a young couple who had just had their first child and were celebrating the birth when the knight was summoned to the castle by the king.

"You must lead my army to the holy land," the king said, "and make true believers out of the Saracens."

"But your highness, we have just had a son," the knight said.

"What is more important to you, your son or your king?"

"Sire, you know that I am loyal to you," the knight replied, "and I shall always serve the kingdom."

"Well, then you will lead the army," the king demanded.

"But sire, why must we conquer the holy land, which is thousands of miles away? Why can't we leave the Saracens in peace?"

"I see that marriage has made you soft, my son," the king said. "It is our duty to defend our religion, to show all people that the only true way to God is ours! Will you not go, or must I send Sir Albert to lead my forces?"

The knight sadly nodded and agreed to go, and when he returned to his wife, he told her the news and promised her that he would return within three years. As she sobbed, he said, "Take care of little Rob," for that was the name of their son. "And if anything should happen to me, make sure that you keep him far from the king's court. I fear that our king will use me and all his knights to satisfy his own glory."

The next day the knight left and led an army of five hundred brave men to the holy land, and for the next three years, messengers brought news to the king that his forces had slain thousands of Saracens and taken three of the major fortresses in the holy land. It seemed that nothing could stop the valiant knight, who fought in the name of his king and country. But one day, toward the end of the third year, a messenger returned from the holy land and reported to the king that the knight and his army of five hundred had been massacred, and not a soul had survived.

"Those savages!" the king exclaimed. "I shall send more and more until we kill them all."

When the sad news reached the knight's wife, she did not weep, nor did she say a word when the king sent his condolences and offered to raise her son at his court. It seemed strange to the king that she did not thank him for his offer, and when he sent a messenger a second time, she was nowhere to be found. She had disappeared with her son. Nobody knew where she had gone.

During the next eighteen years, the knight's wife, Lady Amber, lived deep in the forest with her son and two servants. It was there that she raised young Rob, and she forbade her servants to talk about the king, about weapons, and about war. Rob was not allowed to hunt or fish. His mother taught him to cherish the lives of all the animals in the forest, and they cleared the land in front of their small cottage and grew vegetables and planted fruit trees. Rob learned how to ride horses, plow the land, and swim in the deep lakes. He learned reading and writing and played the guitar, and his mother was content. If anyone chanced upon their isolated dwelling in the forest, her servants would chase them away. She refused to hear news of the outer world. She was especially frightened of the king's knights, who might come and take her son off to war.

One day, when Rob had turned twenty-one, he went swimming in a lake at the edge of the forest, the only place that strangers dared to approach, for they thought the forest was enchanted. While Rob was swimming, three knights approached on horseback. He watched as they got off their horses, refreshed themselves, and let their horses drink from the lake. Their armor glistened in the sun, and their swords and lances sparkled. Rob got out of the lake and asked them who they were. They laughed at the tall, strong boy, who seemed so naive and innocent.

"Knights," they said. "We're the king's knights."

"What's a knight?" Rob asked.

The knights laughed again, for the boy was truly unaware of how important they were.

"The best and most glorious thing in the world!" they said. "We'll show you what we can do."

The knights got back on their horses, raised their lances, and began to duel with one another in a nearby clearing. They made sure not to hurt each other, and when they rode over to Rob, one of them said, "You have the makings of a knight. Perhaps you'll come to the king's court one day and join us."

And off they rode, leaving Rob to stare after them with envy. As he looked to the ground, he saw a mandrake root and remembered that it had magical powers. So, he pulled it from the ground and said aloud, "I wish, I wish with all my might that I could become a knight."

All of a sudden he heard a yell.

"Help! Help!"

In the middle of lake, a strange little man with a yellow beard was screaming for help. Rob rushed into the water and swam toward the man, who could barely keep afloat. What made his situation even worse was that a gigantic fish was pulling at his tiny feet.

"Help!" the little man cried. "I'm drowning."

Rob caught hold of him, pulled his feet away from the fish, and brought him ashore. When the little man dried himself off, he said to Rob, "You should be ashamed of yourself!"

"What?" Rob replied. "I saved your life."

"You did, and you didn't!"

"What do you mean?"

"I mean, you made a wish with a mandrake root, and you were too close to the lake for my own good. At any rate, I am obliged to honor your wish."

"You mean, it worked!" Rob became excited.

"I mean that I'm the yellow dwarf, and I have three things to give you, but you must never say a word about this to your mother."

Rob promised, and the yellow dwarf led him into a part of the woods that he never knew existed. After clearing the way through some bushes, the dwarf showed him a large dark cave and led him inside.

"There!" the dwarf pointed, as he lit a torch.

Against the wall was a large sword and a glittering white armor. And next to the sword and suit of armor was a huge golden stallion.

"You are to come here every day at sunset for the next three weeks, and I shall teach you what it means to be a knight," the dwarf said. "This sword is magical and will make your arm like steel, and you will be able to vanquish all your enemies. This armor will become part of you, and your body will be like iron. Nobody will ever be able to kill you. And this horse is like the sun. It will always rise and carry you wherever you want. Now, is this what you want? Do you truly want to become a knight?"

Rob's eyes glistened. "Yes, with all my might."

"Let me warn you," the dwarf said. "Once you start acting as a knight, you cannot stop. Once you promise a king your allegiance, you must serve him, or else you will die. So, you must never break your word to a king."

"I understand," Rob said solemnly.

For the next three weeks, Rob stole into the woods and learned how to become a knight. Though his mother noticed something strange about his behavior, she had no idea where he went and what he did at sunset every night. Finally, when three weeks had passed and Rob was dressed in his white armor and sitting on his golden horse, he heard some bugles in the distance.

"The time has come," the dwarf told Rob. "You must take your leave and go to the king's court. Do not say farewell to your mother. Do not look behind."

Rob wanted to see his mother one more time, but the dwarf slapped the back of the horse, and off Rob went. When he arrived at the king's court, the people were amazed at the handsome knight, and when Rob approached the king, he dismounted and announced, "I have come to serve you, your highness. I am the Iron Knight."

"For years I have been fighting my holy wars," the king said. "But my forces have been dwindling. Try as we might, we cannot defeat the Saracens."

"You will, your majesty. I can assure you," said Rob.

"Iron Knight, if you succeed, you will have my daughter Miranda as your wife," the king said, and he pointed to a lovely young woman dressed in a long white gown.

Rob's heart was touched, and he felt more than ever how glorious it was to be a knight.

"I pledge my allegiance, sire," Rob said. "Give me three years, and I shall return."

"Three years," the king said. "And you shall have Miranda and half my kingdom."

With an army of five hundred, just as his father had many years ago, Rob rode off to the holy land. When the knights began the battle with the Saracens, Rob was everywhere to be seen, slashing, cutting, piercing, trampling. His steel sword was like a machine that riddled the bodies of his enemies. Blood splattered on his white armor, but nothing could penetrate it. His golden horse carried him into the thick of the battle, and like fire, it blazed a way through the enemy forces. Soon Rob was no longer called the Iron Knight by the saracens, but the Holy Terror. No one and nobody could slay him, even though the knights in his own army died. Days turned into weeks, weeks into months, months into years. The Iron Knight killed thousands of Saracens, and even if they surrendered, he slew them. To his horror he could not stop his arm and sword from killing. His own men became afraid of him and ran away. His armor became caked with blood, and each night when the sun set, and he had to rest, he resolved to make peace with the Saracens the next day and stop his arm from killing. But when the sun rose, he began riding his golden horse and slaying anyone who came near him.

When three years had ended, Rob returned from the holy land and announced to the king that the Saracens had fled to some other country, that the holy land was theirs, and that he wanted to marry Miranda and live in peace.

The king smiled at him and said, "Marry Miranda you will, but I want you to return to the holy land and push on. There are other lands to conquer, and we must spread our light to the savages. We must civilize them!"

Rob looked at the king with horror.

"No!" Rob said. "I can't go on killing."

"You must!" the king demanded. "You gave me your allegiance."

Rob looked at the king closely, and for the first time, he realized that the king's yellow beard and his eyes resembled those of the yellow dwarf. For a moment he thought he saw the dwarf sitting before him on the throne.

"You must!" the king demanded. "Either you kill, or you die. I shall give you one night to think about it."

After the king spoke those words, he disappeared and Rob was left alone. Suddenly he thought about his mother and the forest. He thought how peaceful his life had been until he had met those knights. He thought about the three years of killing. He thought about what it meant to be a knight.

At this point I stop the story, and of course, there are question marks on the faces of the children. They want to know what Rob did. What happened to him? In response, I ask the children to tell me what choice they think he made and why. We discuss the knight's dilemma, and I encourage them to finish the story for me with all sorts of possible endings. Sometimes we stay with this tale, and the children write out and illustrate their endings. But I also ask them whether they know what a knight is and when knights lived and fought. I ask, Why? What is the difference between a good knight and a bad knight? I ask about other knights like Lancelot or Gawain, and if they know them, I ask them to tell me a story or write a story about these knights. The entire session can turn into storytelling about knights with the children providing a good deal of the material. In turn, this can lead to interesting follow-ups for the teacher with regard to the history of knights.

For instance, in one program the teacher developed a cluster or set of lessons around the Knights of the Round Table, and she brought in an adaptation of Mallory's *Knights of the Round Table* and read it to them. Afterward, she explained the history of King Arthur and the Holy Grail and discussed other famous characters such as Merlin, Guenivere, Lancelot, Percival, etc. After telling stories about how the different characters functioned in relation to the Round Table and the Holy Grail, she asked the children to retell one of her stories and then create their own knight story. Then she asked what the role of the queen was. What roles did the ladies play? Why couldn't they be knights? Could they possibly be heroines? Here she introduced the story of Jean D'Arc by reading an adaptation for young children. Once again, toward the end of the week, she asked the children to retell her story or invent their own with a woman as knight.

Clearly, there are numerous follow-ups that a teacher can develop, depending on what she or he wants to emphasize. In my own storytelling session, I divide the children into three groups and ask them to act out *The Iron Knight*. First, however they must sit down and think up their own ending. Since I have more or less "animated" the children to think about a peaceful ending, their skits tend to be peaceful, but it is difficult to predict what the children will invent, and here the No-Touching Rule is important. In some cases, they may want to kill the king and introduce violence, imitating what they have seen on TV. After each group performs its play, I generally ask why they chose their ending and discuss why they chose a violent ending if they did so. In some sessions, I do not use dramatization but divide the children into groups, where they write and recite their endings. Afterward I ask them to draw some scenes from their stories.

In other sessions that I have developed about peace, I tell two other tales and work with "What If" games. In each session, I tell one or two classical fairy tales that "celebrate" war and male aggression before telling an unusual tale that I hope will raise the children's consciousness of the causes of violence and war. I use two excellent tales for this purpose, and many more can be found in two fine collections: *Weaving Words, Spinning Hope: A Collection of Stories and Teacher Activities to Help Children Explore Issues of Peace, Justice, and Social Awareness*, compiled by Storytellers for World Change Network, and *Peace Tales* by Margaret Read MacDonald. Both of my tales have been adapted from literary and folk sources. The first is based on the Danish writer Carl Ewald's *The Fairy Tale about God and Kings*, and I recite it in this fashion:

For hundreds of years the kings of the world fought wars against one another, but while the kings and their families lived on and prospered, their people died in these battles. They died in the hundreds, the thousands, and the millions, and the wars kept occurring, until finally, the people in many different countries elected deputies and sent them to God to ask for help against the kings. They no longer wanted war and did not know how to stop the bloodshed.

When the deputies arrived at the gates of heaven, they were greeted by one of the archangels and led to a great hall, for there were seven hundred deputies. Soon, God appeared, and the speaker of the deputies stood up and told God all about the perpetual wars and asked God to stop the kings from causing bloodshed. When he finished, everyone in the hall waited to hear what God would say, but God looked at them and shook his head. "I don't understand why you are complaining," God answered. "I never gave you kings."

All of a sudden, the deputies in the hall started shouting and yelling in confusion. They did not understand what he meant by this, and they cried out that the world was full of kings, all of whom insisted that they ruled with God's blessings.

Then God raised his voice, and there was silence.

"I don't know what you are talking about!" he gave the deputies a severe look. "I created you all equal. I may have given you different colors and forms, but I created you all equal! Now I bid you farewell!"

The deputies were stunned. They sat in silence until the archangel came and led them out of the hall and back through the gates of heaven, where they sat down and began weeping. When God heard about this, he took pity on them and invited them into the large hall again. Then he summoned an angel and said, "Fetch the book in which I listed all the troubles that human beings were to have if they sinned, and check to see whether I wrote something about kings there."

The book was very large, so large that the angel needed an entire day to finish his work. In the meantime, the deputies waited patiently and hoped that God would see how things were. In the evening, when the angel had finished, he reported to the Lord that he had found nothing, and God turned to the deputies and stated. "I don't know a thing about kings. Good-bye."

But the poor deputies, who had been sitting the entire day, began to weep and lament, and they looked so desperate that God took pity on them once more. And again he summoned the angel and said to him, "Get the books in which I've recorded everything that human beings must suffer for their foolish prayers so that they might learn that my teachings are wiser than theirs. Check to see whether I wrote anything about kings there."

And the angel did has he was commanded, but since he had

twelve thick books to read, it took him two weeks to finish the work. In the meantime, the deputies were given rooms in the heavenly hotel, and each day they waited impatiently for God to appear and tell them that he would help them. Finally, the angel reported to God that he had found nothing, and God asked the deputies to assemble in the large hall.

"There's nothing I can do for you," he told them. "I have searched my soul and checked all my writings, but kings are evidently your own invention, and if you are tired of them and their wars, then you must seek your own solution!"

Upon saying this, God dismissed the deputies for the last and final time.

This tale also leads to many questions about the responsibility for war and peace that lend themselves to "What If" games, but before I discuss these possibilities, I want to present the other tale that I tell on different occasions. It is a version of a Japanese folk tale entitled *The Three Strong Women*, and I first told it in Milwaukee when a teacher confided that she was having trouble with some of the boys, who were picking on the girls or being disruptive. She felt that I might have some effect on their behavior because they rarely saw a male teacher in elementary school, so I was a kind of a role model. After I told the tale, the boys were somewhat stunned, and there was a change in their behavior that day, although of course it takes more than one day and one tale to bring about real change. On other occasions, this tale has prompted a debate between the boys and the girls over which gender was superior. Though the children became somewhat vociferous and began teasing one another, they were also compelled through the Japanese tale to realize that fairy tales are not always about strong men who like fighting and winning women as rewards. In my version of *The Three Strong Women*, I sometimes change the setting and characters using different countries and people. I have used Native Americans, Russians, Africans, etc. Though fairy tales may reveal racist or sexist tendencies, many are color-blind, and they can be used to appeal to all ethnic groups.

Here is my version of *The Three Strong Women*.

The Three Strong Women

Hundreds of years ago, the Great Emperor of Japan held a wrestling tournament once a year, and the strongest and fiercest wrestlers arrived to compete for a huge pot of gold. The wrestlers were gigantic, and they often broke each other's bones. Some were tossed out of the ring and died from the fall. Some were trampled and suffocated. The more brutal and exciting the fights were, the more the Emperor liked them. And each year he looked forward to his tournament, which lasted one week. At the end, despite the fact that many wrestlers lost their lives or were crippled for life, the Emperor was happy to crown a champion, and the champion was happy because he would have enough gold to last him the rest of his life. The champion never thought about the wrestlers he killed.

One year, Big Bear, a champion wrestler from a small island off the coast of Japan, decided to enter the tournament, and he left his home to travel to the mainland. When he arrived, he had two months to practice for the tournament, and he decided to go up into the mountains to train for the contest. When he went into the woods and began to climb a mountain, Big Bear noticed a young woman carrying a large pitcher of water on her head that she held steady with one hand. Since Big Bear was a fun-loving guy who liked to play jokes, he thought he would sneak up behind the young woman and tickle her under the arm so that the pitcher would fall. So he crept up behind the woman as quietly as he could, stretched out his hand, and said,

"Kitchey koo! Kitchey koo!"

However, to his great surprise, the young woman brought down her elbow and squeezed his hand until it was stuck in her armpit, and she reached up with her other hand to hold the pitcher in place. Her elbow and arm were like a vice, and Big Bear could not free his hand as the young woman kept walking and dragging him along with her.

"Stop!" Big Bear yelled. "I don't want to hurt you."

But the young woman kept walking up the mountain, dragging Big Bear along. Try as he might, he could not free himself.

"I'm warning you," he shouted. "I don't want to use all my strength. You could really get hurt!"

The young woman kept walking with Big Bear talking. He yanked and yanked, but his hand remained trapped.

"It was just a joke," Big Bear said, trying to humor her. "I really didn't mean anything by it. Can't you take a joke?"

The young woman kept walking with Big Bear talking, and he talked his way to the top of the mountain, where the young woman finally released his hand.

"White Lily," a voice called out to the young woman from the inside of a cabin, "is that you?"

"It is me, mother, and I have brought a guest."

Just then, a woman came out of the house carrying a stove and bathtub piled on top of one another above her head. Big Bear was amazed, and he gasped as he watched the woman carefully put the stove and bathtub down on the porch. She waved to him and said, "Just doing some spring cleaning," as she disappeared back into the cabin.

All of a sudden, Big Bear heard another voice coming from over a hill. "White Lily, is that you?"

"It is me, grandmother, and I have brought a guest."

Much to Big Bear's astonishment, a tiny old woman appeared on the ridge of the hill carrying a cow in her arms. As she descended the hill, he heard the grandmother say, "The poor darling hurt its leg, and I've decided to nurse it in the shed next to the cabin."

The grandmother waved at White Lily and walked past her and Big Bear on her way to the shed.

"What's going on here?" Big Bear said.

"What do you mean?" White Lily replied

"I mean, how come you're all so strong?"

"It runs in the family," White Lily explained. "You see, we love the mountain air up here. It calms us and gives us strength."

"But where are the men?"

"Dead. The Emperor needed soldiers, and they were forced to fight in his wars. They lost their lives, and ever since then we have lived alone. But we are not afraid. We've learned to exercise and become strong. We've watched the animals and birds, and tonight we'll show you what else we can do."

Later that evening, as the sun began to set, the three women began to dance in a clearing as Big Bear watched. Then suddenly they began to wrestle with each other and toss each other high into the air. Sometimes they caught each other. Sometimes they did triple and quadruple flips. One time the grandmother flew fifty yards through the air, and White Lily caught her and gently set her down. Another time, the mother jumped back and forth over the cabin. Their wrestling was like a dream dance, and Big Bear could not believe what he was seeing.

The next morning, Big Bear went to White Lily and asked, "Will you teach me how to wrestle? Will you teach me how to become strong?"

White Lily looked at him, and Big Bear pleaded, "I want to win the Emperor's tournament."

"All right, but you will have to help us around the farm. We will begin lessons with grandmother, for she is the most tender among us and will not hurt you."

For the next two months, Big Bear helped the women on the farm and watched them carefully. He breathed the mountain air and took walks in the woods. And each night he learned the gentle art of wrestling and how he could use his power in extraordinary ways to defend himself without destroying his opponent. Wrestling became a dance of harmony. He found himself wanting to use his power in harmony with the three women.

When the time came for Big Bear to leave the mountain, he was sad, and yet he had dreamed of winning the Emperor's tournament. So, he departed, and after arriving at the Emperor's castle, he was immediately called upon to fight. As he entered the ring, the crowd laughed at him because Big Bear was dressed in simple brown shorts and was not as fat and ferocious as all the other wrestlers. But when the first match began, the crowd became silent, for Big Bear was so fast and quick, so agile and nimble, that the wrestling game turned into a dance, and the other wrestler found himself wanting to dance in harmony with Big Bear. At one point, Big Bear grabbed the other wrestler, who weighed at least 300 pounds, flipped him high into the air, and then caught him gently so he would not hurt himself. The crowd was enchanted, and the other wrestler smiled, bowed, and retreated from the ring. And each time a wrestler entered the ring to fight Big Bear, he ended by dancing, leaping into the air, and gracefully retreating from the ring.

In the end, Big Bear was declared champion, but the Emperor was furious. He could not stand the gentle dances. He wanted action, fierce fighters, broken bones, dead bodies. He wanted excitement and raw power.

When he gave the pot of gold to Big Bear, he told him, "Never return to my tournament. If you do, I'll see that you will be killed!"

Big Bear took the gold, and before he left the Emperor's court, he shared the gold with the other wrestlers. He saved three coins for himself and quickly departed for the mountain of the three women.

Some say, when the ground begins to tremble and rumbling can be heard high in the mountain, it is not really a storm or an earth-quake. It is only Big Bear and the three strong women. They are wrestling and shaking the mountain. They are dancing, and there is no cause to feel afraid.

The emphasis in the writing and drawing activities that follow all these tales is on "What If" games. Either I place my own "What If" questions on the board, or I solicit "What If" questions that pertain to the tales. Some examples:

The King of the Golden Mountain
What if the black dwarf had captured the son?
What if the king had not used the ring to wish his wife and son to appear before his father?
What if the queen had not married another man?
What if the king had returned to the queen and made peace with her?

The Blue Light
What if the king had paid the soldier good wages?
What if the witch had turned out to be a lovely peasant woman who wanted to share the blue light with the soldier?
What if the soldier had not wanted revenge?
What if the blue light had failed to work at the end of the story?

The Iron Knight
What if Rob had never wished to become a knight?
What if the king's daughter had decided to save the Iron Knight?
What if the king had been convinced that wars were not necessary?

The Fairy Tale about God and the Kings
What if God had not decided to listen to the deputies?

What if the people refused to fight in the wars?
What if God decided to help the deputies and end all wars?

The Three Strong Women
What if Big Bear had been stronger than White Lily at the beginning?
What if Big Bear had decided not to enter the wrestling tournament?
What if Big Bear had lost the wrestling tournament?

All of these questions, as well as those raised by the children, lead the story in the direction in which the children themselves desire to take it. The questions also bring out details that are important to remember, or contradictions in the tales themselves. Often the children's questions are imaginative and revealing and shed light on possible interpretations of the tale that have very specific meanings for the individual children.

Though I intend to use this session to lead to a discussion of peace and war and heroism, I do not want to preach a particular ideology. That is, my standpoint on peace will be made known through the stories, and I want to encourage a free discussion and discover what the children think about these issues. If asked direct questions, I shall, of course, be as honest as I can. Sincerity is important in all my discussions with children, and a good storyteller should never hide his or her convictions. If the storytelling is done with teenagers, it is obvious that there can be lengthy discussions about the issues raised by the tales, and I am more apt to reveal my own particular position from the beginning, why I feel the way I do, and how the stories have taken on a personal meaning for me. However, in my target age group of six to ten, I prefer to prompt the children to express their opinions. I do not want to intimidate them, nor do I want them to please me. At a certain point I am there to listen, and they must feel this, or else I am doing something wrong.

Exploring Genres

ৡ 5 ৡ

The Wisdom of the Beasts

Animal Tales and Fables

The focus in this session is on different kinds of animal tales, with an emphasis on the fable as a distinct genre but one that is related to the fairy tale, as all the short narrative forms such as the legend, myth, and anecdote are related to one another. To create transition, I generally tell the wonderful tale *How Six Made Their Way through the World*. Once again there are many different versions of this tale, and I shall discuss it at length when I talk about creative dramatics and the fairy tale.

In brief, the Grimms' story is about a soldier who is discharged from service with three pennies and vows to get revenge on the king if he can find the right people. He travels into the forest and meets and recruits: 1) a strong man carrying a bunch of trees; 2) a sharpshooter who can hit a target two miles away; 3) a man blowing windmills with his breath two miles away; 4) a runner who can run faster than any bird can fly; 5) a man who wears a cap that freezes everything if it is worn straight. These five men help the soldier defeat the king's daughter in a foot race. But the treacherous king and his daughter want to cheat and kill the soldier and his helpers, who are, however, too clever for these deceitful people. In the end, the soldier and his five helpers leave with the king's treasury, which they share with one another, and the soldier does *not* marry the princess.

Now this tale bears a great resemblance to the popular *Bremen Town Musicians*, which I want to record here in its entirety because it is pivotal in this session.

The Bremen Town Musicians

A man had a donkey who had diligently carried sacks of grain to the mill for many years. However, the donkey's strength was reaching its end, and he was less and less fit for the work. His master thought it was time to dispense with him and save on food, but the donkey got wind of what was in store for him. So he ran away and set out for Bremen, where he thought he could become a town musician. After traveling some distance he came across a hunting dog lying on the roadside, panting as if he had run himself ragged.

"Why are you panting so hard, you old hound dog?" asked the donkey.

"Ah," the dog said, "because I'm old and getting weaker every day. Now I can't even hunt anymore, and my master wanted to kill me. Naturally, I cleared out, but how am I going to earn a living now?"

"You know what," said the donkey, "I'm going to Bremen to become a town musician, and you can come with me and also join the town band. I'll play the lute, and you, the drums."

The dog agreed, and they continued on their way. Soon after, they encountered a cat sitting on the roadside, making a long and sorry face.

"Well, what's gone wrong with you, old whiskers?" asked the donkey.

"How can I be cheerful when my neck's in danger?" the cat replied. "My mistress wanted to drown me because I'm getting on in years. Moreover, my teeth are dull, and I'd rather sit behind the stove and spin than chase after mice. Anyway, I managed to escape, but now I don't know what to do or where to go."

"Why don't you come along with us to Bremen? You know a great deal about night serenades, and you can become a town musician."

The cat thought that was a good idea and went along. Then the three refugees passed a farmyard where a rooster was perched on the gate, crowing with all his might.

"You're crowing gives me the chills," said the donkey. "Why are you screaming like this?"

"I've predicted good weather for today," said the rooster, "because it's the day my mistress does her washing. Still, she has no mercy.

Tomorrow's Sunday, and guests are coming. So she told the cook to cut off my head tonight because she wants to eat me in the soup tomorrow. Now you know why I'm screaming my lungs out, while there's still time to scream."

"That's foolish, redhead!" said the donkey. "You'd be smarter if you came along with us. We're off to Bremen where there are better things than death. You've got a good voice, and if we make music together, it's sure to be a good thing."

The rooster liked the proposal, and all four of them continued the journey together. However, they could not reach the town of Bremen in one day, and by evening they came to a forest, where they decided to spend the night. The donkey and the dog lay down under a big tree, while the cat and the rooster climbed up and settled down in the branches. To be on the safe side, the rooster flew to the top. Before he went to sleep, he looked around in all directions, and it seemed to him he saw a light burning in the distance. He called to his companions and told them there must be a house nearby, since he could see something shining.

"Well, this place is not all that comfortable, so let's get moving," said the donkey.

The dog thought some bones and meat would be just right for him, and they all set out toward the light. Soon it began to grow brighter, and it got even more so once they reached a brightly lit robber's den. Since the donkey was the tallest, he went up to the window and looked inside.

"What do you see, gray steed?" the rooster asked.

"What do I see?" replied the donkey. "I see a table covered with wonderful food and drinks and some robbers sitting there and enjoying themselves."

"That would be just the thing for us!" said the rooster.

"You're right," said the donkey. "If only we could get in!"

Then the animals discussed what they would have to do to drive the robbers away. Finally they hit upon a plan. The donkey was to stand upright and place his forefeet on the window sill. The dog was to jump on the donkey's back, and the cat was to climb upon the dog. When that was done, the rooster was to fly up and perch on the cat's head. After they put their plan into action, the signal was given, and they all started to make music together: the donkey brayed, the dog barked, the cat meowed, and the rooster crowed. Then they crashed into the room, shattering the window. Startled by the horrible cries, the robbers were convinced that a ghost had burst into the room, and they fled in great fright into the forest. Then the four companions sat down at the table, gathered up the leftovers with delight, and ate as if there were no tomorrow.

When the four minstrels were finished, they put out the light and looked for a place to sleep, each according to his nature and custom. The donkey lay down on the dung heap in the yard, the dog behind the door, the cat on the hearth near the warm ashes, and the rooster on the beam of the roof. Since they were tired from their long journey, they soon fell asleep.

When it was past midnight and the robbers saw from the distance that there was no light in the house and everything seemed peaceful, the leader of the band said, "We shouldn't have let ourselves be scared out of our wits."

He ordered one of the robbers to return and check out the house. When this man found everything quiet, he went into the kitchen to light a candle and mistook the cat's glowing fiery eyes for live coals. So he held a match to them to light a fire, but the cat did not appreciate the joke. He jumped into the robber's face, spitting and scratching, and the robber was so terribly frightened that he ran out the back door. However, the dog was lying there and bit him in the leg. When the robber raced across the yard, he passed the dung heap, and here the donkey gave him a solid kick with his hind foot. All this noise woke the rooster from his sleep, and he became lively again and crowed "Cock-a-doodle-doo!" from his beam.

The robber ran back to the leader as fast as he could and said, "There's a gruesome witch in the house! She spat on me and scratched my face with her long claws. At the door there's a man with a knife, and he stabbed my leg. In the yard there's a black monster who beat me with a wooden club. And on top of the roof the judge was sitting and screaming, 'Bring me the rascal!' So I got out of there as fast as I could!"

Since that time the robbers have never dared to return to the house, but the four Bremen Town musicians liked the place so much that they stayed on forever.

In using *How Six Made Their Way through the World* and *The Bremen Town Musicians*, I try to bring out the nature of collective heroism and solidarity. Both tales concern individuals who work hard and serve a master, only to be treated in a dishonorable way. As individuals, they are weak and cannot attain justice. However, they learn that, when they pool their talents, they are strong, and they employ their skills and strength not to kill their adversaries, but to satisfy their notions of justice and establish the lives they want to lead.

It is obvious to the children that *The Bremen Town Musicians* is filled primarily with animals as heroes, animals who talk and think. They are accustomed to talking animals from many other stories and films in their childhood, and they rarely pose the question, how can animals talk? Nor do they think about the fable or other types of animal tales such as the trickster tales and *pourquoi* tales as genres, and rarely do they discuss the symbolic nature of the animals and their actions. This is why I try to stimulate them to think about the different meanings of the animals in the tales. In this case, I suggest at one point that we can look at the animals as old people, and I try to reveal how the tale concerns "ageism," or the manner in which we discard old people when they are no longer of use to us. Or, I talk about the animals as common workers who do not have an organization like a union to help them when they are forced to retire or are fired. Finally, I also suggest that the tale can be understood on a "literal" level, and I discuss the special attributes of animals and how we perceive or do not perceive the rights of animals in our society.

As animal tale—and there are many other genres that use animals—the fable has a history that goes back thousands of years, and the most important collection, even today, is *Aesop's Fables*. It has been said that Aesop was a freed slave who told his fables in a coded language using animals as symbols to conceal his subversive messages. The fact is, however, that we are not certain who Aesop was and exactly why he told his tales. He never printed them, nor did he leave a clear record of his life behind him. His fables were spread by word of mouth and were only transcribed hundreds of years after his death. Though Aesop remains a "mysterious figure," the tendency of the fables collected under his name is clear: they are a repository of social knowledge that assumes the form of proverbial wisdom, and that employs animals (as well as humans) in familiar social situations to give practical advice about how to survive and be successful in the face of stupidity and arbitrary power. The proverbial wisdom of the traditional fable, emanating from the historical repository of everyday knowledge, cannot be fully separated from religious teachings. However, the morality or morals in the fables are not bound systematically to one religious or ethical code. The fable does not convey ethical instructions or commands but practical knowledge about the way the world is, works, and operates, and how to survive or get through life. Depending on who the fabulist might be—and every society has produced great writers of fables like Phaedrus, La Fontaine, Roger L'Estrange, Gotthold Ephraim Lessing, Joel Harris, Leo Tolstoy, Rudyard Kipling, Robert Louis Stevenson, William Saroyan, and James Thurber—she or he will depict a typical everyday occurrence as a problem, along with a way to solve the problem. An exemplary situation is portrayed, and the reader or listener is to learn from this example. That is, there is a lesson to be drawn and wisdom to be gained from the example, which is often summarized at the end in the form of a proverb. The fable intends to motivate the reader to apply and use this wisdom in similar everyday situations so that the wisdom becomes second nature or habitual.

Given the significance of Aesop's fables, I generally follow *The Bremen Town Musicians* with a telling of *The Hare and the Tortoise* and *The Shepherd Boy and the Wolf* to demonstrate the different structure of the fable: brief, to the point, didactic:

The Hare and the Tortoise

A hare laughed and made fun of a tortoise because it moved so slowly. But the tortoise just looked at him calmly and said that he would run a race against the hare and beat him any day he would name.

"All right, you fool," said the hare, "I'll leave you in my dust!"

So, without further ado, they agreed to start. The tortoise began jogging at his usual steady pace without stopping for one solitary moment. The hare treated the entire matter very lightly and said he would first take a little nap before overtaking the tortoise. Meanwhile the tortoise plodded on and the hare overslept. When he finally awoke and headed for the finish line, he arrived only to see that the tortoise had crossed it before him.

Slow and steady wins the race.

The Shepherd and the Wolf

A shepherd boy, who tended his flock not far from a village, used to amuse himself at times by crying out, "Wolf! Wolf!" His trick succeeded two or three times, and the whole village came running to his rescue. However, they were only rewarded with laughter for their pains. One day the wolf really did come, and the boy cried out in earnest. But his neighbors thought that he was up to his old tricks and paid no attention to his cries, enabling the wolf to devour the sheep. So the boy learned, when it was too late, that liars are not believed even when they tell the truth.

In both instances, the structure of the fable enables the children to see how an everyday occurrence—the challenge, the assignment—is turned into a predicament. One tale has a happy conclusion, while the other ending serves as a warning. The children will probably have heard or seen some version of these fables. The most classic one is *Peter and the Wolf*, and I ask them if they know similar fables. If there is some difficulty in recollecting a fable—and sometimes the children have not been exposed to many fables—I ask them to tell me an incident with a pet or an animal. Were they almost bitten by an animal? Did they ever save an animal? What lesson did they learn from their experience? Several children generally raise their hands, and I ask them for their stories. Then we *swap* tales, so to speak, with one child's tale leading to the next.

The *swapping* of tales is very important, and I encourage this throughout all the sessions. When they are finished, I ask them if they want to hear another kind of animal tale that they have never heard before. Here I introduce the genre of the *pourquoi tale*, which generally illustrates how a particular animal has developed a certain characteristic. For instance, there are many *pourquoi* tales about bears and why they lost their long tails. In the Grimms' collection there are several tales, such as *The Wren*, *The Owl*, and *The Flounder*, that explain how animals were either rewarded or punished for their behavior by developing a certain trait. As my example, I use the following tale which I have created from different folk motifs:

The Elephant and the Mouse

Women are afraid of mice, so they say, and so are elephants, too. If you want to hear, I'll tell you why.

There was a time when elephants did not have long trunks or big ears. They were sleek and slim, tall and trim, and when they walked through the forest, they were so proud that they trampled everything and every animal in sight.

"We are the kings of the jungle!" the elephants used to announce as they ran through the jungle in herds knocking over trees and squashing all the tiny animals that could not get out of their way fast enough. The frogs, squirrels, ants, rabbits, and moles lived in fear for their lives, not to mention the poor little mice.

Now in those days many mice lived in the jungle, and many of them had been crushed to death by the haughty elephants. Every beast in the jungle, including the lions, was afraid of the elephants because they had large sharp teeth and big jaws and liked to eat other animals. They were so fierce and strong, and their skin was so thick, that it was practically impossible to hurt them. Moreover, they had extra long trunks that they used to grab the other beasts and devour them with their huge jaws. So the lions, the tigers, the panthers, and the other great animals of the jungle avoided the elephants. They, too, lived in fear of these huge monsters.

But one day, after the elephants had run wild in the jungle, pulling up trees, destroying flowers, and killing many a tiny animal, not to mention some snakes and some leopards, the mice called for a meeting of all the animals of the jungle.

"We cannot go on living like this," said the leader of the mice.

"What do you propose to do?" asked the panther.

"I propose that we form an army and fight them!" said the mouse.

"No!" roared a lion. "They cannot be beaten. We have tried in the past, and have lost."

And all the other animals agreed.

"But what are we to do?" croaked a frog. "They are becoming more and more vicious."

All of a sudden, a young mouse stepped forward. "I shall stop the elephants!" he declared.

But all the other animals laughed at him. "You! How can a pipsqueak like you stop the elephants? They'll kill you for sure."

But the little mouse was not afraid.

"They almost trampled me to death the other day," he said, "but I think I've found their weak spot. Trust me. You have nothing to lose."

And the animals looked at each other and realized that the little mouse was right. They had nothing to lose, and so they promised to help him as best they could.

The next day, the little mouse went to the elephants and cried out, "Send me your king. I have come to challenge him!"

The elephants looked and looked to see who had cried out this challenge. As we know, elephants cannot see very well, and they depend more on their ears than their eyes. Finally, they saw the little mouse standing at the edge of their herd, and they all began to laugh until the great king of all the elephants came and asked them why they were laughing.

"Do you see that little pipsqueak over there? He has come to challenge you."

When the king of the elephants turned his gaze to the tiny brown mouse, he laughed so hard that his huge stomach began to rumble.

"Go away, little one, before I grab you and eat you for a snack!" the elephant roared.

"I won't go away until you accept my challenge!" the mouse replied.

"Are you crazy?" the elephant bellowed.

"Are you afraid?"

"Me, afraid of a mouse?" said the elephant. "You must be kidding."

"You must be afraid. Otherwise, you would accept my challenge."

"All right," the elephant said. "What is your challenge?"

"You must try to trample me tomorrow," the mouse said. "I shall be waiting for you at the middle of the jungle road. If you fail, you and the elephants must stop killing the animals and tearing up the jungle."

"And if you fail, you will be dead just like the other measly mice we've killed," the elephant said.

"But I won't," the mouse said.

"I should kill you now for your insolence, but I'll wait for tomorrow," the elephant answered angrily.

The next day, all the animals gathered deep in the jungle, and the mouse stood alone in the middle of the road. When the elephants started to approach the road from the river, there was fear in the air. The ground began to rumble. Soon the king of the elephants was about a hundred yards from the mouse, and the little mouse called out, "Come and get me, you coward!"

The elephant could not see the mouse very well, but he heard him and was enraged.

"Your time has come, little one!" the elephant blared with his trunk up high and his jaws opened wide. He looked ferocious as he began his charge.

"You'll never catch me!" the mouse said as he began to run.

The elephant increased his speed, and he began to gain on the poor little mouse. All he could think about was how much he wanted to trample the little pest, but the mouse kept running and taunting him, saying, "Come and get me!"

Then, suddenly, the mouse stopped, and the elephant seized the opportunity to leap into the air intending to squash the little mouse once and for all, but as he came down, the mouse jumped to the side, and the elephant crashed through some branches that were covering a gigantic hole in the ground. Down, down, down he went, until his head could hardly be seen. The elephant was caught in a trap that the animals had dug the night before, and they all came out of the jungle, cheering the little mouse.

"No fair!" cried the elephant.

"Do you think what you do is fair?" answered the mouse. "Unless you and the other elephants promise to stop destroying us and the jungle, we shall build traps all over, and we shall cover you with dirt!"

"No, please not that!" whimpered the elephant, who could barely see the mouse leaning over the edge of the hole.

"Promise!"

So, the elephant gave his promise, and ever since then, the elephants only eat leaves and vegetables and walk on the ground as tenderly as they can for fear of holes and mice. They no longer have large teeth and jaws, nor do they see very well. But they see enough to know:

Little things can always make the great take a big fall.

There are a number of animal tales centering on the fox, wolf, and bear or lion that make for good storytelling sessions. There are also numerous Native American cycles of tales about the coyote as trickster, just as my little mouse has some of the trickster in him. By focusing on one animal, I have developed an entire cluster of tales in a session or two and, in collaboration with the teacher, followed the clusters with games and activities during the week. Two examples come to mind involving the cat and the rabbit.

By taking the cat in *The Bremen Town Musicians* as a starting point, I ask the children if they know of any cat stories. Do they know cats? Do they have cats at home? Can they tell me about their cats? We swap tales, and then I tell a version of *Puss in Boots*. There are numerous classical versions of *Puss in Boots* by Gianfranco Straparola, Giambattista Basile, Charles Perrault, and the Brothers Grimm. I generally combine the elements I like best to form my own story, although sometimes I read directly from a book and show the pictures. After telling the tale, I ask the children why they think the cat is a he. Aren't most cats feminine? Do we know anything about the history of cats? Can we do some research about the history of cats? They were once worshipped in Egypt as powerful goddesses, and later they became associated with witches. Why? There are not only fables about cats but myths, legends, and fairy tales, and I have at times spent two weeks with children exploring the fables, fairy tales, myths, and legends about cats. An interesting comparison can be made between *Puss in Boots* and Madame D'Aulnoy's *The White Cat*, two tales written at about the same time, one about a cunning male cat and the other about a clever female cat. And, of course, this comparison can lead to a presentation of Lloyd Alexander's tales in *The Town Cat and Other Tales* and/or his novel *The Cat Who Wished to Be a Man*.

One excellent follow-up activity with cats that my wife used in a fourth-grade class was to ask the children to draw a cat in the middle of a piece of paper and then do the following:

1. Write the name of the cat on the upper left-hand corner.
2. Write what is special about the cat in the upper right-hand corner. Does it catch mice? Does it climb trees? Does it play with yarn?
3. Write where the cat lives in the lower left-hand corner.
4. Write the name of the cat's worst enemy in the lower right-hand corner.

5. Turn the page and write a short story about how the cat used its special gifts to defeat its worst enemy. When you are done with your story, please draw an illustration for your story on another sheet of paper.

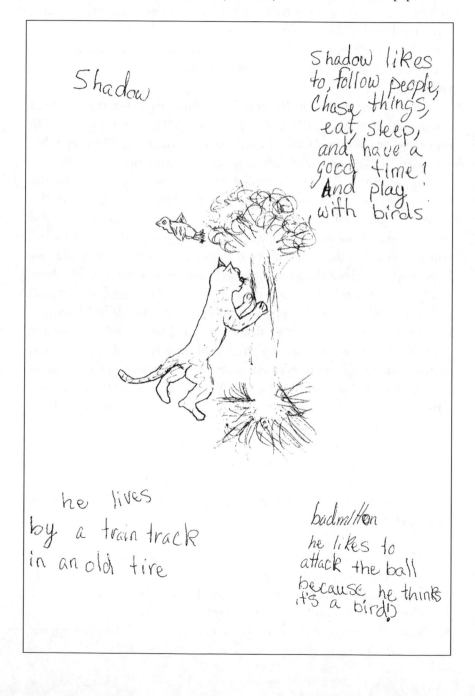

Shadow

Shadow likes to, follow people, chase things, eat, sleep, and have a good time! And play with birds

he lives by a train track in an old tire

badmitton
he likes to attack the ball because he thinks it's a bird!

This activity can also be used with rabbits and hares, and there is a wonderful tale in Peggy Appiah's *Tales of an Ashanti Father* that I like to tell when I focus on hares because it raises the question of community and collective action.

The Tortoise and the Hare

The Lion, King of Beasts, once called all the creatures of his kingdom together, and when even the smallest and slowest had arrived he addressed them thus:

"My people, I have long been concerned by the lack of unity and cooperation among the animals. Not only do we suffer the depredations of hunters and trappers, but animal attacks animal in the forest and you, my people, have ceased to help each other. Were we all to work together no hunter would be able to attack us, and when groups of men tried to come into the forest we would have adequate warning and would be able to keep out of their way, and even to destroy them. What suggestions have you so that we will work better together?"

One animal after another stood up and talked, some making suggestions and some complaining that it was not their fault. The little tortoise sat at the feet of the King and watched and listened. After a bit the hare jumped up, and when the King had nodded that he could speak he said, "I, O King, do not need help. I can run and jump and am quite capable of looking after myself. As you know, I am the swiftest animal in the forest. If anyone starts to chase me I can tire him out. When any of us are caught it is just by accident. I am quite happy with things as they are."

Then the animals started to talk at once and the King was obliged to silence them. He caught the eye of the little tortoise, and seeing that he wanted to speak, he lifted him up on a stool so that the other animals could see him.

The tortoise looked around the crowd and turned to the hare. Then he began to speak: "You hare, you are a foolish animal. Have you not heard the King advise us to work more together? You think you are safe but even I, the little tortoise, could beat you in a race and therefore teach you the importance of unity and cooperation."

The hare was furious and shouted back, "You silly little creature.

You know quite well that you could not even begin to race me. I am the swiftest animal of the forest and your are known for you slowness. You insult me by your talk. You had better take back what you said."

The tortoise smiled. "If you are so sure of yourself then I will race you and show you that I can win," he said.

The hare, angrier than ever, addressed the King who was smiling broadly at the idea of the tortoise racing.

"O King," said the hare, "I challenge the tortoise to prove what he says or else he should be punished. I ask you to arrange for a race tomorrow."

The King agreed and soon the animals were marking out the course of the race and talking and laughing about the tortoise's challenge. Indeed, they laughed so much that the sound could be heard in the next village.

The time was fixed for the race and the animals went home. The tortoise hurried to his house and sent out messengers to fetch all the members of his family, young and old. When they had arrived and the doors of the yard were closed against the strangers, the tortoise addressed them thus:

"Members of my family, elders and friends, you will have heard of the rudeness of the hare and of my challenge to him. I have called you together because this is a matter that affects not only me but the honor of every tortoise. If I win, then glory will go to our family as a whole; if I lose, as I do not intend to do, then we are all disgraced. Will you help me so that I can win?"

The largest and oldest of the tortoises replied, "What you say is true and we will all help. Nonetheless we think you very unwise to challenge the hare in this matter for you cannot possibly beat him."

"There, Grandfather, you are wrong," replied the tortoise. "With your help I shall win. Listen now to what I have to tell you, and do as I say. Will all the tortoises of my size and color please come to this side."

There was a scuffling and a large body of the tortoises moved across the yard. "Each one of you has a part to play. I will give you all numbers and you will know your order," said the tortoise, and he numbered them all.

"Now number one," he said, "you go and hide in the bush some fifty feet from the beginning of the course. When the race has started and you see the hare approaching, step out into the path and start going along the path. At the same time I will disappear into the bush, so that when the hare turns around he will see no one on the path. Number two, you go some forty feet further on..." And the tortoise gave them all their places along the route. To the last one he gave special instructions to make sure he crossed the line ahead of the hare. Then he told them to go and take up their positions under cover of dark. He also told them that they should sing the following song when they saw the hare coming so that the next one of them would be ready to come out of the bush.

> *"Me de boko-boko be duru abrokyire."*
> "With patience and diligence, I shall reach far off places."

The following day all the animals were out early to watch the race and there was an air of festivity. When they saw the tortoise they laughed: "He, ho, ho, hee, hee, hee, ha, ha, ha." But the tortoise only smiled back at them.

The hare had been so angry at the insult that he had not slept all night. He had lain fuming on his bed, unable to eat or sleep. Now he was longing to be off and to prove once and for all what a fool the tortoise was.

The King had appointed judges and some stood at the beginning, some at the end of the course. At last, they were ready to start. The hare shot ahead without looking back, and then, thinking it was stupid to get hot when the tortoise could not even do more than amble along, he slowed down.

About forty feet from the start, the hare turned around but was surprised to see no sign of the tortoise. Then he looked ahead again, and there in the middle of the path was the tortoise, going along for all he was worth.

"So, you have magic," thought the hare, and he started to run more swiftly. When he turned to look again there was no tortoise behind him. He looked ahead and there in the path were the tortoise, singing a song and so bespattered with dew that it looked as if it was sweating profusely. The hare began to get angry and hurled insults at the tortoise as he passed.

Then he really began to get worried. He ran as swiftly as he could, but always ahead of him in the path was the little tortoise, singing as he went:

"With patience and diligence, I shall reach far off places."

Making a final effort, the hare threw himself across the winning line, but just before he did so he heard a great cheer and people began to shout, "The tortoise has won, the tortoise has won." The hare collapsed groaning on the ground while the judges clustered round the tortoise congratulating him.

"That was nothing," said the tortoise. "I am not even hot."

The judges went at once to tell the King the result of the race. At first he did not believe them, but with so many witnesses he could not fail to be convinced. He laughed heartily and again called together all the animals so that he could honor the tortoise.

When the animals had come together they called for the tortoise. In he came at the head of all his family and relations. They waddled proudly in, each one feeling and looking like a small chief. The tortoise's victory had made them proud and confident.

The King called the tortoise to come up beside him and then called on the people to cheer the victor. When the crowd was again silent the King asked the tortoise how it was that he had managed to beat the hare who was the swiftest animal in the forest.

"It was the triumph of unity and cooperation," said the tortoise. "We won because we all stuck together."

"*We* won?—You mean you won," said the King.

"Well, yes, Your Majesty, I won. You see every member of my family gave me their support so that we were able to win."

"Why do you keep saying *we*?" asked the King. "It was surely you alone who won the race? Now we will call on the hare to congratulate you," he said, and he turned to look for the hare.

The hare had been so ashamed of himself that he had slunk home and had not come to the meeting. When the King saw that the hare was absent he sent for all the members of the hare family to come quickly.

Very soon, with his head bowed, the hare came into the courtyard. The other animals tittered and smiled behind their paws. Behind the hare came all his people looking angry and ashamed.

One by one they were made to come up and congratulate the tortoise and his family on the victory. Then the King asked the tortoise again to say how he had won the race. "All my friends helped me," said the tortoise.

The King, being wise, did not ask any more questions in public, but you may be sure that by evening he had heard the whole story. In the meantime he again addressed his people: "The tortoise," he said, "has showed us the value of unity and cooperation. Let us learn from him. If you cannot all work together, at least let those of the same family help each other."

From that day many of the animals started to move together in herds for their mutual protection, the birds flew in flocks, and the ants, who already knew what could be done by mutual help, moved into even greater colonies. Only the hare, embittered by his experience, continued to live alone and to rely on his speed to save himself from his enemies.

Like the cat, the hare has also been worshipped as a god by different tribes throughout the world. In North America, the Great Hare, or White Hare, is supposed to have shaped the earth, and he is the major protagonist in many trickster tales. In the Southeastern United States the rabbit, known as Cottontail, is considered a benefactor of humankind among different Native American tribes and is also considered a trickster. His role has also been significant in Africa, and in numerous African tales mixed with Native American tales in the nineteenth century. Here I ask what the children know about rabbits and hares. Is there a difference between the two? Where do they live? Why are they generally associated with males? Has the hare always been as conceited and arrogant as in *The Tortoise and the Hare*? Where does the expression *scared as a rabbit*, come from? Was the rabbit also treated like a god the way cats were? Why not? These are some of the questions I raise in a session about rabbits, and once again, after telling one or two fables about rabbits, I ask the children whether they know any tales about rabbits that they might want to share, and whether any of them has ever had a rabbit as a pet.

After the swapping of tales, I may tell a tale from Uncle Remus or a tale similar to the one that J.J. Reneaux tells in *Cajun Folktales*. It is entitled *The Theft of Honey* and begins, "Lapin was the smartest critter in all of Louisiana. That rabbit was such a smooth-talkin' rascal that he could charm the whiskers off a cat and sell bacon to a pig. Lapin was full of trouble for true, and he just loved to play his tricks on all the other animals, especially his neighbor, Bouqui." Bouqui turns out to be a fox, and Lapin makes a fool out of him by stealing his honey from a jug and pretending that the ground soaked it up. This tale is similar to the Grimms' *The Companionship of the Cat and the Mouse,* and it is worth comparing the two because the cat eats the mouse in the end, whereas the rabbit does not resort to violent ends. Why not? What is the difference between the cat and the rabbit? These are questions that I explore with the children, and, of course, with older children, it is possible to move to a reading of Richard Adams's *Watership Down* and study other tales and novels in which rabbits are the protagonists.

Whatever cluster of animal tales I present, the tales all lend themselves remarkably well to creative dramatics. Before I ask the children to act out some of the stories, I begin with a charade game. I ask the children to form an audience, and I explain that each one is to act out an animal in pantomime while the others have to guess which animal it is. Whoever guesses the animal is next in line to perform. Nobody is allowed to perform twice. Once most of the class has presented an animal, I divide the class into two or three groups. One group is asked to perform a dramatic exercise while the other two watch. In this warm-up drill, I ask the children to begin walking about slowly in a circle without touching each other. Then I call out the name of an animal, and they are supposed to move in and out like this animal in slow and fast motion. At one point, I yell, "Freeze!" The children are to stop in their tracks, and I ask them to feel the animal and to adjust their statue if they do not feel that they represent it the way they want. After the children do this two or three times, I ask the other groups to do the same. The point of the exercises is to loosen the children up and prepare them to act out the fables. They will use some of the movements and gestures in these exercises in their improvisations.

After the skits, I ask the children to draw their favorite animal and tell me a story about this animal. Sometimes I begin by asking them to tell me a story about animals and then illustrating it. Here I pose some questions that may help them find a story line: Where does the animal live? Is it a danger-ous animal? Does it mix well with other animals? Do humans hunt this animal? Does the animal help humans? I suggest possibilities for stories: Imagine a group of animals who decide to live together. Imagine an animal that no longer wants to be the way its master wants it to be. Imagine two animals like a cat and dog that decide to live together. Imagine being trans-formed into an animal and how it would feel to be the animal.

The best follow-up activities responding to fables can be found in a booklet published by Karen Kennery and Herbert Kohl.[1] As we have seen, the fables contain a wealth of proverbs and morals such as "In unity there is solidarity" (*The Bremen Town Musicians*); "Slow and steady wins the race" (*The Hare and the Tortoise*); "Don't believe liars even when they are telling the truth" (*The Shepherd and the Wolf*); and "Little things can always make the great take a big fall" or "The bigger they are, the harder they fall" (*The Elephant and the Mouse.*) Kennery and Kohl recommend that the teacher or storyteller create lists on the board such as the following (and here I am revising their topics somewhat).

Morals
Be good or you'll be lonesome.
You can't eat your cake and have it too.
Don't kick a man when he's down.
You never lose money taking a profit.
Beggars cannot be choosers.
I wouldn't trust him farther than I can throw a bull by the tail.
Don't count your chickens before they hatch.
You get nothing for nothing.
When the fox preaches, beware of the geese.

Reversing Morals
Children should be seen and heard.
With friends like you, I need enemies.
Kick a man when he is down.
Nothing's fair in love and war.
Let he who has sinned cast the first stone.
When in Rome, do as the Americans do.
Miracles always cease.

Warning Morals
Fools tread where wise men fear to enter.
Don't play with fire.
Never trust a dog.
Don't put all your eggs in one basket.
It is not so easy to fool little girls nowadays as it used to be.

General Truths in Morals
Show me a man's friend, and I'll tell you who he is.
Everything has its time and place.
Art consists in concealing art.
Big fish eat little fish.
As a priest is, so is the parish.
Too many cooks spoil the broth.
It takes two to tango.

Cynical Morals
With friends like you, I don't need enemies.
Every dog is allowed his first bite.
He is low enough to crawl under a snake's belly.
There is no safety in numbers, or in anything else.
Life's hell, and then there's death.

The children can be asked to add to these lists and, using one of the morals, to write a fable with the moral at the end.

For another activity, Kennery and Kohl suggest creating a list on the board about the origins of people, places, things, or habits. For instance, with the help of the children, the storyteller can write the following on the board.

Why are elephants afraid of mice?
How did the camel get a hump?
How did language come into being?
Why were rules of language invented?
Why were armies created?
Why do pigs like mud?
How did the spider get to make a web?
How did the leopard get its spots?
Why are there two sexes?
Why do dogs and cats hate each other?

In all of these activities, children learn how to regard animals metaphorically and to create stories that pertain to their lives. Of course, fables do not rely entirely on animals, and it is often through animals that children begin to learn something about themselves. There is, however, a certain danger in encouraging children to use animals in their fables.

In one of his essays in *On Seeing*, John Berger talks about how we have come to view animals as inanimate objects without feelings. In particular, he criticizes the manner in which stuffed animals as toys represent false images of animals and lead children to believe there is nothing wrong in hunting animals and making trophies out of their skins. The stuffed animal can be thrown around, put on the shelf as a trophy, and placed in bed as a snuggly item. The animals are thus domesticated as objects and treated as though they have no feelings. They are deprived of their habitat and nature, and we lose a sense of nature and our own nature by making animals into commodities, a point that is also addressed by Marsha Kinder in a slightly different way in her study of the depiction of animals on television.[2]

Of course, it is possible to argue that Berger fails to recognize that stuffed animals (without the real skin of the animal) enable children to overcome their fear of a strange creature. Through contact with the imitation, a child can develop an affection for and attraction to the other kinds of species. The stuffed animal can be used in games in which the child works through anxieties, just as he or she does with dolls of all kinds.

Nevertheless, Berger's point is well taken. We have "de-naturalized" or "de-humanized" animals in our society to such an extent that we arrogantly believe those "other" animals are on earth to serve us. Our ancestors used to worship animals, while we tame them and destroy them as though it were our right. Fables tell us otherwise, and some remarkable fabulists like the French writer Jacques Prévert try to remind us that our humanity depends to a great extent on how we sensitize children and ourselves to the deep feelings and needs of animals. So I want to close this chapter with Prévert's provocative *The First Donkeys*.

The First Donkeys

Once upon a time the donkeys were completely wild. That is to say, they ate when they were hungry. They drank when they were thirsty, and they ran in the grass whenever they desired.

Sometimes a lion came and ate a donkey. Then all the other donkeys ran away, whining like donkeys, but the next day, they stopped thinking about it and began again to bray, to drink, to eat, to sleep.... In short, except for the days when the lion came, they had a fine life.

One day, the masters of the universe (that is the way men love to speak about themselves) arrived in the land of the donkeys, and the donkeys, very happy to see the new people, galloped to meet the men.

The donkeys (while galloping): "They are funny pale animals. They walk on two feet. Their ears are very small. They are not very good looking, but even so, we must give them a cordial welcome.... That is the least we can do."

And the donkeys performed some funny acts. They rolled in the grass and moved their hoofs. They sang the song of donkeys, and just for the fun of it, they pushed the men and made them fall on the ground a little. But men do not like jokes when they are not the ones who play them, and only five minutes after their arrival in the land of donkeys, the masters of the universe tied up all the donkeys like little hot dogs on a string.

All except the youngest, the most tender. That one they killed and roasted on a spit. The men sat around the donkey with knives in their hands. The donkey was cooked just right. The men began to eat and make sour faces. Then they threw their knives on the ground.

One of the men (to himself): "It's not as good as beef! It's not as good as beef!"

Another: "It's not good. I prefer lamb!"

Another: "Oh, it's really bad!" (He cries.)

And upon seeing the man cry, the captured donkeys thought that it was remorse that made the man cry.

They are going to let us go, the donkeys thought. But the men got up and began talking together, all the while motioning with their hands.

Chorus of men: "These animals are not good to eat. Their cries are unpleasant. Their ears are ridiculously long. They are certainly stupid, and they do not know how to read and add. We shall call them asses because we can do whatever we like with them, and they shall carry our baggage. After all, we are the masters here. Onward!"

And the men led the donkeys away.

Here is a story that depends on an ironic reversal, and since children generally have difficulty with irony, it is important that the storyteller and teacher work carefully with the children in pointing to some of the major issues raised by Prévert in this tale. For instance, by making clear that Prévert is using the men and donkeys in this tale to talk about colonization, the storyteller can raise the following questions.

1. Why have the men come to the land of the donkeys?
2. What are the differences between the men and the donkeys?
3. Who do the donkeys represent?
4. Why is there a misunderstanding between the donkeys and the men?
5. Why do the men attack the donkeys?
6. What will the men do with the donkeys?
7. Must the donkeys always be slaves?

These questions lead to a discussion of colonization, and here the teacher can do a follow-up by developing a lesson cluster about colonization with questions concerning the colonization of America, the colonies, and how the colonies freed themselves from the British. And, of course, it is important to discuss how the "Americans" colonized the West.

Colonization is an important topic in storytelling because stories themselves have been used to "colonize" the minds of children. Each story that a child hears is like a settlement. That is, the narrative settles in the child's psyche and occupies a role, some narratives more important than others. The child will be occupied by particular stories, and it is important at a certain time to help children grasp why they are "occupied" by certain stories and to demonstrate that they can change them. The point here, as is the point of most fables, is not to preach a new value system or message to the children, but to make them aware through the practical wisdom of the fable how they can escape the dangers of "colonization" and lead fuller and freer lives.

Paying the Piper, or
How Legends Lead People On

There is a fine line between legends and rumors. Let us take the example of *The Pied Piper*, a legend that originated in the small town of Hamelin, Germany, during the Middle Ages. The earliest source is a stained-glass inscription from about 1300 that reads, "On the day of John and Paul 130 children in Hamelin went to Calvary and were brought through all kinds of danger to the Koppen mountain and lost."

About 150 years later, the monk Heinrich of Herford recorded this event in the Latin *Lüneburg Manuscript*, in which he states that a thirty-year-old man came and led the children from the town of Hamelin playing a flute. The next record we have of this event is a 1553 diary written in German by Hans Zeitlos, the mayor of Bamberg, and it is followed by a similar short version in 1556 by the theologian Jobus Fincelius. Up until this time, rats had never been mentioned in any of the accounts, and it is only in 1565 in the *Family Chronicles* of Count Froben Christof of Swabia that rats enter the picture and are linked to the children of Hamelin and to a pied piper dressed in a colored garment.

There are numerous other sources in Hamelin itself, such as the front of a house erected in 1602–03 that has the stone engraving "In the year 1284 on the Feast of Saints John and Paul, the 26th of June, 130 children were led astray by a pied piper and led out to Calvary by the Koppen where they all disappeared." Another house built in 1610 bears the engraving "In the year of Our Lord, 1284, 130 children from Hamelin, in the custody of a piper, were led out to the Koppen, and there they disappeared." Again no rats, but they were in other versions and eventually became standard fare in the Pied Piper Legend by the time the Brothers Grimm wrote their own in 1816.

The Children of Hamelin

In the year 1284, a peculiar man appeared in Hamelin. He wore a bright multicolored coat, and this is why he was allegedly called Brightman. He said he was a ratcatcher and promised to free the town of all the mice and rats for a certain amount of money. The towns-people reached an agreement with him and guaranteed to pay him a particular sum for his work. Thereupon, the ratcatcher pulled out a little pipe and began blowing. All at once, the rats and mice came crawling out of the houses and gathered around him. When he thought there were none left in the homes, he started walking out of the town fol-lowed by the entire pack. After reaching the Weser River, he took off his clothes and went into the water. All the animals followed, and when they plunged into the river, they drowned.

Once the townspeople were freed from their plague, however, they regretted that they had promised to pay the man, and refused to give him any money. Instead, they made up all sorts of excuses so that he went away angry and bitter. On the 26th of June, the feast of St. John and St. Paul, at seven o'clock in the morning, or at noon according to other people, he reappeared, now in the form of a hunter with a terrifying face and a strange red hat, and he began playing his pipe in all the streets of the town. This time no rats or mice appeared. Instead, the children, boys and girls from four and up, came running in large numbers, including the grown-up daughter of the mayor. The entire flock followed him, and he led them out of the town to a mountain, where they all disappeared together. A nanny had seen all this from a distance, for she had been drawn there with a child in arm, then turned around, and brought the news back to the town. The parents ran in crowds through the gates and searched for their children with heavy hearts. The mothers were miserable and shrieked and wept. Messengers were sent at once by sea and land all around the region to inquire whether the children, or even only a few of them, had been seen, but everything was in vain. Altogether, 130 children were lost. Two are said to have returned somewhat later, but one of them was blind and the other deaf so that the blind child was not able to show the place where the piper had taken the children and could only tell about it, while the deaf child could show the place but had heard nothing. A little boy had run along with just a shirt and had turned around to fetch his jacket, thereby escaping the misfortune that had befallen the others, for when he had run back to join them, the others had already disappeared into the hole in the side of the hill that is still shown today.

The street on which the children ran through the gate to leave the town was called the Street of Silence even in the eighteenth century (as It is still called) because no dancing or music is allowed there. Indeed, when a bride is brought to the church with music, the musicians must stop playlng the Instruments when they reach this street. The mountain near Hamelin, where the children disappeared, is called Poppenberg, and on the left and right two stones have been erected in the form of a cross. Some say that the children were led through a cave and came out on the other side in Siebenbürgen.

The townspeople of Hamelin documented this event in the town records and took care to note the year and day of the loss of their children. According to Seyfried it was the 22nd of June not the 26th of June, that is given in the town records. The following lines are inscribed on the town hall.

In the year 1284 A.D.
130 children born in Hamelin
were led out of our town
by a piper and lost in the mountain.

And on the new town gate, one can read:

Centum ter denos cum magnus ab urbe puellos
duxerat ante annos CCLXXII condita porta fuit.

In the year 1572 the mayor had the story painted on the church windows with the appropriate inscription, which has become for the most part unreadable. There is also a coin with the inscription on it.

What is going on here? How do we begin interpreting this evidence and examining all the tales, poems, and documents that eventually culminated in the famous poem by Robert Browning "The Pied Piper of Hamelin" (1842), which itself was based on a 1605 English version by Richard Verstegan?

Most scholars agree that two different tale types merge and blend by 1565. The first concerns the actual incident of a mass emigration by children in 1284. Some historians believe that the children might have actually been lured away from Hamelin long before the year 1284 to take part in the Children's Crusade of 1212, while others think that the legend concerns a plague or epidemic in 1284, and that it was death that carried the children off. Perhaps the best explanation concerns the social and economic situation of the town at the end of the thirteenth century: due to poverty and the lack of jobs, the young people of Hamelin did not have much of a future, and documents reveal that a professional recruiter, looking for people to colonize German parts of Eastern Europe, came to Hamelin between 1250 and 1285 and convinced a large group of young people to resettle in the East. Whatever the case may be, it is apparent that the townspeople concealed the reasons why so many young people left Hamelin and that, out of shame, they invented stories to make it seem that "children" were taken away from them through magic or a demonic figure.

As the story developed and spread like a rumor, storytellers embellished it with the second tale type, which concerned ratcatchers. Due to the diseases carried by rats, a real profession of ratcatching developed during the Middle Ages, and as with all professionals—shoemakers, tailors, soldiers, spinners—stories circulated among and about these ratcatchers and their craft. Therefore, at one point in the oral tradition, a storyteller made the piper into a ratcatcher, and new elements were added to the legend of the strange mass exodus from Hamelin.

Though we still cannot be absolutely certain about the actual incident today, we do know that something traumatic and significant happened in the town of Hamelin in or around 1284. It was of such magnitude for the people of this town and others who heard about it that they continued to tell the tale and interpret it in their own way up to the present.

Here we have the basis of a legend, which is a story about a crucial event in the development of a group, community, nation, or religion, and which becomes distorted and expanded in many different ways and for different reasons so that it bears little relation to the actual event and yet generally serves an ideological purpose. In contrast to the legend, a rumor is a story about something that did *not* happen and yet could have happened and thus is often taken for the truth. What is interesting about the distinction between rumor and legend is that the rumor, as Patricia Turner has superbly demonstrated in *I Heard It Through the Grapevine*, is often used to get at the truth, to expose some insidious threat to a community, while the legend will often cover up a defeat, a crime, a shame and then celebrate it as a magnificent event. We see this in all types of heroic and religious legends. Just think of the manifold heroic legends about King Arthur, Roland, Barbarossa, Joan of Arc, Napoleon, George Washington, Abraham Lincoln, Davy Crockett, Buffalo Bill, Billy the Kid, Geronimo, Columbus, etc. Every nation, community, and religion has its legends as do most families. What makes them so appealing is their exaggeration, their concealment of the facts, their creative play with the facts. They offer us the chance to tell *our own version* of an important incident, to play with perspective, to justify ourselves and our interpretations of actuality, and to record the incident historically and become part of history.

But let us return to *The Pied Piper*, for I begin this session with this version.

Long ago, I believe it was the year 1284, in the town of Hamelin, in the country of Germany, there were rats, big, ugly, monstrous, disgusting rats, and these rats carried diseases, and the diseases caused plagues, and thousands of people died in these plagues. But a thousand people did not die in Hamelin. Nobody died at all because the town found a way to get rid of the rats. Some people say that the town was very lucky, but other people say that Hamelin's luck was not worth the price the townspeople paid. Now I shall tell you why.

"We must get rid of the rats!" the mayor of Hamelin announced at a town meeting. "If we do not act soon, there will be a plague, and we shall all die."

"But we have already paid large sums of money to three ratcatchers," someone said. "Why aren't they doing their job?"

"They are," the mayor said. "Yesterday, they caught ten rats."

"And the day before, we caught fifteen rats," said a ratcatcher said, who was attending the meeting. "But they keep coming! There is very little we can do to stop them. We're leaving town at sunrise, and we'd advise you to do the same."

The townspeople were shocked and began yelling at the mayor, "Do something! Do something!"

"Quiet!" the mayor said. "There's no need for panic. Let us sleep on this, and tomorrow we'll make a decision."

The next day, the ratcatchers left town, and the mayor met with the other councillors.

"We have three weeks to find someone who can help us," said the mayor. "Otherwise, we may have to do what the ratcatchers said and leave the town to the rats."

"Let us send our messengers and offer ten thousand gold coins to anyone who can help us," said a councillor.

"But we only have a thousand gold coins in the treasury!" said another.

"We must save the town," declared the first councillor, "and no self-respecting ratcatcher would take the job on for less than ten thousand gold coins. So, if we must lie, we must lie. Let's put it to a vote."

Well, the town council voted to offer a reward of ten thousand gold coins to anyone who could rid the town of the rats. That very day messengers were sent out all over Germany and then throughout Europe. After one week passed, the townspeople were disappointed that nobody appeared to help them. Then the second week came and went. And finally, toward the end of the third week, a strange young man was sighted at the edge of the town. He was dressed all in blue and had a cape with stars on it, and his pointed cap was graced by a bright green feather. He camped beneath a large oak tree and played a flute while he cooked a meal over a small fire. As he played his pipe, some rabbits came out of their holes and began to dance around the fire. It was a merry sight, and some farmers who were heading into town saw it and told everyone about the mysterious stranger who could charm rabbits with his magical pipe.

The next day, the piper appeared before the mayor and the town council.

"I've come to collect the reward," the young man said.

"You have, have you?" asked the mayor. "Well, how do you plan to rid our town of rats?"

"That is for me to know, and you to find out," he declared.

"You'll receive no money," the mayor said, "unless you drive the rats out forever."

"The rats will disappear," said the piper, "and I shall expect ten thousand gold coins."

The mayor and the town council promised the piper that he would have his money, and crowds of people formed at the town hall to watch the stranger, who was tall and solemn. He did not smile or nod to anyone, and when he left the town hall, the people backed away from him in fear.

Later that day when the clock struck twelve, the piper appeared at the town square, and this time he was wearing a multicolored cape that sparkled in the sun. He put his lips to his flute, and the people waited to hear his music. But there was nothing to be heard except some high shrill hum, and even the hum could barely be heard as the piper began strolling through the streets. Though the people were still afraid of him, they laughed and said, "He's more a jokester than a ratcatcher! Someone should fix his pipe! He's full of hot air!"

All at once, however, the rats started to pour out of the cellars of the houses and out of all the nooks and crannies of the buildings. Wherever the piper strolled, the rats followed him as if in a trance, down this street, into that alley, over the hill, and through a boulevard. Hundreds of rats, all sizes and all colors, marched behind the piper until he had gone through the entire town twice as if to make sure that all the rats were with him.

The people were stunned. They watched the piper lead the rats down to the river. When he arrived at a dock, he stood aside and kept playing as the rats plunged into the dark water and drowned. Thousands of big, ugly, monstrous, disgusting rats dove into the water and drowned.

It was sundown when the piper went to the town hall and demanded his reward.

"Here it is," the mayor said, and he handed the piper a bag of gold coins.

The piper looked inside and remarked, "But there can't be more than one thousand coins here."

"That's the reward," said the mayor. "That's what we promised."

"You're lying," said the piper.

"Lying? Am I lying?" the mayor turned to the other councillors.

"No, not at all!" they said in unison.

"You're all lying!" the piper said angrily, "and if I do not have the ten thousand gold coins by tomorrow at sunrise, you will lose the most valuable treasure of your town!"

The piper turned briskly and left the town hall. He did not even bother to take the bag of gold coins.

"Don't worry," said the mayor. "There's nothing he can do to harm us!"

"And he even left the money, which we certainly can use," said one of the councilmen.

"He'll make a laughing stock out of himself," said another.

When the sun rose the next morning, the pied piper stood in the middle of the square. He appeared to be waiting for the mayor and the councillors, but they did not dare to go outside. Everyone hid inside and watched him from their windows, from behind curtains. The piper looked at the sun. He looked all around him. The entire square was empty and silent. Then the piper put his flute to his lips and began playing. Again, nothing could be heard but a strange ripple that went through the air like a startling vibration. A slight breeze crept through the doors and windows of all the houses, and the breeze resounded in a sweet lull. All of a sudden, all the doors and windows flew open, and the children began to move from their rooms out onto the streets. There were hundreds of children, girls and boys, all the children of the town, and they began to dance toward the town square where the piper kept playing. The people of the town could not budge. It was as though they were paralyzed, and when they tried to scream and warn their children, all they could push from their lungs was air.

The children gathered in the square with smiles on their faces, and when the piper began to move down the street that led out of the town, they followed him, singing and rollicking. They followed him into the country toward Mount Koppen, and then they disappeared.

Later that day, at noon, when the townspeople could move again, they rushed out of the town, but they could not find their children. Nor did they ever hear anything about what had happened to them. Some say that the piper was the devil and sold the children into slavery. Others believe that the piper was an angel and punished the townspeople for their lies. Whatever the truth may be, the children left Hamelin in the year 1284, a year the people will never forget.

After telling this tale, there are often questions like; where are the children now? Did they die? Why didn't the piper lead the adults out of town? Was the piper really the devil? At a certain point, I ask the children whether they can imagine a different story. How could the town have gotten rid of the rats without the piper? Did the mayor and councillors have to lie? Couldn't the parents have protected their children? Was there a way for the children to escape? Couldn't the piper have returned the children? If it is a true story, can we change it?

Can we write our own legend?

The Piper's Magic Flute

A long time ago, there was a country filled with starving and needy people. It was a country that had many kings, queens, and generals, but they did not really care about their people, until it was too late.

When the people cried out for better jobs, better homes, and better food, they were ignored by their kings, queens, and generals, who said that there was nothing they could do for them, and that if they wanted new leaders, they should vote for a new government. But the kings, queens, and generals did not think the people would ever vote against them, or that they would ever lose their power.

Now, just at that time, a young man arrived at the capital. He had once been a valiant soldier, and he had a voice as sweet and smooth as a flute. When he spoke, the people were almost hypnotized by the sound of his voice, and he promised them that he would lead them to glory and fame, if they would follow him.

"Better jobs! Better homes! Better food!" he said. "You'll all be equal! You'll all be rich and powerful! You won't need kings, queens, and generals anymore! They are corrupt!"

So marvelous were his words that the people called him the Piper, and the Piper wore a handsome uniform with a mysterious insignia. Everyone thought it was a magic sign that gave the Piper special powers. "That was why he wasn't killed in the war," they thought. "That is why he will live forever." And in the next election, they voted for him, and he became their new leader.

Now the people wore smiles on their faces, and they all began to dress like the Piper and wear a band with his magic sign. He gave them jobs, homes, and food, and they adored him and followed him and all his commands. They built whatever he told them to build. They destroyed whatever he told them to destroy. And the more power he had, the more power it seemed that the people had. Whenever he spoke with his magic flute-like voice, it seemed that they themselves were speaking. He told them how great they were and how pure, and that they had to make themselves even purer.

One day, he told them that there were rats infecting their country, that these rats were redheads, and that they must get rid of the redheads because they were infected by the devil. The Piper ordered his police and soldiers to round up all the redheads and to do away with them. And the people thought this was good.

When the Piper told the people that the country was now pure, they were happy and rejoiced that they were pure. But the Piper said their work was not done yet.

"We must go to war," he said. "There are redheads all around us. We must purify the rest of Europe and then the world!"

And the people believed him, and the Piper led them out of their country to fight wars. But the more the Piper led them into war, the more the people began to suffer at home. The soldiers were dying. There was little food. And people's homes were destroyed by bombs. The other countries were stronger, and they began sending messages that made the people wonder who the real rats were. They began to realize that they may have been misled, and the magic voice of the Piper began losing its power.

"We must get rid of the Piper," the people thought to themselves, but they were too scared to say this aloud or to do anything because the Piper had spies and police everywhere. So, the people continued to follow the Piper's orders until the Piper himself lost his voice and killed himself.

When he died, the people were suddenly free. The magic of the Piper's voice had lost its hold on them. But they had been so accustomed to hearing his voice as their own that they could not find their own voices. It seemed to many that the Piper's voice was still inside them, until they suddenly began to hear their own children singing freely for the first time in their lives. The music resounded through the streets, and thanks to the songs of their children, the people began once again to think and speak for themselves and to listen to the music in their hearts.

I have used *The Pied Piper* as one example of the work I do with legends, and it lends itself nicely to dramatic improvisation. However, I have used other legends, either local or national legends, and I have rewritten and recited "counter-legends" to demonstrate to the children that the legends are not true though they contain truth. Or, I have adapted a legend to address another historical figure such as Hitler to bring up the question of conformity. Finally, I have told legends about Johnny Appleseed, Paul Bunyan, and Iron John, who represent common people, to suggest that it is not important to be rich and famous to become a legendary figure.

In one class with older children I once explored the different legends of *Robin Hood*. We began by writing down on paper all that we knew about Robin Hood, the books and comics we had read about Robin Hood, the different Robin Hood films we had seen, and the Robin Hood games we had played. Once this was done, we read our papers and shared memories of Robin Hood. Then I asked the children whether we could discover who the "real" Robin Hood was, and we decided to begin a research project. For the next two weeks, the children read different books about Robin Hood (including comics) and brought in different book versions and tales of Robin Hood. I also brought in material for us to read together, and sometimes we enacted scenes from the stories to obtain a better idea of Robin Hood and his merry men. Then we made comparisons with Robin Hood figures like the famous Mexican hero Zapata or Billy the Kid, and we talked about the motif of "stealing from the rich to give to the poor," or about protector-of-the-poor figures like Zorro. Finally, we watched several films about Robin Hood, Billy the Kid, and Zapata, and I asked the children either to write a report about the true Robin Hood, Zapata, or Billy the Kid, or to write their own story about these legendary figures. In our final session, we shared the reports and stories on a "legendary day."

Most of the "legendary heroes" are known or will become known to the children, so it is important to stress that there are also legends about "unknown" people, and these people are just as important as the "known" or famous people. In a collection of tales, *Upstate Downstate*, edited by Moritz Jagendorf, I came across the following legend, which illustrates my point.

The Great Sacrifice

Folks in Pennsylvania tell stories of hex and haunt and tales tall as heaven, but they also tell tales of men and places with love and veneration in their hearts. One of these men is George Washington, and one of these places is Valley Forge, where even frozen bodies could not cool the fire of burning freedom.

It is told around fireside and camp that there lived in Valley Forge that winter of the Revolutionary War a man who forgot that he had fled Germany to America for freedom's sake.

His name was Manheim and he was a Tory, so he spied for the English, but his daughter Elizabeth was on the American side. She had a sweetheart on General Washington's staff to whom she spoke of plots and treachery hatched by Manheim and his friends. In that bitter winter she became ill but kept up her patriotic work just the same.

One fierce, cold winter morning her father learned that General Washington would pass by Valley Forge that very afternoon and might even stop there. Here was a chance to kill the leader of the American War!

Manheim summoned at once some Tories living nearby, and together they hatched a plan to kill the general.

Elizabeth heard it, but she was too sick to go to camp. She prayed to God to give her the chance to warn Washington when he came.

Manheim and his men waited tensely, playing and drinking. So did Elizabeth, with burning face and parched lips. The day was getting on. A dull and hazy sun shone angrily in the sky and an icy wind whipped the trees and houses when a lone, tall horseman came down the road. He came to Manheim's house and the horse slowed down. The rider, General Washington, looked up at the sky, stopped, and knocked at the door.

Manheim watched behind the window.

"It's him," he whispered loudly to the men who were in the side room. "He can't get away this time. Shut the door and wait."

He opened the front door, and a cutting wind rushed in.

"How can I serve you, sir?" said Manheim, smirking. Elizabeth stood behind him.

"May I rest here for a short time and have some feed for my horse?"

"Both, sir, and with pleasure. I'll take your horse to the stable."

"I'll not trouble you, sir," said Washington. "I'll put it up."

The general saw the horse settled comfortably and then returned.

"This time we'll catch that big buzzard. I must get him to lie down in my room, and there we'll finish him quickly," Manheim said to his daughter. The girl did not answer. Her throat and her lips were dry, and her eyes burned.

The general was at the door, and Manheim led him into the room next to where the conspirators were.

"Would you like something to eat, sir?"

"No, thanks, all I need is a little rest."

"Then just have a glass of spirits. Elizabeth, fetch the bottle and glasses."

Elizabeth got a bottle and glasses, and Manheim filled them and gave one to Washington. He raised his own high and said, "General, here's to the success in our undertaking."

"To our success," said the general.

"Now, sir, if you will, you may rest in the upper floor in my room. You can stay as long as you wish. There's a bed there, sir, and you can look upon it as your own. Elizabeth, take the general into my chamber."

They walked into the hall, Manheim holding the candle high and talking all the time, till they came to the head of the stairs.

"Now, Elizabeth, show the general to my room."

Elizabeth began walking up the stairs.

"This way, sir," she said. Her father still stood at the head of the stairs. The girl's head was swirling, and she could hardly walk.

"I can't warn him, my father is standing there," she kept thinking. "What shall I do?"

Now she was at the top of the stairs; her father's room was the first door, her own the second. Without even thinking, she led the general to her own door instead of her father's, opened it, and said in a low voice:

"Here, sir, make yourself at home."

George Washington went in and closed the door.

Elizabeth could hardly walk down, and her father noticed.

"Daughter, you are ill. Go to your room and lie down; it will do you good."

"I think I will," she said. Her teeth were chattering.

Manheim went into the room where the Tories were waiting. Elizabeth walked up the stairs slowly, stopped for a moment, and then opened the door to her father's room, went in, and lay down on the bed.

All was still.

Manheim was with the two Tories in whispering conversation.

"He's in my room now and shortly will be asleep. We'll throw dice to see who should finish him. No one will look for him till the morrow, and by then we'll be safe with the British and well rewarded."

The dice were thrown, and they were against Manheim.

The German did not flinch. "I'll do it," he said. "We'll wait a little to make sure he's asleep."

They sat silent for a time. It was so still in that house that you could hear hearts beat. Outside, the wind screamed in wild fury.

Soon Manheim rose. He took off his boots and walked slowly up the stairs. It was pitch black, but he knew his way.

The first door was his room; he had told Elizabeth to take the general there. He had not seen her lead him to the second door, her own room....

He opened slowly the first door, the door to his room. It was dark, but he knew well where his bed was and he saw a figure on it.... He moved up to it. There was a swift movement in the dark! A moaning cry!...

Manheim came down quickly to where his men were drinking.

"We must set out at once; it is dark. I'll go fetch Elizabeth."

He ran up again, this time with candle in hand. Just as he reached the landing, the door of his daughter's room opened, and there stood General Washington!

"Host," he said quietly, "I want to thank you for your hospitality. I must set out. I will see that you are paid by my adjutant." He walked slowly down the steps and out. Manheim stood stock still, unable to speak! Then he rushed into his own chamber and—there was a piercing cry!

The Tory traitors ran up and through the open doorway; there Manheim stood still as stone and ghostly white, for on the bed lay his daughter, whom he had murdered. She had given her life to save Washington for America.

This legend can be either read or recited from memory to the children, and it is significant because it is seemingly about Washington but really about Elizabeth Manheim. Nobody may ever remember her, yet this legend gives her a due place in history. It opens the door to many questions that can be explored with children, questions both general and specific:

1. Must legends always be about famous people?
2. Who were the Tories?
3. Why were the Germans in America at that time? Whose side were they on during the Revolutionary War?
4. What happened at Valley Forge?
5. Have there been other wars that divided families? The Civil War? The Vietnam War?
6. Did Elizabeth want to sacrifice herself? What could she have done otherwise?
7. Is it important to remember people like Elizabeth?

The Great Sacrifice can lead to important follow-up activities on American history and perhaps to research about other "heroes" and "heroines" who have made sacrifices. The children can discuss what makes a hero and when and why it may be necessary to make a sacrifice. One suggestion for a writing exercise is for the children to imagine one of their real-life heroes placed in a dangerous sitation in which he or she may have to make a sacrifice. Their stories should illustrate what might happen if...

There are many other follow-up writing and drawing games that the storyteller and teacher can use with legends. For instance:

1. If *The Pied Piper* is used for the session, I ask the children to draw a picture and describe how the townspeople get rid of the rats without the help of a ratcatcher. Or, I ask them to show how the townspeople prevent the ratcatcher from leading the children from the town.
2. The children can also write and illustrate their own "What If" stories. Here I ask them to give me their questions, which I write on the board. "What if the mayor and town councillors had not lied? What if the town had been filled with tigers instead of rats? What if the Pied Piper had been a good fairy? What if the Pied Piper had led the children to paradise and their parents had joined them? What if the town councillors had admitted to lying and had told the Pied Piper they did not have enough money to pay him?"
3. Aside from the "What If" game, I ask the children, who do you think

might be a Pied Piper today. Can you imagine any person in your life—a politician, a movie star, a general—who might be regarded as a type of Pied Piper? Why? Can you draw that person as a Pied Piper and tell a story about him or her?

4. If I do not focus on *The Pied Piper*, I ask the children to give me important historical dates, and I write them on the board. For instance, if I focus on American history, some of the dates might be: 1492, 1620, 1779, 1810, 1865, etc. In many cases, the children do not know these dates, and this is a good time to introduce them. Once they are on the board, we may talk briefly about Columbus and the discovery of America, the arrival of the Pilgrims, the American Revolution, the War with England, and the Civil War. I do not put too many dates on the board, perhaps five or six, so that there is adequate time for discussion, and I ask each child who gives a date to say something about it. After the discussion, I ask the children to choose any date from the board and to try to write their own legend about that date. If they do not like any of the dates on the board, I tell them they can choose their own date from, local or personal history. In either case, I also ask them to illustrate the date. Once these stories are written, they are shared with the rest of the class. This activity is best combined with follow-up lessons in history by the teacher. Or, if the storyteller knows in advance that the teacher is planning a history cluster, the legend can be based on particular historical events or heroes.

5. Instead of dates, I ask for legendary heroes ranging from George Washington to Martin Luther King. I write the list of names on the board, and this list may be longer than the list of dates because the children have many different heroes and heroines who may include rock and movie stars, sports figures, or local people. At one point, after twenty or so names, I stop, and I ask the children to tell me what makes these people so important and legendary. Then I ask them to tell me a story about them and to illustrate the story. Again, if they do not find a name on the board that they like, they are free to choose their own name and write a story about their own legendary figure.

6. For older children, I have developed a follow-up activity with teachers that involves historical research. They are to take their birthday and write a brief report about who else was born on this day, what events have taken place on this day in the past, and what saints or legendary figures might be associated with this date. After writing the report, they

are to take one aspect and try to develop it into a legend by exaggerating the events. Younger children might want to write a legend about somebody famous or notorious in their family. They can do simple research by asking their parents or relatives about somebody who is "legendary" in the family.

7. In 1988, Richard Shenkman published a useful book entitled *Legends, Lies, and Cherished Myths of American History*. Among the truths that he establishes in contrast to the legends are:

    The story of Columbus discovering that the world is round was invented by Washington Irving.

    Most American presidents did not pull themselves up by their bootstraps. They came from well-to-do families.

    The popular image of the frontier as a place of violence is only partly due to the fact that the place often was violent. Many more people have died in Hollywood westerns than ever died on the real frontier. There is no evidence that anyone was ever killed in a frontier shoot-out at high noon.

    Shenkman exposes the falsehood of more than one hundred legends and myths, and his "exposures" can be used by older students as the basis for research stories and papers. Why and how did certain legends come into being? What is the difference between history and legend?

8. If the class or school happens to be focusing on a special historical event or figure, as many schools did with Columbus in 1992, I try to find appropriate material for my legend so that we can explore different perspectives. It is also possible to enhance cultural understanding in a class by discussing the famous legendary figures of different countries, ethnic groups, and ancient tribes. The children can be asked to research a particular date or legendary figure from another tradition in the library. Depending on the age group, they can be asked to compare different versions of a legend or to write their own legend about a historical incident or figure.

History is an art form. It is not a natural science or a social science. Reports on the past depend on the communicative skills and perspective of the historian, and historians must be good storytellers. They must develop narrative strategies and artfully bring together facts, documents, diaries, newspapers clippings, etc. in a manner that will convince their readers that their version of past events is "truthful" to the degree that we can establish truth. Historians must imagine events and depict them as a painter might portray them on a canvas. Historians can choose from a variety of narrative conventions and practices to convey *their* sense of history, and their versions of history form the basis of legend or are often legendary themselves.

Children are born historians. They return constantly to the important and traumatic events of their lives and record them in their subconscious and conscience. They are eager to learn about their birth and their history. At one point they want to know all about their prehistory: their grandparents, great grandparents, and so on. They want to belong to a community and to have a sense of their own importance. They want to make legends out of their own lives, they daydream about becoming important, and though they may be misled by certain legends, they can also learn how to make legends serve their own histories.

❧ 7 ❧
Mythmaking

One way to begin a session about myths is to tell either a legend or a fable about how powerful "legendary" figures sometimes call upon a god for help. Aside from making a connection between genres, the story helps make the simple and quick points that there are supernatural creatures whom we call gods or divinities, that tribes and societies have believed in these gods, and that many still do. These gods play different roles for different people, and they have been worshipped for different reasons. There are gods and goddesses of war, peace, hunting, harvesting, drinking, playing, music, wisdom, etc. Let us take Jupiter, for example, in one of Aesop's fables.

Zeus and the Bee

A long time ago, when the world was young, a bee stored her combs full of rich honey and flew up to heaven to make an offering as a sacrifice. Zeus was so delighted with the gift that he promised to give her whatever she requested. Therefore, she responded immediately and said, "Oh glorious Zeus, my maker and master, poor bee that I am, please give your servant a sting so that when anyone approaches my hive to take the honey, I may kill him on the spot."

Now Zeus was horrified, for he had not expected the tiny bee's viciousness. Moreover, out of his love for humans, Zeus became angry and answered her, "You shall have your sting, but your request will not be granted the way you wish. When anyone comes to take away your honey and you attack him, the wound shall be fatal, not to him but to you, for your life shall go with your sting."

Then there is Aesop's fable about the great goddess of love, and here we see a cat playing another important role.

Aphrodite and the Cat

Once a cat fell in love with a young man and prayed to Aphrodite to change her into a beautiful young woman, hoping to gain his affections. The goddess had compassion for the cat and transformed her into a lovely woman. As a result, the young man fell in love with her and soon took her home as his bride.

When they were sitting in their room, Aphrodite came to visit in an invisible form to see if she had changed the cat's nature by changing her shape. So she set a mouse down before her. Forgetting her new condition, the young woman jumped from her seat, pounced on the mouse, and would have eaten it on the spot if her horrified husband had not stopped her. Disturbed by such a frivolous act, Aphrodite immediately turned her into a cat again.

Try as one may, it is impossible to deny one's nature.

When I tell these fables, I always stress the unique nature of the Greek gods and explain how gods differ from humans in these fables. They have very few weaknesses and are stronger than both animals and humans . In fact, they determine the destinies of both animals and humans, who are often depicted as helpless without the gods. Then I ask the children whether they have ever heard of any other Greek gods and, if not Greek gods, any other gods and their remarkable qualities. If they have difficulty, I might suggest names such as Zeus, Diana, Odin, Thor, Heda, Mercury, Hercules, Prometheus, Varuna, Samitar, and others, and as I name these gods, I write them on the board and say something about their special powers. As soon as they volunteer a name, I ask about the powers that this god or goddess may have and, if possible, for a story or brief account about the god or goddess. Invariably, popular "gods" like Superman, Batman, Wonder Woman, and others are mentioned. I am not concerned about this confusion at this point because the children are making important connections. After all, is there a great difference between Zeus and Superman? For children, Superman is just as mythic as Zeus, and the storyteller can make important associations with popular heroes. On the other hand, I hope to point to some differences by illustrating the "religious" nature of the myths.

We use the word *myth* in many different ways, and one way is to indicate the difference between a true story and fiction. If I say, "that's just an old myth," I generally mean that nobody believes the story anymore or that it has been made up, is perhaps a lie. A mythomaniac is someone who cannot stop lying and exaggerating. We dismiss mythomaniacs and stories that are apparent falsehoods. Yet we also stand in awe of many of the ancient myths because we know that they held power over people at one time. They were sacred and linked to religious beliefs and rites, and their symbolic language still has a great appeal for us today. Moreover, we all want to believe in the supernatural and identify with the supernatural, especially children. They need to believe that there are powers that will intercede in their lives and protect them, not only from inimical forces outside their homes and communities but from problems within them.

As I tell myths, I try to bring out their paradoxical nature. On one hand, they can help children understand the significance of humility by showing that human beings depend on gods and must obey their laws and worship them or else be punished. On the other hand, myths "humanize" the gods, bring them down to earth, and reveal that they are no better than humans, or, put more positively, humans can be like gods. There is divine potential in each one of us. We can become like a god, if we follow certain rites of passage.

The rites of passage are at the basis of most myths throughout the world. And the narrative structures of the myths that I tell are clearly different from the fables that I introduce at the beginning of the session. Whereas fables deal with everyday life, concern the survival of the common person, use animals metaphorically, and always end with some kind of moral, myths concern the extraordinary, use gods metaphorically, and seek to explain why the world has become the way it is. Fables serve as a transition for introducing myths and for demonstrating similarities and differences. In particular, Aesop's fables are didactic and celebrate the omnipotence of the gods, as do many other Greek and Roman fables; they are also similar to warning tales. After establishing the awesome power of the gods through the fables, I move in the other direction to "humanize" them. Here it is important to recall the sacred nature of myths.

One of the great scholars of religion and myth, Mircea Eliade, shed a great deal of light on this aspect of myth, which, he believed, "narrates a sacred history; it relates an event that took place in primordial Time, the fabled time of the 'beginnings.' In other words, myth tells us how, through the deeds of Supernatural Beings, a reality came into existence, be it the whole of reality, the Cosmos, or only a fragment of reality—an island, a species of plant, a particular kind of human behavior, an institution."[1] Since myth narrates the deeds of supernatural beings, it sets examples for human beings that enable them to codify and order their lives. By enacting and incorporating myths into their daily lives, humans can have genuine religious experiences. Indeed, it is through recalling the gods of the past and bringing them into the present that one becomes their contemporary and at the same time is transported into primordial or sacred time. This transportation is also a connection, for a mortal can gain a sense of his or her origins and feel history as the present and time as divine.

What interests me when I tell myths is how these stories intend to reveal the mysteries of the world though initiation scenarios and the portrayal of exemplary heroes. Time and again, no matter what the ancient society was (and we can still see this aspect in viable contemporary myths), its myths contain initiatory ordeals. They present battles with monsters, apparently insurmountable obstacles, riddles to be solved, and impossible tasks, such as descent to the underworld or ascent to heaven. Other myths explain the origins of the world, how good and evil forces developed, and in what ways the gods are models to be emulated and or questioned.

Zeus and the Great Flood

Thousands of years ago, there was nothing but chaos in the universe, and out of this whirling chaos was born Eros, the spirit of love, and from this spirit came Uranos and Gaea, heaven and earth, and Erebos and Nyx, night and day. And as love moved and soothed the turbulent forces, order was brought about in the universe, and soon Eros peopled the heavens with mighty and immortal gods and the earth with mortal humans and animals.

The rulers of the heavens were magnificent gods, and the greatest of the gods were Zeus and Hera. Zeus was the father of gods and humans, and, as the bringer of light, he possessed every form of power imaginable. It was he who controlled day and night, the seasons, and the winds, and it was he who watched over the earth and judged the actions of human beings. He demanded and rewarded truth, faithfulness, and kindness, and punished falseness, faithlessness, and cruelty. He could be generous and merciful or hard and wrathful. His wife Hera was no less powerful, and she, too, protected the virtuous and punished the sinful. It was she who helped women at childbirth and was honored at harvest time. It was she who opposed the forces of darkness on the earth and often tempered Zeus's anger with her mercy and wisdom.

The heavens where Zeus and Hera made their dwelling were called Olympus, and the most powerful gods lived in this abode: Poseidon, god of sea; Hades, god of the underworld; Ceres, goddess of agriculture; Apollo, god of the sun; Artemis, goddess of the moon; Hephaestus, god of fire; Athena, goddess of storms and battles; Ares, god of war; Aphrodite, goddess of love; Hermes, god of animals and cunning; and Hestia, goddess of the hearth. They all had their temples and priests on earth, and they all ruled their realms of the world in harmony, although they sometimes fought among themselves, and sometimes wrought chaos on earth and caused mischief among the humans who were driven to sin.

Indeed, the human race was once nearly destroyed by Zeus, and would have been if it were not for Philemon and Baukis, a kind old couple, poor but pious, who honored Zeus every day in their poor cottage in Phrygia. Now, Zeus was a master of disguises, and he could take the shape of man or beast, and he often came to earth unexpectedly to see what his people were like and how they were behaving. So, one day, he said to Hermes, "Come with me, my swift messenger, we shall disguise ourselves as beggars and visit the earth, for we have not been there many a year, and rumor has it that chaos may return to the world. And if chaos returns to the world, then the entire universe will be threatened."

Hermes, who was always faithful to Zeus, agreed to accompany the great god, and they disguised themselves as two beggars, father and son. Once they arrived on earth, they could move with the speed of light and appear wherever and whenever they desired. When they did, they heard,

"Away, you wretches!"

"Get out of here!"

"Send the dogs after them!"

"Beat them!"

"You have one hour to leave this land, or you die!"

"You disgusting, dirty creatures!"

Wherever Zeus and Hermes went on earth, they were cursed and turned away. They saw war and starvation, greed and cruelty, rich against poor, man against woman, and all the people killing animals and tearing up the earth. There was so much crime and chaos that Zeus made up his mind to stop it by doing away with all of humankind. That is, until he came to the city of Phrygia. At first, he and Hermes went begging at the doors of the rich, and at each of the villas and houses, they were turned away with mean words. They were about to return to Olympus when a wealthy landowner said, "Get out of my sight! If you want help, go to Philemon and Baukis. They may be the only ones stupid enough to give you some crumbs!" And he pointed to a tiny cottage on a hill outside the city and slammed the door in front of the two beggars' faces.

When they reached the cottage of Philemon and Baukis, they stood in front of the small dwelling which had no door. Then Philemon came out and said, "Welcome to our hut."

"You must be tired," Baukis said, and she prepared a warm bath for them and asked them to rest.

After they were refreshed, Philemon told them he was going to kill a goose for their dinner. It was their last goose, but he told them that it didn't matter, for somehow, with the help of the gods, they would find a way to survive and to help those in need, especially beggars like Zeus and Hermes.

With that, Zeus had heard enough, and he and Hermes suddenly revealed themselves as the great gods that they were. Philemon and Baukis were terribly frightened, but Zeus told them, "The good have nothing to fear in life!"

And his words were like lightning and thunder, and the skies became dark and violent. When Zeus waved his hand, the cottage was transformed into a golden temple and the hill into a large mountain, and below, the people of the city came running out of their homes. When they saw the golden temple and Zeus and Hermes standing next to Philemon and Baukis, they began offering sacrifices to the gods and worshipping them. But it was in vain. Zeus would not accept their false sacrifices, and he waved his hand again, letting loose a monstrous flood to cleanse the entire world of sinners. Only the temple on top of the mountain and Philemon and Baukis remained, and when the flood began, Zeus spoke to the kind couple, whom he transformed into a priest and priestess.

"Take these stones," he said, giving six each to Philemon and Baukis, "and throw them from the mountain."

The couple did as they were told, and their stones went flying hundreds and thousands of miles in all directions from the mountaintop, and wherever they hit the water, land began to emerge again. Eros swept down from Mount Olympus, and soon the force of love created life once more.

Philemon and Baukis lived to a ripe old age, and people took journeys to visit them, celebrate peace on earth, and honor Zeus and Hera and all the gods. When the time finally arrived for the kind Philemon and Baukis to die, they were changed into two trees, an oak and a linden, and they stood on either side of the temple for thousands of years to come.

Since some children may be uneasy about myths that concern religious topics and beliefs, I purposely use Greek and Roman myths because they are part of our classical Western heritage but do not touch directly on the children's lives. Moreover, they are related to other myths and religions in the world, and by telling a myth that depicts the origins of the world, I can give the children a sense that many cultures have different gods and unusual versions of how the world began and how people have sinned. I do not want to correct the children's own "religious" versions. Rather, the use of the Greek myths can foster tolerance for other types of religions and customs. Since the Greek and Roman gods are so fantastic and distant, they free the children to contemplate what it means to be divine, what is just and noble, and why there are different explanations for the origins of natural phenomena.

Following the "origins" myth, I generally tell a heroic myth that depicts significant gods and figures who are bound to be recognizable to the children either through comics, TV serials, or popular films.

How Fire and Hope Came to the Earth

For many years Zeus refused to let humans know the source of fire, and it remained a mystery to them. To be sure, they learned to make fires in their huts and caves to keep them warm during the winter. They needed fire to cook their meals and make their weapons. They lit torches to worship the gods and to bring light into dark dwellings. But at the beginning of the world, they did not know where fire came from, for it quite often burst from the skies like lightning and set forests and land ablaze, and other times it exploded from volcanoes as though it came from the bowels of the earth. People were frightened of the flames, especially when the fire spread and destroyed forests and dwellings. Each time sparks flew through the air and blazing flames appeared, they prayed to Zeus for help, for they did not know how to control fire or use it effectively to create energy and power.

Zeus liked it this way because he did not trust humans. If they learned the source of fire, he felt, they would become arrogant and use it for destructive purposes.

"No, that is not the case," said Prometheus, the noble Titan, who had come to plead with Zeus. "Please, you must trust humans. They will make great progress if they know how to use fire."

Hera, who admired the handsome Prometheus, also spoke in his behalf. "Perhaps he is right," the Queen said. "Perhaps we should aid them with fire."

"They will only create more and more weapons and destroy the earth if they learn the secret of fire!" Zeus said angrily. "What you call progress is death and destruction!"

"But fire can help cure and heal people. Like the light of your wisdom, fire can illuminate ways toward a better life," Prometheus pleaded.

"You have heard my answer!" Zeus said. "I said no, and I mean no."

But Prometheus was courageous and stubborn, and though Titans are only demi-gods, they can perform extraordinary feats. So, when Zeus had retired for the evening, Prometheus bravely stole some fire from Zeus's hearth and disclosed the secret of fire to humankind. The people rejoiced when they learned what fire could do for them, and they worshipped Prometheus as a god.

However, Zeus was enraged and summoned Prometheus to Olympus.

"You have disobeyed me!" Zeus roared. "Just who do you think you are?"

"I have only tried to champion the cause of humanity," Prometheus said humbly.

"Well, my champion of humanity," Zeus said, "you will pay mightily for your crime."

"Have mercy," Hera said. "Perhaps it will turn out not to be a crime! Prometheus meant well."

"Yes, I shall have mercy," said Zeus. "He will not die, but he will learn what it means to be insolent, and he will be reminded each day what it means to steal fire from the gods!"

"I am ready," Prometheus said nobly.

But Prometheus was not really ready for the horrible punishment. In his anger, Zeus condemned the hero to be chained alive to a rock in the Caucasus Mountains, and every day a gigantic vulture came and ate his liver. But Prometheus was not to die, for Zeus had his liver grow anew each night so that the vulture could feast on his liver again the next day.

The noble Prometheus suffered for a long time, and he would have suffered even longer if Hera had not taken pity on him. She told her husband that justice that is cruel is not justice, and that she, too, had a say in this affair. She summoned Heracles, another great Titan, to take his bow and arrow and shoot the vulture, which he did. And when the vulture lay dead, the powerful Heracles carried Prometheus on his shoulders back to Olympus, where Hera honored him and made it known to the humans that Prometheus was the bringer of light.

However, Zeus was angry at Hera and resented the fact that the human race was now enjoying the benefits of fire. So he ordered his son Vulcan to create a beautiful woman out of clay, and he named her Pandora. Then Zeus ordered Athene to teach her all the domestic skills that women must know, until she was perfect. He ordered Aphrodite to teach Pandora how to be graceful and artful, until she was the epitome of beauty. Finally, Zeus commanded Hermes to train her to use her speech to flatter and charm, to convince and demand, until she was the perfect speaker. When all the gods had put their touch on Pandora and she was finished, there was no one, god or man, who could resist her charms and beauty.

Zeus was extremely pleased with the final product, and he called upon his trusty Hermes and said, "I want you to take Pandora to Epimetheus, the brother of Prometheus, as a gift. Do this now without fail!"

When Prometheus heard what Zeus was doing, he warned his brother that this might be a trick, but Epimetheus thought that Zeus was trying to atone for the cruel manner in which he had punished his brother. Besides, he fell in love with Pandora at first sight, so striking was she, and he married her the next day.

Now, Pandora had a beautiful jeweled box with her that Zeus had given her, and Zeus had told her that it was never to be opened. It was only to be admired. When Epimetheus asked her what was inside, she said, "Never, never open it."

"But you must trust me," Epimetheus said.

"Of course I trust you," Pandora replied. "But even I do not know what is inside."

"Don't you want to know?"

"No," she replied. "I fear to disobey the gods."

But the longer the box stood in her room, the more beautiful and attractive and mysterious it seemed, and one day, Epimetheus could not restrain himself. Despite Pandora's warning, he took the box from her and demanded the key, but as soon as he opened it, he was shocked—all the diseases, maladies, troubles, and plagues that were to trouble humankind forever came rushing out of the box. Epimetheus was horrified and ashamed, and he would have killed

himself, but Pandora pointed out to him that Hera had also put something else into the box that would also stay with humankind. It was
Hope, she pointed out to him; Hope that humans would eventually
triumph over the worst of catastrophes.

And so it was, and so it is.

I purposely choose a heroic myth that conveys a sense of comedy and
tragedy so that children can begin thinking about stories in these terms.
Depending on the age group, the storyteller can talk about tragedy, comedy,
and tragicomedy. Possible questions:

Who is a hero?

What is a tragic hero?

What are gods?

What are titans?

What are nymphs?

Why are there so many different kinds of myths?

Sometimes I tell a Scandinavian and an Irish myth and compare the
two. Other times I introduce African and Oriental myths. If I want to illustrate what tragedy is—and I like to present concrete examples in discussions, since they often lead to stories—I might tell the Oedipus myth. But
my favorite tragic myth is an Egyptian myth:

A young man eagerly wants to know all about truth, and he
becomes a disciple at the temple in Sais, where the great goddess Isis resides. Isis is not only a moon goddess; she also represents
Truth, and only those who are ready to face Truth can see her, for she
wears a veil. Very few have ever seen her face. The young disciple is
told that he must be patient and learn how to read the mysterious
symbols of nature before he can be initiated and allowed into the
temple of Isis. However, he loses his patience, and one day he steals
into the temple and takes off the veil of Isis so that he can see her.
However, face-to-face with Isis, he is turned into stone, for Truth is
both sublimely beautiful and terrifyingly ugly.

The face of Isis's face in this myth is like the face of Medusa: if you are not ready for the truth, it can be so horrific that it can kill you.

The tragic story of this disciple can be contrasted with a myth of successful initiation concerning a young man or woman. Here I often tell a myth about moon worship that may be related to *Cinderella*, for it deals with the reincarnation of a mother who successfully guides her daughter through different (lunar) phases of her life. There are some fine collections of myths that storytellers and teachers can use and vary in storytelling and follow-up sessions. In each case, I make sure that the children become familiar with the functions of the gods and their connections to certain rituals. I also ask the children if they know any myths and want to share them with the rest of the class. Since there are numerous definitions of myth, we discuss them and try to come to a consensus.

Once we complete this discussion, or once we reenact a myth, I write the following on the board:

Zeus, king of the heavens and all-powerful god
Hera, queen of the heavens and all-powerful goddess
Poseidon, god of the sea
Hades, god of the lower world
Persephone, goddess of vegetation
Demeter, goddess of agriculture
Hestia, goddess of the hearth
Ares, god of war
Hephaestus, god of fire
Apollo, god of the sun
Artemis, goddess of the moon
Aprhodite, goddess of beauty
Athena, goddess of wisdom
Hermes, god of speech, messenger of the gods
Dionysos, god of drink and spring
Themis, goddess of hospitality

After all the names are on the board, I ask the children to imagine a story that involves one or more of these gods, and then to illustrate it. I discuss what sort of help humans might ask from these gods and why.

What functions do the gods serve?

Explanation of function

Illustration of powers and qualities of gods

Discussion of rituals and celebrations

Do humans always receive help?

Types of help

Forms of initiation

What must humans do to receive help from the gods?

Interdependence of humans

Gratitude of humans

Do the gods always agree among themselves?

Discussion of different belief systems

Explanation of conflicts on earth due to gods

Should one always obey the gods?

Discussion of authority

Absolutism and faith

Once we break the myths down through questions and discussion, the children can better see how the stories are constructed, and they can choose one of the questions as the basis for their stories. They share their short myths at the end of the session, and, of course, the teacher can pursue numerous follow-ups with the Roman and Greek myths.

Many other writing games can be played with the gods. Most children are already familiar with these games, but they can be useful in a different context.

1. Card game—Cards are distributed, and each child chooses a god or goddess to illustrate. The cards are collected by the storyteller/teacher, mixed, and redistributed. The children must tell a story based on their new card and must create a new illustration for the story. Groups of five children are then formed, and each receives five cards. Each group must retell one of the storyteller's myths in its own way. The groups must use the cards they have, but they can expand and embellish the myth any way they desire. When the groups are done, they form a circle, and each group takes a turn reciting or performing their myth.

2. Salad game—The names of three to five gods are written on the board, and are then mixed with other words. Based on the words on the board, the children write and illustrate their own myths.

As a follow-up to the introduction of myths, the teacher can introduce the children to other mythic figures in Celtic, Norse, German, Egyptian, Brahmanic, African, Vedic, or Native American mythologies. Depending on the school, the teacher can work with a librarian or with parents to discuss the natures of different mythologies, and can ask the children to look up myths in encyclopedias and dictionaries and write small reports. If the children are old enough, they can do more extensive research reports and recite their findings in class. They can also write myths based on their findings.

Not only do children learn about ancient societies and religions through myths, but they begin to explore the idea of history and how the past may be related to the present. They take hold of the myths, mold the myths, and, in the process, render mythmaking more than just an exaggeration. Mythmaking extends our imaginative way of living and helps us touch the mysterious forces that we want to fathom.

❧ 8 ❧
Tall Tales

In Minneapolis, after I had held a series of storytelling sessions at the Andersen Open School, I walked into the classroom one day and told the children, "No more fairy tales or myths." I announced that I was going to tell them a real story, and I proceeded to recall the following anecdote.

When I was about seventeen years old, I had a big fight with my parents. I had told them that I needed their car to go to school and meet some students in the evening to rehearse a play, but I really went to a party. When my father and mother found out, they yelled at me and grounded me for lying to them. Well, I was so hurt and so mad that I stole the car after they went to bed. It must have been around midnight, but I didn't care. I just wanted to run away, and I headed up north.

As I was driving, it began to snow. I should have checked the weather report, but I hadn't had time. Well, the fact was, I was driving into a blizzard. I drove and drove until I could go no further. When I got stuck, I knew I shouldn't stay in the car or I would freeze to death. So I got out and started walking. I couldn't see anything. My coat was covered with ice and snow. I was shivering and on the verge of tears, but even my tears froze, and I kept wishing that I had never left home. I could barely move, but I knew I shouldn't stop or I would freeze in the snow. Suddenly, I came upon a cave and rushed inside. It was pitch black. I couldn't see a thing. I was still cold, but at least I was protected from the snow. At least, I thought I was safe until, all at once, I heard a roar. Not a plain roar, but a ferocious roar. I turned and blinked. Standing before me was a huge, five-hundred-pound grizzly bear looking right into my eyes. I was paralyzed with fright! I was so scared that I think my heart stood still. What was I going to do? I had no weapons with me, not even a knife. I couldn't run out into the snow. I wasn't stronger than the bear. I certainly wasn't faster. Finally, I remembered—bears could be hypnotized if you kept still and looked into their eyes for three minutes, straight into their eyes without blinking. So, I summoned my courage. While the bear was trying to make up his mind whether or not to eat me, I stared at him, straight into his eyes. After a while the bear seemed to be humming and in a trance.

"Bear," I said. "Sit up!"

The bear sat up.

"Bear," I said. "Turn over!"

The bear turned over.

You can't imagine how happy I felt. I looked around, and I saw that it was beginning to get light outside. So I said, "Bear, lie down!"

I got on top of the bear, and I said, "Bear, carry me home."

And the bear left the cave, and I directed the bear through the snow toward my home early in the morning. When I got there, my parents were astonished. At first, they wanted to run and get the police, but when I jumped off and ran to them, they realized there was no danger. Still, they had been very worried about me, and they made me promise never to lie or run away again. As for the bear, who was still hypnotized, we gave him to the zoo, and if you want to find out whether I'm telling the truth, you just have to go down to the Minneapolis zoo and ask old Mike the zookeeper, who's in charge of the grizzly that carried me home and sort of saved my life in the blizzard.

After telling this tale, I was surprised at first to see how many of the children actually believed it. They wanted to know more about the bear, how mad my parents were, where all this took place, whether the bear was still at the zoo, etc. Some of the children, however, were doubtful and began asking me how I had hypnotized the bear. They said it was impossible, and anyway, how could a bear understand English? How did I stay on the bear's back in the snow? Eventually, after it became obvious that I was not telling the truth, I explained to the children that I had told a "tall tale," that is, I had stretched a short anecdote in my life to make it sound like something big. I told them that I had run away from home one time and that my parents had been worried because I had taken their car, but that I had never met a bear and had returned after a day because I missed my parents and did not want to hurt them. In my imagination, I said, I like to think of what might have happened, or I like to make some events of my life more exciting.

The tall tale is closely related to the legend and the myth because they involve actual events and beliefs, exaggerated and told in many different versions depending on the social and temporal context. In the case of the legend, the story is generally based on an actual event. In the case of the myth, the story is generally based on a real belief system and practiced rituals. In the case of the tall tale, however, there is an important shift in emphasis and theme. Instead of focusing on a hero or god, the narrator generally tells a story based on an incident in his or her own life, or an event in a friend or acquaintance's own life. The common person becomes the hero; everyman and everywoman can become a hero. The ordinary becomes extraordinary, and the distortion is a means by which we can laugh at ourselves or dissect an event to understand what happened or why we did what we did. The tall tale is often based on a simple anecdote that needs to be repeated because it is not as simple as it seems; otherwise, we would not remember it. The anecdote keeps coming back to us in different forms until it becomes part of family or communal lore. It may be related to a wish, a wish for something that did not happen and that we still desire. It may also be related to a desire to celebrate some talent or gift that we find lacking in ourselves and wish to possess. Or the anecdote might deal with a talent of ours that has not been recognized; we insist through the tale that we are greater than we seem. Finally, the tall tale often contains burlesque humor, and openly exposes human weakness without harming the target in the way that ironic, cynical, or sadistic humor might.

Tall tales were often told on the American frontier to overcome fear of the unknown, and to provide laughter when dread and anxiety threatened to depress people. Tall tales are optimistic because they are about escape and about how common people use their cunning to outwit hostile forces. They are also about luck and about learning how to grab hold of an opportunity. In this respect, they are related to the Hans and Gretel tales in the Grimms' collection or the British and American Jack tales. One tall tale I am fond of telling is:

Clever Gretel

There was once a cook named Gretel who wore shoes with red heels, and when she went out in them, she whirled this way and that way and was as happy as a lark. "You really are quite pretty!" she would say to herself. And when she returned home, she would drink some wine out of sheer delight. Since the wine would increase her appetite, she would take the best things she was cooking and taste them until she was content. Then she would say, "The cook must know what her own food tastes like before she serves it!"

One day, her master said to her, "Gretel, tonight I'm having a guest for dinner. Please prepare two chickens for me and make them real tasty."

"I'll take care of it, sir," Gretel responded. So she killed two chickens, scalded them, and stuck them on a spit. When evening arrived, she began roasting them over a fire. The chickens began to turn brown and were almost ready, but the guest did not make his appearance. So Gretel called to her master, "If the guest doesn't come soon, I'll have to take the chickens off the fire. It would be a great shame if they weren't eaten now while they're still so juicy."

"Then I'll run and fetch the guest myself," responded the master.

When the master had left the house, Gretel laid the spit with the chickens to one side and thought, "If I keep standing by the fire, I'll just sweat and get thirsty. Who knows when they'll come? Meanwhile, I'll hop down into the cellar and take a drink."

She ran downstairs, filled a jug with wine, and said, "May God bless it for you, Gretel!" Then she took a healthy swig. "The wine flows nicely," she continued, "and it's not good to interrupt the flow." So she took another long swig and carried the jug back upstairs to the kitchen, where she placed the chickens back over the fire, basted them with butter, and merrily turned the spit. Since the chickens had been roasting a long time, she thought, "I'd better taste them to see how they are." She touched one of them with her finger and said, "Goodness! The chickens are really juicy! It's a crying shame not to eat them all at once!" She ran to the window to see if her master was on his way with the guest, but when she saw no one coming, she returned to the chickens and thought, "That one wing is burning, I'd better eat it."

So she cut it off and enjoyed eating it. When she had finished, she thought, "I'd better eat the other wing or my master will notice that something's missing." After she had consumed the two wings she returned to the window and looked for her master, who was nowhere to be seen. "Who knows?" it suddenly occurred to her. "Perhaps they've decided not to come and have stopped somewhere along the way to have a drink." Then she said to herself, "Hey, Gretel, cheer up! You've already taken a nice chunk. Have another drink and eat it all up! When it's gone, there'll be no reason for you to feel guilty. Why should God's good gifts go to waste?"

So, she took a drink of the wine from the jug and ate the chicken with relish. When she had eaten one chicken and her master still had not returned, Gretel looked at the other bird and said, "Where one is, the other should be too. The two of them belong together: whatever's right for one is right for the other. I think if I have another drink, it won't do me any harm." So she took another healthy swig and began sending the second chicken to join the other in her stomach.

Just as she was in the midst of enjoying her meal, her master came back and called, "Hurry, Gretel, the guest will soon be here!"

"Yes, sir, I'll get everything ready," answered Gretel.

The master checked to see if the table was properly set, and he took out the large carving knife and began sharpening it on the steps in the hallway. While he was doing that, the guest came and knocked politely at the door. Gretel ran to answer it, and when she opened it, she put her finger to her lips and whispered, "Shhh, be quiet! Get out of here as quick as you can! If my master catches you, you'll be done for. Listen to him sharpening his knife! He's going to cut off your ears!"

The guest heard the sharpening of the knife and dashed from the house as fast as he could. Gretel wasted no time and ran screaming to her master, "What kind of guest did you invite!!" she cried.

"Goodness gracious, Gretel! What's going on? What do you mean?"

"Well," she sobbed, "he snatched both chickens just as I was about to bring them to the table, and he's run away with them!"

"What's got into him?" said her master, was upset by his friend's behavior and especially by the loss of the fine chickens. "At least he could have left me one of them so I'd have something to eat."

He then ran out the door and began chasing his guest and shouting at him to stop. But the guest pretended not to hear. So the master continued running after him with the carving knife still in his hand, screaming, "Just give me one, just one!" meaning that the guest should at least leave him one of the chickens. But the guest thought that his host was after one of his ears, and to make sure that he would reach home safely with both ears, he ran as if someone had lit a fire under his feet.

I use this tale try to set a narrative model for the children. At one time, *Clever Gretel* was probably just an amusing anecdote about an incident between a master and a cook, exaggerated through different tellings and changed into a tall tale. The protagonist is a cook, and the incident concerns the common act of cooking, which is turned into a preposterous tale of "rebellion." There are numerous tall tales concerning cooking and food. We spend a good deal of our time in kitchens and eating, and we tell many a tale while eating at a table. We also tell tales while cooking together in the kitchen if someone is with us. Many tales are also about food, the lack of food, appetites, and hunger. It is not by chance that there are so many tales about food, since we depend on it so much and never seem to get enough, never seem to have it when we need it. An entire cycle of tales originated during the Middle Ages about the "Land of Cokagyne," or the "Land of Cocaigne," in which everything is turned upside down and everyone has plenty to eat and drink. The designations "cokagyne" and "cocaigne" stem from the Italian word "cucania," which meant a kind of cake or cookie in the Middle Ages. Therefore, as the tales spread to different countries, the name changed but still indicated the topos: the "Land of Cockagne," "Land of Cocaigne," or, in German, "Schlaraffenland" was a sweet land, a paradise in the common Medieval imagination, where there was an abundance of good things to eat and no laws or rules to deprive people of what they desired. Throughout the Middle Ages and up to the present, tall tales about turning the world inside out and feasting were especially common during Carnival and have become associated with holidays. Amid the famines and general poverty of the Middle Ages, food became a symbol of liberty and joy.

In *Clever Gretel*, the cook emancipates herself, so to speak, by drinking her master's wine and taking her master's food. She does this innocently, but she does it out of a great desire to have a good life. We all want good lives—even common cooks—and even in kitchens, there can be a kind of rebellion, or a wish for change. Turning the table on her master, Gretel links a tall tale to change and to transformation, and the narrative structure of the tale itself follows the principle of transformation. What begins as a common, seemingly realistic event with a common character is gradually exaggerated and changed into a fantastic event: the protagonist seizes an opportunity to fulfill a wish or desire, or somehow stumbles into good fortune. This is especially true in the Jack tales and the Hans tales, which are not always tall tales but are certainly related to them.

Soon after telling *Clever Gretel*, I ask the children if they want to hear about something else that happened to me, and I promise with my fingers crossed that, this time, I'll tell them a true story. Then I proceed with:

The Snake Pond

One winter I was visiting my cousins in a little town called Pleasantville, New York. It was early winter, and though there was snow on the ground, most of the lakes and ponds were beginning to freeze. We wanted to play in the woods, and since my parents knew that we liked to play ice hockey, even without skates, on the Snake Pond, they warned us not to go near the pond because it was probably not solid ice yet. We promised to do as they said, but we were somewhat wild at that time, feeling our oats, my two cousins who were ten and eleven, my brother, who was also eleven, and me, the oldest at twelve.

Snake Pond was a pond we loved to play hockey on with sticks and a stone. We never went swimming there because it had the worst snakes, lizards, and other reptiles you can imagine. Some people even said there were strange sea monsters in the water. But we never believed them. We knew they were just trying to scare us.

When we got there, we saw that the pond was frozen, so just for the fun of it, and to test the ice, we began throwing rocks on it. The more we threw, the more we realized that the pond was frozen solid. We picked up the heaviest rocks imaginable to make one final throwing test. The ice remained frozen. So we decided to go out on the ice for the very final test before we began playing hockey.

As usual, since I was the oldest and tallest, I went first, and behind me, single file, were my brother and two cousins on their tiptoes, a little afraid. I was calm, and I turned my head to them as we inched our way to the middle. "It's okay, you chickens," I told them. "Just follow me." But when I reached the middle, the ice started to crack. My brother and cousins jumped with fright, turned, and ran off the ice, and there I was, left alone in the middle with the ice cracking. I made a desperate attempt to follow them, but the ice split, and I plunged into the water. Down I went, deep, and I could barely hold my breath. As I rose to the top, I cried out, "Get a branch! Quick! Quick!"

One of my cousins found a long branch and flung it out onto the ice, and while treading water, I grabbed hold of it. They grabbed the other end and pulled and pulled, until I began to emerge. Just as I was climbing out of the water onto the ice and beginning to crawl, however, a huge hand grabbed at my leg.

"No!" I screamed. "Help!"

The hand was pulling me back into the water. There was a tug of war between my cousins and brother and the monstrous hand. Finally, I reached into my pocket and pulled out my hunting knife and began stabbing the gruesome hand until it let go. I reached the shore, shivering. We ran home, and my father gave me a good talking-to and grounded me for a week. But I couldn't forget the hand. Nor could my cousins and brother. Nobody believed us. They said it must have been weeds or a snake or some animal.

But that summer, when I was visiting my cousins again, we went to Snake Pond to fish. We took out a rowboat, and when we got to the middle of the pond, we threw out our lines. I was the last, and when I cast my line, a hand shot up, a monstrous hand, and tried to pull me in.

"Let go!" my cousins cried out. "Let go! It's tipping the boat!"

But before I knew it, I was dragged from the boat and pulled deep into the water. When I opened my eyes, I was face to face with a hideous creature. I knew it was going to be a struggle for life or death.

And just as the monster was about to strangle me, an octopus grabbed his legs, one after the other, and dragged him away. I don't know what happened to the monster, but I rose to the top and climbed onto the rowboat, and my cousins set a new world record for rowing us to the shore.

Since then I've never returned to Snake Pond, and I don't think I ever will.

After the second tall tale, I admit to the children that I have not kept my promise but have told a "whopper." But, I explain to them once again that my story is partially true and is based on an incident from my childhood when I almost drowned by walking on the ice of a pond when I shouldn't have. It is a story I like to tell, I say, because it reminds me that I should be careful in dangerous situations. And, of course, my cousins and brother like to tell the story because they can tease me about the incident.

Once I demonstrate how I can use a real event in my life as the basis for an exaggerated story, I ask the children whether they have any "tall tales" or "whoppers" to tell. Instead of doing creative dramatics this time, I try to develop a "story swapping session." If at first there are no responses, I ask the children leading questions such as:

1. What about a fishing trip? Did a big fish get away? Did a canoe or boat almost tip over?
2. What about a skiing trip? Did a monster appear in the mountains? Did you have to ski through great mountains?
3. What about just going into a cellar and encountering a ghost? Or perhaps a buried treasure?
4. What about simply taking the bus and seeing the bus drive off to a strange place and not to school? The bus driver loses his or her way and takes you to another country.
5. What about going shopping and buying a cheap ring for a quarter? Then, when you rub the ring, a geni appears and grants you three wishes.
6. What about a doll or stuffed animal that suddenly comes alive?
7. What if you went to your locker and you were cleaning it out when, all of a sudden, you heard a noise at the back of the locker? You look carefully, and the back of the locker opens up. You step into your locker

and go through the back door. What do you see? What happens?

8. What if you have gym and you have forgotten your gym shoes? The gym teacher sends you to the lost and found where there is a box of old gym shoes. You have to put on a pair of strange gym shoes. Suddenly, the shoes begin dancing or flying. The shoes are magic. What happens?

I ask the children to think about real events in their lives and how they might change them or exaggerate to make another kind of story out of them. I try to get them to play with their daydreams because, unlike the nocturnal dreams that tend to have nightmarish qualities and are more related to anxiety and dread, daydreams are filled with hope and anticipation. They are projections of possibilities and alternatives that indicate how life can be changed. I want to exploit the children's daydreams in a positive way, exploit them in the sense of mining and using the rich material and stuff of these daydreams that may illustrate for the children the direction they want their own lives to take.

By swapping tales in a circle, we are also exchanging information about ourselves, revealing and sharing moments of our lives. Swapping tales is a form of building community and creating trust, even if the starting point is the tall tale, because the tall tale contains more truth about ourselves than we realize. By no means should a storyteller or teacher put pressure on *all* the children to tell a tale; the swapping must occur on a voluntary basis. Once the children are encouraged, there are usually many volunteers to fabricate fabulous tales on the spot, especially if you begin with a suggestion like discovering a door at the back of the locker. For instance, my wife used this motif to begin a chain story sitting in a circle with each child making a contribution to the narrative. She began the tale by telling how she opened the door at the back of her locker and entered a strange world. Then she stopped and had each child add a short incident as my wife became a character and wandered in a strange land like Alice in Wonderland or like the children in Narnia.

Swapping tales is just the beginning of this session. I go on to introduce several writing and drawing games to enhance the children's communicative skills.

1. I ask the children to take any event in their lives—happy, sad, cruel, kind, etc.—and change it in an exaggerated way. Since we have already done the swapping, they have the confidence to take common and

ordinary happenings and to play with them in their imagination. I ask them to pretend that something happened when it did not happen, or to take a true story and change it into a lie, or to take a lie and change it into a true story. All of these stories can be illustrated.

2. While we are swapping stories, I ask the children whether they want to play a sort of game with tall tales and true tales. I ask for a volunteer to tell a story, but *not* to tell us whether it is true or not. We are then supposed to guess whether the tale is a tall tale or a true tale. Here I try to show how a story can be told either tongue-in-cheek or sincerely. The children use their vocal powers and gestures to disguise, conceal, convince, persuade, and invent. Then, after a few more volunteers tell tales, I ask everyone to write this type of story and illustrate it. The stories are then read to the rest of the class, and we must guess whether each story is true or not.

3. Depending on the children's age, I bring in old newspapers or magazines appropriate for their reading level. It is important that these newspapers and magazines contain short reports and articles about the latest news in the city or world. The children read two or three short accounts, cut one out, and paste it on a piece of paper. This "true" account of an accident, catastrophe, crime, marriage, ball game, etc., serves as the basis for a tall tale. That is, the newspaper account is stretched into an imaginative story that plays with the "truth." This game or exercise can be used during the session or as a follow-up with the teacher. If it is used as a follow-up, the children are asked to read a newspaper at home, cut out an interesting account, paste it on a sheet of paper, and bring it to school the next day. In class, the children can read the events to one another and talk about them. Then, on the basis of their newspaper account, they can write their own "tall" version. Another possibility is to collect all the newspaper accounts, mix them, and redistribute the accounts. they are to Each child writes a "new" version based on the articles he or she receives. If possible, the results of these writings are shared with the other children.

4. We distribute old newspapers and magazines, and the children cut out scenes and figures in any way they want. They take their cutouts and paste them on a large sheet of drawing paper to form their own picture or montage. I generally tell the children they can use advertisements or pictures of politicians, actors, policemen, etc. The scenes can depict any incident. Then, based on the photomontage they create, they tell a story

to "illustrate" their illustration. The purpose here is to alter their perspective and to shed new light on a particular "objective" photograph. By playing with the image, the children are encouraged to take their own work seriously, and to narrate their own pictures and fantasies.

In one storytelling session that I conducted with adults in New York, I concluded a day-long workshop by asking the participants to talk about their most traumatic experience, their most joyful incident, or their most persistent daydream. I began by talking about the time I ran away from home, about my daughter's birth at the Flower Hospital and almost fainting while watching my wife have a caesarian, and finally about how I had persistently imagined myself as a star basketball player. We then moved around the circle—there were about ten or twelve participants—and a young man talked about his alcoholism and fights with his father; a young woman talked about her parents dying in a nursing home; another young woman talked about her exclusion from a party and how she suffered while her brother mocked her; an old man talked about finding his son, who had gone off and left him many years ago; a grandmother talked about her trip to India to visit a guru and how she found herself. These are just a few of the stories I recall. Once we made the rounds, the participants took pen in hand, and I asked them to transform the incidents into tall tales or fantastic tales. The purpose of this exercise was to see if they could gain sufficient distance from the event to reshape it as a different story that might be shared in a public setting. Since I did not want complete stories, I asked them to stop writing after ten minutes and to share their "beginnings." We used these beginnings to talk about where their stories might go and why, and the participants were free to suggest alternatives and to take off with someone else's beginning. Here it was important to keep the beginnings "alive," to pay more attention to beginnings given our usual tendency to become too absorbed in how a story ends. We stress closure too much or, if not closure, alternatives to the ends of stories. We tend to forget that the initial settings of our lives may already be our end; that is, most of our actions are predicated on how we begin our lives. Without understanding our beginning and how our beginning prescribes us, we cannot alter our behavior, and we can become discouraged and believe that our "fates" are determined for us. One way to explode the overwhelming sense of fate is to retell our beginnings, to exaggerate, and to grasp their import through humor.

Tall tales and swapping stories can be effectively used in many different settings such as youth centers, camps, hospitals, and old age homes. Here I want to suggest that schools and storytellers have not done enough to work with older people, especially those who are in old age homes. I once conducted an experiment with a group of elderly people in an old age home. Initially, I had been invited by the director of this home to stimulate the participants to record the memories of their past for their families. I was to help them learn how to record their "oral histories" on paper or tape them with cassettes. However, I discovered that many of them were hesitant to tell their stories because they had difficulty recalling all the facts, names, events, and truths of incidents, and they did not want to tell the stories if they could not remember them exactly as they were. Moreover, some of the stories were embarrassing or painful. So I began telling them a few tall tales related to my life, and I told them that instead of hearing their "true" histories, I told them I wanted to hear scandalous or hilarious whoppers, the stranger the better. The result was a stream of remarkable stories that combined legend, anecdote, and fairy-tale motifs. We swapped these tall tales, and some of the participants began writing them down for their children and friends. Some began recording them. Then, I made contact with a local school where I had been working, and I asked two of the elderly people to help me in two sessions on tall tales.

When the man and woman, both in their late seventies or early eighties, arrived, they told a series of tall tales based on their lives in the chilren's own neighborhood, and the children were captivated. When the elderly couple asked the children to share stories with them, the youngsters, who had already had one tall-tale session, felt confident sharing their tales. As exchange began, it occurred to me that much more work could be done with elderly people both inside and outside schools.

When I finished this session, I asked the children to contact one of their older relatives during the next week and to bring in a family story, an anecdote, a tall tale, a legend to share with me and the rest of the class. Here it was most important that I had the help of the teacher, who had worked with the children during the week to help them gain a sense of family oral history and why it is so important. After all, we keep family together through story, all types of stories. We circulate these stories to remember and be remembered. Our hope for immortality lies in story.

Somewhere over the Rainbow

Utopia and Wishing Tales

Fairy tales are born out of dissatisfaction, frustration, and discontent. We seek to make the best out of the negative in our lives, to negate the negative through magic, to use our imagining creatively to play with forces that distress us. We wish, dream, desire, search, struggle, and lie to make our lives more bearable than they are. More than any other oral or literary genre, the fairy tale embodies the utopian *gestus* of our lives through the wish. By *gestus* I mean the way our behavior, actions, and thinking gesticulate toward one goal, and this goal is a place that we do not know concretely. It is no place and yet a better place. It is a place we know intuitively, and we call it utopia.

Of course, the fairy tale is not the only genre that can be called utopian. As we have seen, many genres, like the legend, myth, and fable, incorporate utopian motifs and features, and we can consider the utopian novel its own genre. We have created all these genres as though it were natural and necessary because there is something within us that compels us to look forward and struggle for a better life, and we mark this down in script and record it with words. However, it is only by setting out and searching, as the fairy tale often recommends, that we can begin to distinguish what utopia may look like. At the beginning we may be misled, distracted, or deceived into believing that gold, power, and glory constitute utopia, and indeed, they may make us happy. Yet the best of tales signal that material wealth and power are not sufficient; if we want to find utopia, which literally means "no place," we must go beyond material wealth. Moreover, we often learn that utopia is impossible unless everyone is happy, and that individual happiness depends on communal happiness, which is extremely difficult to engender given the way the world is today. Therefore, the "true" utopian tale keeps us yearning, dreaming, thinking. It impels and compels us to contemplate where we are and why we are heading in a certain direction. It makes us examine and re-examine our wishes, for there are good wishes and bad wishes. Take that wonderful story *The Three Wishes*, which Charles Perrault, among numerous others writers and storytellers, shaped into a fairy tale that in some form or another has become known to all of us.

The Three Wishes

Once there was a poor woodcutter named Pierre, whose life was so hard that he sometimes longed to die and rest in peace. This tormented man complained that the heavens had not been kind to him, for despite his honest living, neither the gods nor the fairies had ever granted him a single wish.

One day he was grumbling to himself in the forest when Zeus appeared with a thunderbolt in hand. It is impossible to describe how frightened the good man was. Indeed, he threw himself on the ground and cried, "Forgive me, sire! I don't want a thing. No wishes. No thunder, my lord. Just let me live in peace!"

"Have no fear," Zeus responded. "I've come because I've been moved by your complaints, which have troubled me. You will now see how just and powerful I am, for I'm going to grant you three wishes. You shall have three and only three. But I warn you, make sure you know what will bring you happiness. Think carefully before you make your wishes!"

With these words, Zeus disappeared like lightning, and the woodcutter was not sure whether he had been dreaming or awake. He longed to make his first wish to find out. So he picked up his bundle of wood and rushed home to tell his wife. As he was running along, he said to himself, "I've got to be careful. Haste makes waste! But I can't wait to tell my wife what's happened."

Upon entering his cottage, he called, "Lizzie! Let's make a large fire, my dear, and drink some wine! We're going to be rich. You won't believe what happened to me today!"

And he told his wife what had happened, and when she heard the story, she began making a thousand different plans in her head. However, like her husband, she realized that they had to be wise about all this.

"Pierre, my dear," she said to her husband. "Haste makes waste. Let's mull over in our minds what the best wishes for us might be. I suggest that we sleep on it and put off our first wish until tomorrow."

"I agree," said her husband. "But now, get some of the good wine from the cellar, and I'll get the fire started."

After she had fetched the wine, they drank it by a large fire and smiled at each other. Then Pierre leaned back in his chair and said, "I'd like nothing more with this fine wine and warm fire than a nice sausage. That would make the evening perfect!"

No sooner had he finished speaking than his wife was astonished to see a very long sausage approaching her from the corner of the chimney like a snake. At first she screamed, but then she realized that it was in fact a sausage and that her husband had wasted one of his wishes by his foolish remark. Now she was furious and began scolding him.

"You can become rich as a king and have all the gold, pearls, rubies, and diamonds that you want," she said, "but all you think of is a measly sausage!"

"I know, I know. I should have been more careful," he replied. "I made a bad choice. I'll do better next time."

"How stupid can you be!" she said. "Now I know why the gods granted you the wishes. You'll waste every one of them!"

"That's not true," Pierre answered. "I was just daydreaming."

"That's your problem," Lizzie exploded. "You dream too much, and we have nothing."

"And your problem is your mouth!" he exploded. "Yack-yack, yack-yack, you never shut up. I wish the sausage was hanging from your nose. Maybe that would shut you up!"

Once again, the woodcutter's wish came true, and within seconds the sausage was hanging from his wife's nose. Now, if the first mistake made Lizzie angry, you can imagine how the sausage dangling from her nose made her feel, especially since she was a pretty woman with grace and charm. She wanted to give Pierre a piece of her mind, but the dangling sausage prevented her from speaking easily, and her husband was somewhat relieved.

"I still have one wish left," he thought to himself. "So, I could make myself king, and maybe Lizzie would feel better if she were queen and would forgive me for giving her a sausage for a nose. On the other hand, people would make fun of her nose, even if she were a queen, and she would never let me hear the end of it. I had better ask her whether she wants to be a queen with a horrible nose or a woodcutter's wife with a pretty nose like she had before."

Lizzie knew that if she became queen, she would have a lot of power and could force people to ignore her sausage of a nose. She could even make them compliment her nose. Yet, after thinking about it carefully, she realized that nothing could really be better than to be the person she really was, and she decided to keep her own nose rather than to become an ugly queen.

So the woodcutter made his last wish a wise one, and his wife had her own nose restored to her. Afterwards, they kept dreaming of the three wishes and imagining what their lives would be like if they could wish again. It is said that they kept themselves happy by imagining and working hard until the very end of their days.

Wishing wisely does not come easily to us and certainly not to children. Joking with a group of children one time, I told them I had the power to grant their wishes, and I remember being astounded when I heard some wish for a chocolate bar or doll when they could have wished for a thousand dollars, possibly because they thought that a chocolate bar or doll costs more than a thousand dollars. But the fact is, children do not know how to wish wisely, and yet their wishes are not unwise; they are based on immediate gratification, lack, or immediate need. They value what they do not have, and in this respect, they are very much in touch with their utopian yearnings. They know what they do not have and what might give them pleasure, and though they may not know what utopia and utopian mean, I try to explore the utopian *gestus* of their lives so that they may glimpse its contours.

This session on utopian tales focuses on wishes gone astray and wishes fulfilled, so the children can learn what it takes to become a "discriminating" wisher and how to give shape to their own daydreams. I generally follow *The Three Wishes* with another well-known tale, *The Fisherman and his Wife*, because it alters the theme and plot of "wishing wisely" in a significant way. After the fish is caught and tells the fisherman that he will grant him all his wishes for returning him to the sea, the fisherman's wife takes over and states exactly what she wants. First it is a cottage, then a great stone castle. The fisherman hesitates to ask the fish for anything more, but his wife persists, for she wants to become what women can rarely become— a king, emperor, and pope. Each time the fish grants her wish, until she wants to be like God. Since it is impossible to satisfy her avarice and ambition, the fish returns the couple to their dirty hovel, where they live to this very day.

Instead of telling the traditional Grimms' version of this tale, it is also possible to tell the wonderful version created by the British storyteller Mike Dunstan.

Kidhus

Once there lived a fisherman and his wife. They were very poor, and they lived in small tatty cottage by the seashore. Every morning, whilst his wife stayed at home doing spinning work for the local sheep farmers, the fisherman went out to sea in his small rowing boat, dropped his nets over the side, and hauled them in at the end of the day. He then went back home, gave some fish to his wife to cook that evening, and sold the rest to the neighbors. And that was how life was for that couple, who often barely managed to keep starvation at bay. They were so poor that they only possessed one thing of any value and that was a small golden ball, which the fisherman's wife used as a weight on the end of her spindle as she worked.

One morning, as she watched her husband making his way down the beach to his boat, the fisherman's wife, seeing what a beautiful morning it was, with the warm sun shining in a cloudless sky, decided that she would go out onto the lawn and work in the fresh air. However, she hadn't been at work for more than a few minutes when the thread on the spindle broke, and the golden ball fell to the ground and rolled down the slope and under some bushes at the bottom of the garden. Of course, the fisherman's wife immediately got up and went to look for it, but she searched high and low, and low and high, and she couldn't find that golden ball anywhere. It had simply disappeared.

As you can imagine, the old woman was very upset to lose the golden ball because it was the one thing of any value the couple possessed, and she was still crying when her husband came home that evening.

"What's the matter?" he asked her as he saw the tears on her face, and she told him the sorry story of how she had come to lose the golden ball.

Now, it just so happened that near their cottage there was a hill, and in that hill lived a troll by the name of Kidhus. Kidhus was very well known for being a little bit light-fingered, and whenever anything was missing, it was always Kidhus who got the blame. So, when the old man heard his wife's story, he immediately put two and two together and said that he would go that very minute and see Kidhus to demand the return of the golden ball. "And if he won't return the golden ball," said the fisherman, "I will demand something of equal value in its place." And with these words he put on his hat, took on a large stick from behind the door, and set off up the hill.

When he got to the top, he thumped the stick three times upon the ground, and a loud voice thundered from inside the hill:

"Who gave my house such a thwack?"
"It's I, Kidhus, your neighbor back,
My old woman must be repaid
For the golden ball which she mislaid."

"What is it you want, then?" thundered Kidhus.

The fisherman tried to think of the one thing that would improve life for him and his wife, and finally he said, "We'd like a cow ... a cow that gives one hundred gallons a day."

"Very well," said Kidhus, and when the fisherman turned around, there was a large, black and white cow standing right next to him. The old man led the cow back down the hill to the cottage, and his wife was well pleased with their new acquisition; she could already almost taste the sweet milk on her lips.

In the morning the fisherman got up as usual, had some breakfast, and took his boat out fishing. His wife had her work cut out at the cottage milking the cow, because it takes a lot of time to hand milk one hundred gallons of milk from a cow, and by the time the old man came home that evening she had just about finished.

"Now then," she said to her husband, "tonight we're going to have something different for our tea. I'm sick and tired of eating fish every single day. Tonight we're going to have pancakes."

So she measured out the milk into a large bowl … and suddenly realized that there was something else she needed before she could make pancakes: eggs. She didn't have any eggs at all.

"Never mind," said the fisherman, "I shall go and see Kidhus and ask him for some eggs, because a golden ball is very valuable and must be worth some eggs!"

So he put on his hat and took the stick from behind the door. He climbed up to the top of the hill and hit the ground three times with the stick. Immediately Kidhus's voice thundered from inside the hill:

"Who gave my house such a thwack?"
"It's I, Kidhus, your neighbor back,
"My old woman must be repaid
For the golden ball which she mislaid."

"What do you want, then?" replied Kidhus.

"Well," said the fisherman, "what we'd really like is a hen … a hen that will lay one hundred eggs each day."

"Very well," said Kidhus, and when the fisherman turned around, there by his foot was a large brown hen. The old man picked it up and carried it back down the hill to the cottage. His wife was well pleased with her new hen; she could already almost taste the warm yolk running down the back of her throat.

In the morning the fisherman got up as usual, had his breakfast, and went out to sea in his little rowing boat to do a full day's fishing. Meanwhile, his wife stayed at home and worked all day milking the cow for another hundred gallons of milk, and then searching all of the garden until she had collected one hundred eggs. By the time the old fisherman came home that evening she had just finished her work.

"Right," she said to her husband, "tonight we shall have our pancakes!" She measured out all the milk into a large bowl, then broke the one hundred eggs into the milk and beat them together ... and suddenly realized that there was something else she needed before she could make pancakes: flour. She needed some flour to make the pancake batter, and she hadn't got any.

"Never mind," said the fisherman, "I'll go and see Kidhus and ask him to give us some flour, because a golden ball is very valuable and must be worth a bit of flour."

So he put on his hat, took the stick from behind the door, and set off up the hill. When he got up to the top, he hit the ground three times as hard as he could with the stick, and Kidhus bellowed from inside the hill:

"Who gave my house such a thwack?"
"It's I, Kidhus, your neighbor back,
My old woman must be repaid
For the golden ball which she mislaid."

"What now?" bellowed Kidhus impatiently.

"Well," said the fisherman, "what we could really do with is some flour ... about one hundred sacks should just about do the trick."

"All right then," said Kidhus, and when the fisherman turned around, he saw a huge pile of one hundred large sacks of flour. Well, as you can imagine, it took that fisherman all the rest of the evening to carry those sacks of flour down to the cottage, and by the time he had finished, there was no time left to make any pancakes. But his wife was very pleased with all the flour, and she promised to make the pancakes the following evening; she could already almost taste the little bits of pancake between the gaps of her teeth.

In the morning the fisherman got up as usual, had a spot of breakfast, and went out in his boat to do the fishing. Meanwhile, his wife worked at home and had her work cut out for her, what with another hundred gallons of milk to collect and another hundred eggs to find. By the time the old man returned that evening, she had collected the last egg.

"Right," she said to her husband, "tonight we shall have our pancakes. She measured out all the milk into the large bowl, then broke the

one hundred eggs into the milk. She carefully weighed out the flour
and added it to the mixture. She then beat everything together until
she had the finest, smoothest pancake batter that ever you've seen.

That evening the fisherman and his wife ate pancake upon pancake upon pancake. They ate so many pancakes that they almost
burst, but even when they could eat no more pancakes there was still
a huge amount of batter left over, far more than they could possibly
eat. But on the other hand, neither of them liked to see waste, so they
didn't want to pour the batter down the drain. Then, all of a sudden,
the fisherman's wife had an idea!

Neither she nor her husband were getting any younger, you see,
and in recent months she had started to get a little worried about
what might happen when they both died. So she thought it a fine
idea for them to take the remaining pancake batter up to God,
because surely He was very fond of pancakes too, and their generosity would certainly be rewarded with a place in Heaven for both of
them. And her husband agreed.

"But how are we going to get up there?" asked the fisherman after
a moment's thought.

"Why, that's no problem," said his wife. "You must go ask and see
Kidhus and ask him for a ladder that is tall enough to reach up to
heaven."

"What a good idea!" exclaimed the fisherman. "A golden ball is very
valuable, after all, and must be worth a ladder." And with these words,
he put on his hat, took the large stick from behind the door, and set
off up the hill.

When he finally reached the top, he banged with the stick as hard
as he could three times upon the ground, and Kidhus shouted from
inside the hill:

"Who gave my house such a thwack?"
"It's I, Kidhus, your neighbor back,
My old woman must be repaid
For the golden ball which she mislaid."

"What is it you want now?" snorted Kidhus.

"Well," said the fisherman, "what we could really do with is a ladder
... a ladder so tall that it will reach all the way up to heaven."

"Very well," said Kidhus, "but this is the last thing I'm going to give you. After this the debt will be repaid, and you must come bothering me no more."

The fisherman agreed, and when he turned around, he saw there on the ground was a tiny little ladder, no more than six inches long.

"Hang on a minute," said the fisherman. "How on earth is this going to be of any use to us? It's far too small."

"Look," said Kidhus impatiently, "if I had given you a full-size ladder, you would never have been able to carry it down the hill. All you have to do with this is take it home, lean it against the side of the house, and give it a good watering with the watering can. It will grow as tall as you want it."

So the fisherman put the ladder into his pocket and took it back home to his wife, who was instantly dismissive and scolded him for being such a fool as to bring a ladder that was obviously too small for their purposes. But the old man took her outside, put the ladder up against the wall, and watered it with the watering can. Sure enough, there before their very eyes, slowly but surely, the ladder began to grow.

Soon the ladder had enough rungs for it to reach the top of the house, but still it grew higher and higher until the top of the ladder had disappeared into the clouds and could be seen no more. The old couple were delighted. They rushed inside and strapped a big cauldron on each of their backs to carry the pancake batter in, and when this was done, they carefully began to climb the ladder.

Step by step, higher and higher the fisherman and his wife climbed, and with each rung, they grew more and more excited at the prospect of handing the batter over to God and receiving their reward for their generosity.

Soon they were higher than the house, and then they were higher than the hill where Kidhus lived. Still they climbed, until they were higher than the highest mountains thereabouts. But the higher they climbed, the more difficult it became, as they grew tired, and the wind grew stronger until the ladder was swaying so much that the old couple had to cling tightly to it lest they fall. Onward they struggled until they felt they could climb no more, and they looked down to the ground. Their house was a mere speck, and the hill, a mere bump, but the swaying of the ladder made it look as if the Earth were spinning round and round. Their heads began to swim with dizziness, and they could hold on no longer.

They fell through the air and came crashing down to Earth, where they were killed on the rocks down below.

Now from that day onward, where the cauldrons smashed against the ground and the pancake batter was splashed far and wide over the rocks, that is where the yellow moss grows. And where the fisherman and his wife were killed and their brains were splattered over the rocks, that is where, to this day, the white moss grows.

And that is why these days, when Kidhus sits inside his hill sorting through his belongings and he comes across that golden ball, it still reminds him of the foolishness of the fisherman and his wife, and how there came to be lichen growing on the rocks of the earth.

Dunstan's version of *Kidhus* is based on an Icelandic folk tale, and there is also an English variant entitled *The Old Woman Who Lived in The Vinegar Bottle*. Any of these folk tales, including *The Fisherman and his Wife*, are appropriate for this session, and *Kidhus* is especially interesting because its motifs recall *Jack and the Beanstalk* and a creation myth. Most important, it is about the "failure" of using wishes effectively. All of these versions ask the same question: how can one wish wisely and realize one's dreams? But these stories take place in the distant past, so after I finish telling the Grimms' version of *The Fisherman and his Wife* or a similar tale, I experiment with a contemporary version in which I switch gender roles and emphasize the utopian nature of wishing. In Gainesville, I told the following tale.

Molly and the Fish

Molly was very lonely. She and her brother Clyde lived in a shack near the ocean. They had lost their parents when they were very young, and because they had no relatives, they were left to care for themselves. So, they just went fishing or scavenging along the beach to keep themselves alive. Molly often thought of how life might have been different if their parents had lived, and she often dreamed of moving far away, perhaps to the mountains, where she could find a job, a real job, and maybe become a teacher, marry, and have children. But she and her husband would not die. They would stay with their children.

One time, just as Molly was picturing this, she heard a pounding noise on the beach. Much to her surprise, she saw a gigantic fish flapping its fins, gasping for breath, and springing up and down on the sand. Quickly she ran over to the fish, and, though it was very heavy, she grabbed it by its tail, spun it around and around, and flung it as far as she could into the ocean. And as the fish went sailing, she went sprawling to the ground.

"Molly!" a voice called out, and she looked around her but could not see anyone.

"Molly, look over here!" the voice cried again.

And Molly looked out into the ocean, and the large head of the fish was popping over the waves.

"Molly, thank you!" the fish cried. "And if you ever need any help, just come to this spot and call out to me."

Molly smiled and waved as the fish disappeared into the ocean. When she returned home to the shack, her brother Clyde asked her where she had been, and she told him what had happened.

"What? A talking fish? You're kidding me!" he responded.

"No, I'm not," she insisted.

"Well, if you're not," he said, "prove it to me. Tell your stinky little fish to change our hut into a nice luxury house overlooking the ocean."

"He's not little, and he's not stinky," Molly said.

"You're just a dreamer!" Clyde turned away from her.

But Molly ran down to the beach and walked and walked until she reached the spot where she had thrown the fish into the ocean. Then she cried out,

Where are you, fish?
I need a wish.
My brother doesn't believe in you,
So help me make a change or two.

The fish popped his head out of the water and answered,

Wish wisely, my dear.
There's nothing to fear.

So Molly wished for a luxury house, and the fish told her to return home.

Imagine her surprise when she came across a huge mansion with servants and cars. Everything glittered like gold, and Clyde was stretched out on a terrace like a king, ordering the servants to bring him lunch. The house had twenty rooms, and each was different from the next. The refrigerator was always full, and Clyde invited all his friends from school over and began boasting and showing off. The next morning, however, Clyde was depressed because he had to go to school.

"You know," he said to Molly, "even though we have a chauffeur to drive us to school, your fish could do much more for us. He could make me principal, and you could finally become a teacher. How about that? But of course, your fish can't really do something like that."

Once again, Molly was angry at her brother and went down to the beach and called for the fish,

Where are you, fish?
I need a wish.
My brother doesn't believe in you,
So help me make a change or two.

The fish popped his head out of the water and replied,

Wish wisely, my dear.
There's nothing to fear.

All of a sudden, she found herself being whisked to school, and she was no longer a student but a teacher standing in front of many small children, who were laughing and smiling. But in the hall she could hear her brother, the principal, yelling and ordering the teachers and students about. He made many rules and demanded that everyone listen to him. His favorite room was the detention hall, where he punished anyone who disobeyed him. Nobody could talk to him. Nobody could correct him. He knew it all, and he walked through the halls of the school like a king.

The next day, Clyde told his sister, "I'm tired of just running a school. It's boring, and it's really not important. I'd like to be the governor of the state, that's what I'd like to be, but your stinky little fish could never do something like that!"

Molly was getting tired of Clyde's big talk. But she thought the fish would not mind showing her brother how wrong he was. So she went down to the beach and said,

Where are you, fish?
I need a wish.
My brother doesn't believe in you,
So help me make a change or two.

Once more, the fish popped his head out of the water and replied,

Wish wisely, my dear.
There's nothing to fear.

The next thing Molly knew, she was walking through the gates of the governor's mansion, which was five times the size of their previous mansion. Inside, Clyde was sitting behind a gigantic desk and had twenty assistants and five secretaries. He ordered them to change laws and sign over property so that he would become the richest man in the state. If anyone objected, he had them arrested. He invited all his friends to the mansion and gave them jobs. He stole money from the banks and pretended to use it for the people of the state, but he really needed it to build a race track and buy horses. Soon, however, Clyde grew bored and told Molly, "It was easy for your fish to make me governor, but he couldn't make me into the richest man in the world!"

"I don't care if he could," Molly said. "You've become unbearable."

"You've always thought I was unbearable," Clyde remarked. "You're just trying to cover up for your stinky fish. I bet he can't make me President."

Molly was furious, and she ran down to the beach and called for the fish,

Where are you, fish?
I need a wish.
My brother doesn't believe in you,
So help me make a change or two.

Once more, the fish popped his head out of the water and replied,

Wish wisely, my dear.
There's nothing to fear.

Now Molly could not believe what happened. The entire White

House appeared at the oceanside and replaced the governor's mansion. The White House staff, the military, and all the politicians came to hear Clyde give a talk about how he was going to change America and make it a better place, and how he was then going to change the world. But Clyde was really interested in his own power, and he had pictures and statues of himself made. He ordered the police and soldiers to take over factories and businesses. He commanded everyone to address him as Your Highness, not as Mr. President, and if foreign countries did not honor this, he ordered his armies to attack them.

But Clyde always grew bored. It was not enough to be President, and he called Molly to his Oval Office.

"I have one more challenge for your stinky fish. Tell him to make me God, and then I'll leave him alone."

"What?" Molly said. "You must be insane. I won't do it."

"You don't, and I'll make sure the people suffer!"

Molly had no choice but to go to the beach, where she called out with great hesitation,

Where are you, fish?
I need a wish.
My brother doesn't believe in you.
So show him now what you can do,
To stop his rule.
I've been a fool.

The fish appeared once more and spoke,

Wisely have you wished, my dear,
And now you'll see your way most clear.

When Molly walked back to what she thought would be the White House, she was surprised to see Clyde sitting on the steps of their dilapidated shack. He was moaning and groaning,

"Why, oh why! Why, oh why!"

It seemed as if he were in a daze, and Molly did not say a word to him, but climbed the steps and walked into the house. When she entered the living room, she looked at the barren furniture and realized that nothing had changed except for a small table with a goldfish bowl on top of it. So she walked over to the bowl which had never been there before. When she looked into it, she noticed a sparkling orange goldfish with blue eyes and a little rock cave. The fish darted about and suddenly disappeared into the cave. Molly stooped over and peered into the cave. She was amazed by what she saw. It seemed that all her dreams and wishes were hidden in the cave, and the little fish was trying to show her where they were. The more she looked, the more her face began to shine with a smile that never ended.

Since wishing is central to thousands of fairy tales, the storyteller can choose from a vast selection of stories for use in this session. Many concern a powerful genie or spirit who appears out of a bottle or lamp. Others depict magical animals, who have the power to grant wishes if a good person helps them. Whatever tale the storyteller chooses, it is important to focus on foolish wishes and wishes that go amiss but can be redirected. A utopian tale does not depict the end but the direction toward a golden age, paradise, or contentment. The symbols of the tale are filled and realized by the listeners, who pour their own dreams into the story as it moves along and continues to move in their imaginations.

Utopian tales lend themselves to dramatic improvisation. Children like to be wish-givers and to act out wishes. They like to transform themselves and try out different roles, even if they must play a villain. They are not certain what they want to become, and a wish tale allows them to try out and test certain roles and to feel power and the impact of power. Depending on the children's ages, it is possible not only to act out some of the wish tales but to use "What If" games to alter the tales through improvisation. For instance, I have asked:

What if the fish had been a monster and had not granted the fisherman's wishes?

What if the fisherman had been the one who wanted power, not his wife?

What if the wife had wished to get rid of the fisherman, who was an ogre at home?

What if the fisherman had captured a fish, and it turned out to me a mermaid and he fell in love with it?

What if the fisherman had tried to capture the fish again and punish it with the help of his wife?

What if the woman had been wise, and had been content to live as king and queen and not wish anymore?

I assign the "What If" questions for groups of children to act out through improvisation. I divide the class into three or four groups, and they go into corners to decide more or less what they want to do. Then they try out their play before the other children.

If wishes can be tested and acted out in play, they can also be projected into real situations. They can be projects. They can be drafts for a better life and society. In the writing part of this session, I generally try different experiments to illustrate how change can be "utopian" in contrast to simple change. In Gainesville, I asked a group of seventh-graders how they would change their school if they had three wishes. To begin, I asked, if they could become principal, what changes would they make in the school? If they had a lot of money or could become mayor, how would they change Gainesville? Most of the students were very concrete. They wanted better food in the cafeteria. They wanted to allow chewing gum in school, or be allowed to hold hands. Some wanted simply to destroy the school or get rid of particular teachers. Together we drew up a list of about twenty wishes, which I put on the board, and then the students chose three from the list and wrote their "utopian" tales with illustrations.

In another session, I asked the children, if they had one wish and one wish only, what would they wish for? I wrote twenty-five wishes on the board, and then I said, "Imagine, I am a powerful genie. You have rubbed your magic pencils, and I have appeared. Now, instead of one wish, I am granting you three wishes, and three wishes only. Choose three wishes from the board, and tell me what you will do with them and what happens. Tell me the story of your three wishes!" Here the children generally took their own wish and combined it with two others to produce unusual stories with illustrations.

This session has an important follow-up game. After the children have written their stories and shared them with the class, I remark that most of the wishes have concerned themselves, what *they* dream about and want. Then I suggest that there are people in the world who may be in greater need than they are, who need help, who need wishes. This leads to my next question: Can they suggest groups of people who need help and wishes? In Gainesville, the answers covered some of the following groups: the homeless, the disabled, the blind, the elderly, fourth-graders. I generally asked why they chose the groups and what they thought the groups needed. In one seventh-grade class, we had a long discussion about how the old are treated in American society. After writing the names of various groups of needy people on the board, I ask the children to write a story about how wishes helped the needy to live better. Here I want the children to try and realize what it means to be needy, and that knowing what they want and feeling entitled to it is the first step toward obtaining it. The wish helps to clarify the situation and generates hope. Since there may not be time for children to write during the session, the teacher can continue this project during the week.

I have also done another follow-up in which I ask the children whether they have ever heard of Atlantis, Shangri-La, the Golden Age, or Oz. We talk about lost kingdoms where people shared and lived in peace with one another. I write the names of these "realms" on the board, and we share stories about them (that is, everything we know about them). Then I ask the children to invent their own magical lost kingdom and write a story about how they would go in search of this realm. Again, this is a project that will take more than one session and generally involves work during the week.

In one school, several years ago, I focused an entire session on *The Wizard of Oz* because it is a model of the utopian fairy-tale novel. Instead of having the children read the novel, I condensed and retold of the story with a focus on Dorothy's desperate situation in Kansas and how the tornado somehow answered her wishes because it whisked her off to Oz. The encounters with the Tin Woodsman, the Scarecrow, and the Cowardly Lion represent the typical three encounters in the fairy tale. Dorothy helps and is being helped, and later she uses all that she learns to defeat the nasty Witch of the North and expose the Wizard as a con man. Her experiences in Oz enable her to face the gray reality of Kansas and return to that reality carrying the magic utopian spirit of Oz within her.

After I ended the tale, we did our own improvised staging, and I then asked the children to draw their favorite character and tell me a short story about this character and why it had become the way it was. During the week, the children read the entire novel with the teacher and saw the film on video. When I returned the following week, I told the children that the author of *The Wizard of Oz*, L. Frank Baum, wrote some other Oz novels, and at one point he had Dorothy, Aunt Em and Uncle Henry decide to stay in Oz for good. Since the children wondered how this could have happened, I proceeded to retell Baum's *The Emerald City of Oz*, a wonderful tale about how Dorothy helps Aunt Em and Uncle Henry when they lose their farm to the notorious Eastern bankers. Dorothy *wishes* to help them, and Ozma, the beneficent matriarch of Oz, grants this wish. They are all whisked off to Oz, where Dorothy introduces them to the wonders of their new home. At the same time, the dreaded Nome King has amassed a large army of Whimsies, Growleywogs, and Phanfasms to conquer Oz and destroy its principles of equality and humanism. Fortunately, Ozma, that beneficent matriarch of Oz, invents a fountain for the water of oblivion, which can make her enemies forget their evil intentions and turn them into good intentions. In the end, Ozma succeeds in bringing about peace through this nonviolent tactic.

When I finished telling this new Oz tale, the children wanted to know more about Oz and some of the other Oz books. I told them as much as I could, and finally I asked since they had been reading a great deal about Oz and had seen the movie, would it be possible for them to invent an Oz story for me? We wrote many names on the board, such as

Dorothy   Aunt Em   Uncle Henry   Tin Woodsman   Scarecrow
Cowardly Lion   Wizard   Wicked Witch of the North   Ozma   Gnome King
Whomsies   Growleywogs   Phanfasms   Shaggy Man

Then I asked the children to use whatever characters they liked to compose their own story about Oz and illustrate it. Soon their utopias appeared, their first written conceptions of a lost land somewhere over the rainbow. It was in pursuit of the realization of this land that they began to map out their own utopias. As Oscar Wilde once said, "A map of the world that does not include Utopia is not worth even glancing at, for it leaves out the one country at which Humanity is always landing. And when Humanity lands there, it looks out, and seeing a better country, sets sail. Progress is the realization of Utopia."[1]

❧ 10 ❧
Strange Encounters
with Science Fiction

I f utopian tales bring children closer to their wishes and dreams by
projecting ideal distant lands, then science fiction stories bring them
closer to their wishes by paradoxically transporting them to the future.
Predicated on fact and credibility, science fiction introduces weird characters and places to alienate young readers so that they can learn to accept
difference and to think about alternatives to the present by looking at the
future. Of course, not all science fiction does this. Much science fiction
simply rejoices in technology and natural sciences and maintains that the
world will become a better place through marvelous machines that conquer
nature and space. Then there is the science fiction of gloom that prophesies
doom, that suggests we will become slaves of machines. Indeed, many
science fiction stories and books illustrate how machines will take over the
world and we will lose our souls. In contrast, a "green" science fiction
reveals how we can reutilize machines to prevent the further destruction of
nature and to bring about peace between warring nations and planets. All
science fiction contains inevitable wars and clashes because the world's
future appears to depend on who will control science.

All the wars portrayed in fiction add up to a real war of conflicting
perspectives among science fiction writers, paradoxically because they all

share a concern with peace and the future. They are fascinated by scientific invention that may be used for both good and bad causes or that may accidentally bring about disaster. This is also the bottom-line concern of children. Though children have great difficulty grasping chronology and temporal sequence in science fiction—my nine-year-old daughter still acts as though an hour can pass in five minutes or a year in a week—they can distinguish between past and future, and they certainly know the difference between helpful and harmful machines once they begin touching, using, and playing with them.

Since children generally see the future as immediate and do not grasp long-range plans, their perceptions of life in the future, alien creatures, advanced technology, and foreign planets are very different from those of adults. Steven Spielberg pointed to this difference in his remarkable film *E.T.* Children are apt to believe in fiction as science, and perhaps they are right, for in many ways stories prefigure and anticipate scientific development. They have provided the creative inspiration for many inventors. They are written and spoken experiments that chart a way into the future.

Science fiction became a full-fledged genre in the late nineteenth century as the Industrial Revolution gained force and changed the way we lived, our expectations and our horizons. As writers like Jules Verne, H.G. Wells, Robert Louis Stevenson, and others realized, we needed a new form of fiction to correspond to the fantastic possibilities of the future. In this regard, the fairy tale, legend, and fable were limited despite their utopian *gestus*. Their motifs, topoi, characters, and forms had to be commensurately transformed to address the fears, hopes, and desires of the modern world. Machines and the scientific mind, and their impact on people, became the major themes in science fiction. Would science help us to live better in the future or lead us to destroy ourselves? How do we assume responsibility for the incredible machines that we have created and will create in the not too distant future? Will our planet be habitable? Must we look for other planets and universes in order to survive? Can we receive help from outer space?

In our contemporary space, that is, in my session on science fiction, I draw connections to utopian fairy tales, and I introduce the notion of the "responsible imagination" or "responsible living" through the stories. Responsibility and response are key aspects of building community, and since children are naturally narcissistic, they have difficulty learning what it means to be responsible. Children's play always has a strong impulse of self-gratification, and they often tend to toss their stuffed animals, toys, and other playthings around without care and order them to suit their purposes. Unfortunately, if these objects are destroyed, children see that they can be quickly replaced, and some objects are even manufactured so that they *must* be replaced in a short period of time according to policies of planned obsolescence. Toys and dolls are produced to intrigue, to excite children's curiosity, to make them into consumers. And indeed, children are intrigued by the latest mechanical device, play with it until they are bored, and then discard it. They do not know how it works, and if it does not work, they may smash it on the ground or throw it against the wall. Somehow it will be fixed, or if not, they will buy or obtain a new mechanical toy. This negligent attitude toward toys, i.e., little machines, spills over into our negligent attitude toward animals, nature, and other human beings. In this regard, science fiction stories can instill in children more respect and responsibility for machines and technology, and they can pose the question: how can we humanize machines? How can we relate to machines in a humane way so that they will function effectively and help us fight diseases, poverty, and exploitation? Or, to put it more positively, how can machines enable us to appreciate and take better care of our lives and nature?

One type of science fiction story that children grasp immediately is one that focuses on the mad scientist, who began making a career for himself during the nineteenth century. Mary Shelly's *Frankenstein* was one of the first works to treat the "deranged" scientist, who creates a monster that he is unable to control and that causes havoc in the world. Other writers, like E. T. A. Hoffmann in *The Sandman* and *The Automaton* and Nathaniel Hawthorne in *Rappaccini's Daughter* and *The Butterfly*, introduce mad scientists obsessed by their quest for power and their desire to create a mechanical device that will change the world. The mad scientist is an interesting character because, like the artist and even the shaman, he must be ready to give himself over to an idea; he must transport his body and soul into another realm for a while in order to create something entirely new, something that has never been envisaged, something that comes so to speak from the future. Therefore, though he may be compulsive and obsessive, the mad scientist commands our respect. He is an awesome figure. His ancestors are the alchemists, the wizards, and the witches of fairy tales and legends. He is the male witch of science fiction. Up through the early part of the twentieth century, science was dominated by men, and one of the underlying questions that I pose with science fiction stories is whether the machines are destructive specifically because they have mainly served the needs, fantasies, and aggressive interests of men. Mad scientists are endemic to what we call civilization and progress, and that is all the more reason why I begin this session with a story like this one.

The Mad Postman

Everyone thought William Bent was weird. Even his dog Humphrey thought so. At fifty, he lived alone in a large house on top of Spider Hill. He had inherited this house many years ago when his parents had died, but he never had enough money to keep it in good condition. It was a gray, wooden-frame house with large windows and a green pointed roof that had a rusty rooster for a weathervane on top.

Bent worked as a postman. Tall and haggard, he looked more like a beanpole with leather straps draped around him than like a real post-man. He had a bald spot on top of his head, and his long gray hair touched his shoulders. To match the hair he had a drooping mous-tache that sloped toward his chin, and when he delivered the mail, the young children ran about and made fun of him. However, he took all this in stride and smiled, because Bent was always elsewhere. His mind was always thinking of things he wanted to invent.

"One day, nobody will laugh at me," he would say to himself. "They will thank me and respect me. They won't call me beanpole or Fu Man Chu any more."

But Bent was always too busy to notice the pranks that people played on him. They moved his mail car while he was making his rounds so he wouldn't find it. Or they mixed up the mail so that he delivered it to the wrong address. Bent merely went his way and looked forward to the end of each day, when he rushed home and climbed the stairs to the attic, where he had his laboratory. In fact, the whole house was his laboratory because he had machines, test tubes, cylinders, pipes, wire, and electric components scattered throughout the house in all the rooms. But the experiment he was working on now was the most important: it was called the space divider, and it would allow him to make a slit into space, right into the sky, onto another planet, and walk into the future to another planet. He had built a special platform outside the attic window, and it was from there that he intended to walk into space and through the slit into another world.

$$Z^* +500/ - 678 = A+D - X + Y$$

He had all sorts of formulas written on a blackboard, and chemicals in bottles and test tubes with special labels. The only creature who knew about Bent's experiments was Humphrey, whose only concern was that his master survive so that he could have his chunky cereal and milk every day. Humphrey was a mix of basset hound and greyhound and looked almost as weird as his master. He had given up hunting rabbits and squirrels some time ago, and had accompanied Bent on his rounds as a postman until he had reached the age of ten. Since then, he had become too old and too lazy to do anything, except to remind Bent to feed him, which Bent often forgot to do because he was so immersed in his experiments.

Now on this particular day, Bent had forgotten Humphrey because he was too excited to remember anything but the formula that he had just conceived. He had thought about it while falling over a baby carriage that had been placed in his path as he delivered the mail. When his head hit the ground, the crash caused a shock and sent sensations to his head. Immediately, he knew, and he quickly finished his mail route, ran home and up the stairs to the attic, and wrote the new formula on the board:

$$CD=JZ=HDZ + 100\% \times 100\% = HDZ+? = \{ \quad \}$$

Then Bent began mixing chemicals, and he poured some liquid in and out of test tubes until he had a light blue substance.

"One hour," he said to himself. "It will last one hour, and then I must return."

He set his watch and opened the attic window. Carefully protecting the test tube with the blue liquid, he stepped outside onto the platform as Humphrey watched. Then Bent raised the tube to his lips. Humphrey closed his eyes, and the next second, when he opened them, Bent had disappeared. He had swallowed the liquid.

"No!" Humphrey wailed. "Who's going to feed me now?"

The dog was very unhappy, but Bent was not. He jumped and clicked his heels as soon as he saw the slit in space. His space-divider formula had worked! In a split second, Bent was in another world, one that was green all over: green mountains, valleys, streams, trees, meadows, buildings. Everything was absolutely green!

Bent was standing on a hill overlooking a town. He looked at his watch.

"I have exactly fifty-nine minutes left, and then I must return to this spot," he said, as if to remind himself.

Bent was so excited that he ran down the hill into the town, and all around him were green people, who did not look much different than the people on earth, except that their skin was green. Nor did the houses and streets look much different except that they were all different shades of green. And as Bent walked along the streets, the children and grown-ups acted about the same. They laughed at him, pointed their fingers at him, and tried to play jokes on him.

"Weird!" someone yelled.

"Beanpole!" a young boy screamed.

Bent tried to ignore the remarks. He wanted to speak to the people and find out where he was, but nobody would talk to him. Everyone just mocked him or ran away.

Gradually Bent found himself drawn to a house on a hill that looked a great deal like his own. It was a large, wooden-frame house with a rusty rooster for a weathervane on top. The only difference was that it was green. The door was wide open, and when he entered, he automatically began climbing the stairs to the attic. When he got to the top, he knocked at a door, and a voice cried out,

"Come in, if you dare!"

Bent hesitated for a moment. He was frightened, but he was also curious. So he pushed the door open slowly until he stood facing the strangest creature he had ever seen in his life. She was at least six feet tall, skinny, and had long, curly, green hair dangling down her back. Her eyes were blue and her ears were pointed. She had thin lips and a pug nose. Dressed in some sort of uniform, the woman looked like she might be going to a costume ball.

"Bravo for you!" the woman said. "You dared to enter. Perhaps you're not a fool. How did you get so white?"

Bent was so stunned that he could not answer, and he became

even more stunned when he looked at a blackboard and saw:

$$CD=JZ=HDZ+100\% \times 100\% = HDZ+? = \{ \quad \}$$

It was his formula, the exact same formula.

"Why are you staring like that?" the woman said. "Has the cat got your tongue?"

"That's mine!" Bent exclaimed.

"You must be joking," she responded. "I've been working on this for twenty years. It's my space divider, and I'm about to leave this planet because I can't stand the people here, and they can't stand me. They don't know it yet, but it's their loss!"

Bent looked into her blue eyes, and there was something feisty about the sparkle in her eyes that he liked.

"Well," he ventured spontaneously, "why don't you come with me?"

"Who are you?" she asked.

"I'm William, William Bent from Earth. And you?"

"I'm Domina, Domina from Verdata. But where is Earth?"

"It's another planet, another world," Bent said. "Come with me, quick. You've found the formula just like me, and if you drink a cup, you'll have an hour to spend on Earth. Perhaps you'll be happier there."

Domina smiled, "You're weird, but I like you."

"Come," insisted Bent. "We have no time to lose. We must climb the hill and find the spot where I entered your planet." And that they did. They ran and reached the top of the hill just as Bent's liquid was wearing off.

"Drink the formula, and hold onto my hand," Bent cried out.

And poof! There they were in Bent's attic. Poor Humphrey, who had been sleeping, was frightened out of his wits when he saw tall, green Domina in the attic. He growled, and Bent said, "Oh, be quiet, Humphrey, it's only a friend."

Humphrey was overjoyed to see that his master was there with this strange creature, and he began wagging his tail.

"I had better feed him," Bent said to Domina. "Would you like something to eat?"

"No, thank you," she said. "I'm actually very tired."

"Well," suggested Bent. "Drink some of my formula, and that will allow you to stay as long as you like. Then I'll show you to my guest room, and tomorrow, after you get up and have breakfast, you can see the town when I make my rounds."

"What do you do?" asked Domina.

"I'm a postman."

"You're weird," Domina said, and she went to bed.

The next morning, they all had breakfast together, Domina, Bent, and Humphrey.

"Ready?" asked Bent.

"Ready," said Domina.

It was early in the morning, and Bent drove his car to the post office where he quickly picked up the first bundles of mail that he was to deliver in town. Then he drove to a certain street, where he got out of the car with Domina and Humphrey. He placed Humphrey on a leash, and all three began strolling down the street with Bent delivering the mail at each house. They were quite a sight: the tall, gray-haired Bent with the droopy moustache, the tall green-haired Domina with her blue eyes and pointed ears, and the lean greyhound Humphrey with long flappy basset ears. The people could not believe their eyes. At first they were frightened and called the police.

"Bent's gone crazy!"

"There's a queer mermaid on the loose!"

"They're sick! Just look at them!"

"Weirdos!"

Wherever they walked, Bent and Domina heard the chants of the people and children, and for the first time, Bent realized why he had been trying to invent a space divider.

"Come," he said to Domina, and he practically dragged her and Humphrey back to his house and up to the attic. Then he began mixing liquids into different test tubes. He worked for over an hour until he had a huge supply of blue liquid. Domina watched carefully and did not say a word. When he was done, Bent looked at her,

"You know what I'm doing?"

"Of course," she laughed. "You're weird. Do you want to take Humphrey with us?"

Humphrey barked.

"Why not?" Bent said.

"I don't want to go back to Verdata," Domina said.

"We both know the formula," Bent said. "So we can keep shifting planets until we find the right one."

All three went out on the platform in front of the attic window with the liquid, ready to drink.

"How will we know the right planet?" Domina asked.

"When I find the right kind of chunkies," Humphrey barked.

"When we can be ourselves and not worry," Bent replied.

"Yes," Domina said. "When we can be ourselves."

Then there was a poof! The sky divided for a split second, and they were gone.

I tell a tale like *The Mad Postman* because it raises the question, Are we insane today because we have not gone insane? What is madness indeed when so many sick things occur in today's world, especially when we can do so much good with science and technology? With a science fiction story like *The Mad Postman*, I can introduce questions that deal with conformity, prejudice, the purpose of science, and dreams of outer space. Once again, I do not preach a message but ask the children questions that focus on the nature of a science fiction story and the issues in the particular story. And, of course, I explore any questions that the children raise.

Immediately following this story, I switch the topic to science fiction and war machines. Like many people today, I am distressed by the increase of violence in Western society, and though I dislike the violent comics, TV programs, and games to which children are exposed, I am against censoring them because I do not believe that censorship is the answer to violence or bad art. Censorship is in itself a violent act, an imposition, and there are more creative ways to oppose violence and its causes. The most significant approach to opposing violence and the commercial art that preys on the fantasies and desires of children involves social and economic programs that eliminate poverty, provide jobs, and create possibilities for advancement in all sectors of society. As Penelope Leach has argued in *Children First*, families and communities must not be nourished according to the dictates of a capitalist commodity system or a moral majority that claims to know what is best for the ideal family and community. Rather, families and communities must be provided the means and tools to articulate their own interests and define their own needs with respect to other families and communities. The more autonomous people feel in their families and communities, the less violent they will become, and here storytelling can play a productive role by contributing to a strong sense of community. Storytelling can show children alternatives to violence through different ways of narrating their lives and assuming responsibility for their actions.

In science fiction, whether expressed in literature, films, video games, or oral stories, there is a tendency to glorify war and weapons. Most science fiction films and literature that celebrate battle and power are, bluntly speaking, a disgrace to humanity. But my abhorrence is not about to stop the production of commodities by businesses, especially the culture industry, that socialize youngsters to accept violence and accomodates their whims. I prefer to tell tales of all kinds that make a mockery of war and violence and to suggest that life has greater pleasures than to compete with and vanquish an opponent.

In the course of my storytelling I have combined certain tales and films into one story about war. Some time ago, when I was working on a book of feminist fairy tales, I discovered a picture book entitled *Of Cannons and Caterpillars*, (1977) by Italian feminists Sylvie Selig and Adela Turin, and I used it as the basis for my war story. Then I added important motifs from Jacques Prévert's screenplay for the superb animated film *Le Roi et l'Oiseau* (*The King and the Bird*, 1950), which itself was a contemporary revision of Andersen's *The Chimney Sweep and the Shepherdess*. Finally, two of Hermann Hesse's anti-war fairy tales, *Strange News from Another Planet* (1915) and *If the War Continues* (1915) influenced my conception of this tale, which I call:

How Peace Was Found Again

Well, when Peace left the world in the twenty-first century without anyone noticing its disappearance, there was not a country in the world that had not recently fought a war of some kind, and violence had become a way of life for everyone. The big nations attacked and swallowed up the little ones until, in the year 2085, there were only two countries left in the world, or should I say cities, because all the continents with the exception of North America had been totally destroyed and infected by nuclear bombs and had sunk beneath the oceans. Even North America itself had been turned into a gigantic desert with barren lands and dead corpses spread out from one coast to the next. All that was left on the East Coast was a gigantic modern castle of five hundred floors that stretched high into the sky, and on the West Coast was another castle that also had five hundred stories and towered into the sky. These castles were more like fortresses, and on each one of the floors was a missile with a nuclear warhead pointed at the other castle.

"We shall devastate you!" warned Sir Dominick, the Chancellor of the East.

"We are number One and will destroy you!" responded Henry Kist, the Prime Minister of the West.

But the Chancellor and the Minister were afraid to fire their missiles at each other because they knew that would mean the end of the world. For the time being they carried on their war through words and interviews that they telecast to the remaining people of the world.

But there were not too many people left in the world, and most of them were too poor to own TV sets. There were perhaps a thousand people in the Castle of the East and another thousand in the Castle of the West. They were scattered on different floors of the castle and could not go outside because the ground and air were contaminated by radiation. Both castles were covered with protective glass, and food was produced by chemicals. On the top floor lived the Chancellors and Ministers, then came the generals and their armies, the scientists, the TV journalists, the merchants, the doctors, the lawyers, and the police. The lower one went, the less important the people were, and at the very bottom were the women and children.

Sir Dominick saw his wife once a month and his children once a year at Christmastime, when he gave them toy soldiers, rockets, missile video games, and uniforms. He forgot how many children he had, and he forgot that they were girls, three girls. They all lived on the ground floor of the castle with the other women and children. Sir Dominick saw Prime Minister Kist more than he saw his own family. Once a week, he and his generals, followed by a TV crew, flew to the middle of the country and landed on top of a TV tower five miles high, where they met Prime Minister Kist and his men. It was on top of this tower in a bubble that they held war talks, which were telecast to both cities.

"We have five hundred missiles with bacteriological warheads," Sir Dominick declared.

"We are smarter," said Chancellor Kist. "Our supersonic jets can penetrate your glass and spray poison on your castle."

"We are even smarter," Sir Dominick answered, "because we have hydraulic fans that will blow the poison back to you."

"Our scientists have erected a barrier so that the poison will bounce back to you," replied Chancellor Kist.

"Well, our men have built a higher barrier," Sir Dominick maintained. And so it went.

Each week the two leaders got together and told the other side that they were building new and better weapons. They did not know any longer why they were fighting. Was it for money? Was it because of different beliefs? Was it because of different skin colors? They no longer knew. They just wanted to win. Since no one could remember the days of Peace anymore, everyone was for war.

But one day, deep down in the basement of Sir Dominick's Castle, his ten-year-old daughter Betty went looking for a ball that she had lost, and while she was rummaging about the cellar, she saw something glowing on the ground. Much to her astonishment, she discovered a tiny red flower sprouting from the ground, and next to the flower were books, all sorts of books that she had never seen before, because books were no longer used in her kingdom and few people knew how to read.

"Mother!" she called excitedly as she ran back to the first floor. "Look what I found!" And she showed her mother a big picture book of flowers that she had carried from the basement, and her mother was stunned.

"Where did you find this?"

"In the basement."

And Betty led her mother to the flower and the books, and her mother, whose name was Miranda, knew that something miraculous was happening. So she called all the people who lived on the first floor, the mothers and children and the old people, and they began to read wonderful picture books about farms, gardens, railroads, tiny houses, lakes, and boats. And memories returned to the older people who taught the younger ones how to read and what all these things meant. Slowly the people on the first floor began to dream about leaving the castle and building towns and villages again, and when Miranda visited Dominick that month on the five hundredth floor, she said, "We want to plant flowers and build villages."

"Don't be silly," Dominick answered. "There's a war on. I can't think of petty things like that!"

"Would you mind if we did?" she said.

"You can't." Dominick answered. "The ground is contaminated, and you might get killed. Besides, I can't think about flowers!"

"Would you mind if we tried?"

"Do what you want! I can't be disturbed right now. We're dreaming up a new weapon."

So Miranda left her husband and went down to the ground floor. She gathered everyone together and told them she had a plan that would allow them to build their villages, towns, and gardens.

The next day she sent a messenger to the wife of Prime Minister Kist, whose name was Amanda, and this messenger carried books and a picture of the red flower. Since the ministers and generals never knew what was going on at the bottom of the castles, they did not realize that Miranda had made contact with Amanda. Their children began meeting and playing with one another, while the old people came together and began remembering the peaceful days of long ago. And Miranda and Amanda decided to invite some scientists down from the four-hundredth floor to ask them how they could make the ground safe again and begin planting grass and trees and flowers. At first the scientists were upset because they thought the ground was too dangerous, but when they saw the old picture books with scenes of farms and animals, memories returned, and they began using their brains to think of ways to save the earth. In fact, they stayed on the ground floor with the women and children, and they were not missed because other scientists were busy working on bombs on the five hundredth floor.

Soon, the scientists found a way to grow grass and clean the water so that the desert separating the two cities turned into rolling hills, pastures, and lakes. The workers on the fiftieth floor heard about this and descended to look at the miracle. Miranda and Amanda asked the workers to help build homes and towns and villages, and they agreed, and soon they were followed by technicians from the hundredth floor. Each time people left a floor in either castle, they dismantled their bombs and got rid of them. They left their floors for good and went to live in the new towns and villages. Seven years passed, and by the end of the seventh year, there were no more bombs, and when the generals on the four-hundred-ninety-ninth floor realized this, they stopped being generals and became farmers along with their soldiers.

The only people left in the two castles were Dominick and Kist and their ministers way up high on the five-hundredth floor. They had been completely unaware of what had been happening during the past seven years, and they had just decided it was time to declare the war to end all wars. So they decided to meet as usual at the television tower to prepare their people for the final catastrophe, but when their special jets approached the tower, they found that it had been dismantled. Dominick and Kist ordered their pilots to land on the ground, and when the two men and their ministers touched the ground for the first time in over fifty years, they were astonished.

"It's grass," Dominick said.

"There are villages and people!" Kist added.

"Where are our soldiers and parades?" Dominick was afraid.

"Where is my protection?" Kist cried.

Dominick looked at Kist, "This is a trick! I know it, and you'll pay!"

"Don't try to fool me!" Kist answered. "You're the one who's behind this, you sneak!"

All of a sudden, Miranda and Amanda appeared with hundreds of people, old and young, and two girls ran up to Dominick and Kist with bouquets of flowers.

"This is to thank you!" the girls said as they gave the flowers to the two men.

"Thank us for what?" the men cried out at the same time.

"For letting us do what we wanted to do," Miranda stepped forward.

"Now we don't need you anymore," Amanda said.

And the people began cheering, for Peace had returned to the earth, and as Dominick and Kist looked around, they saw their castles crumbling in the far distance, and they saw smiling faces up close. So instead of declaring the war to end all wars, they surrendered to Peace, and that is why we cherish red flowers and books today, for they will never let us forget how Peace returned to the earth.

Since a science fiction story is always based to a certain extent on fact and scientific possibility, I always try to tell a story that begins with the introduction of a miraculous discovery, person or event, that gives pause for thought. This may mean introducing something from outer space. Whatever the case may be, the exceptional person or event depends on a scientific invention that somehow disrupts the characters of the story and the listeners. This disruption generally raises the question of using science in a responsible way to restore harmony and peace. The ending of the story points either to unresolved problems that science can solve if it is "humanized," or to a resolution due to an awareness that science can be used to everyone's benefit.

I use several writing games to follow the stories.

1. I ask the children to tell me what they think the greatest inventions in the world are and why. As they volunteer, I write the inventions on the board:

   > supersonic jet
   > gigantic computer
   > building crane
   > high-speed train
   > Sony walkman
   > video players
   > X-ray machines

   Once we have about twenty inventions, I ask the children to choose two or three and write a science fiction story about how these inventions have changed somebody's life or life on our planet. Each story should be illustrated.

2. I bring in pictures of machines, instruments, objects, etc. that I have cut out of magazines and newspapers, and I place them on a table. I try to bring in fifty to seventy different pictures. I invite children to choose one or two pictures from the table and paste them on a piece of paper. Based on the picture or pictures they choose, they tell a story of how the machine or instrument has changed somebody's life.

3. We give children drawing paper, and they are asked to draw a creature from outer space or another planet. After they finish drawing their picture, I ask them to tell me a story about the creature or world they have imagined.

4. As a follow-up, depending on the age group, I ask students to study the newspapers during the week and to cut out a story about a scientific invention or event and paste it on a piece of paper. Based on the newspaper story, they write a science fiction story at home and bring it into class. Both the story and the newspaper article are shared with the class in storytelling. Another possibility is for the teacher to collect all the newspaper stories, mix them, and redistribute them in class; depending on the newspaper article that each student receives, she or he writes a science fiction story based on fact and possibility.

One of the problems that storytellers and teachers always confront in sessions where the topic of violence is addressed is that some children write and draw scenes that glorify aggression and power. Such scenes are imitations of images seen on television and film, if not in newspapers and magazines. This is why it is important to set a context or atmosphere of non-violence and to discuss openly with the children why and how violence occurs in different situations. Many children, especially boys, will nevertheless write horror and violent stories based on scientific probability and technological invention, but I believe they will realize in their writing that the machines and alien creatures in their stories depend on *them*. It is this dependence that may help them realize the interdependence of people in the world, especially if the storyteller and teacher are careful to stress the social responsibility of inventors. As little inventors, children should be encouraged to grasp the impact of their "inventions." In this regard, science fiction can bring children closer to the reality of their present situation and at the same time make them realize how much the future depends on their present outlook.

❦ *11* ❦
New Perspectives through Creative Dramatics and Video

Though most storytellers are actors and directors, they rarely make use of creative dramatics and video in working with children. Yet there are important connections to be made, particularly since great advances in technology have enhanced our audiovisual means of communication. Although the movies and TV programs for children in the America and Europe are for the most part deplorable, this new technology is not an "enemy" of children and communal storytelling, as some critics have argued. Theater, film, and video depend on narration, both oral and written, and the mediations between orality, script, stage, camera, and screen can be used in manifold ways to help children develop critical thinking and practical skills. Moreover, since children tend nowadays to be exposed to theater and film narrative as much as to any other form of narration, it is very important that they grasp how plays, videos, films, and screenplays are composed or put together, piece by piece, so to speak.

In showing how plays, videos, and films are made, I also want to work against the negative aspects of television, movies, and video games. Here Marsha Kinder's study, *Playing with Power in Movies, Television, and Video Games* is highly significant for my work. As she has stated,

Narrative maps the world and its inhabitants, including one's own position within that grid. In acquiring the ability to understand stories, the child is situated as a perceiving, thinking, feeling, acting, speaking subject within a series of narrative fields — as a person in a family saga, as a spectator who tunes in to individual tales and identifies with their characters, and as a performer who repeats cultural myths and sometimes generates new transformations. Ever since television became pervasive in the American home, this mass medium has played a crucial role in the child's entry into narrative. My study explores how television and its narrative conventions affect the construction of the subject.[1]

Kinder reveals how, unfortunately for us, Saturday-morning television shows, video games, and films help form a gendered subject who is supposed to believe that she or he can develop protean powers to assimilate the world and buy her or his way into a world more concerned with commodities than with humans. Of course, the boy/girl subjects have clearly delineated roles, the more adventurous and powerful for the boys and the more cheerleading and decorative for the girls. Though it is true that children can develop their cognitive skills through television, movies, and video games, they can also imbibe a false sense of power and aggression that intensifies competition in a capitalist market system. Whatever skills are acquired through television, movies, and video games are acquired at the expense of humanitarian values. Though the narratives of the various TV shows, movies, and videos may seem to differ, they all tend to homogenize child viewers through narrative constructs that frame children as "precocious consumers," as Kinder demonstrates in many examples.

There are few antidotes to commercial television, and movies and Kinder's study does not argue for abolishing these media. Rather the best way to oppose the negative impact of such media narrations is to work with them—to reutilize the media to create different values and a social awareness that leads to more responsible autonomy, not the false sense of power that leads to a colonizing ideology. My own work with children suggests that they are strongly influenced by television and movies, as Kinder indicates, but also that it is possible to animate children into questioning the consumerist subjects they are encouraged to become; we may thus undermine the narratives and messages that they receive daily through television.

As I have demonstrated in previous chapters, I use a great deal of improvisation and creative dramatics in my storytelling sessions. Certainly, I do not always follow my storytelling with a reenactment of the stories. Everything depends on the needs of the teacher and children and the particular topic of the session. However, in some instances, I have actually geared an entire program of storytelling toward producing a play that will later be performed and videotaped. My storytelling was purposely conceived to animate students to make use of technology in staging stories, and I want to discuss two projects that I developed in Milwaukee and Berlin to show how storytelling can effectively develop technical and creative skills while inducing great cooperation among children and creating a sense of community. Neither of these projects was designed to oppose the power of television, movies, and video games, yet both helped the students grasp how they can use narrative to express themselves, their needs, and those of their dreams that have not been entirely manipulated by the intertextuality of television, movies, and video games.

Milwaukee

During the early 1980s, the University of Wisconsin at Milwaukee began an experiment to help "gifted children" during the summer in a College for Kids. For two months, July and August, professors offered courses based on their expertise for youngsters ranging in age from six to sixteen. The courses included mathematics, Italian, biology, art, filmmaking, and much more. The professors aimed to stimulate "gifted" students who might be bored by traditional courses and methods during the school year, and who were allegedly neglected at school because the teachers paid more attention to students who were not as quick to learn skills.

At first, I was hesitant to teach in this program because I thought it might be too elitist. I was also worried about the standards used to determine whether or not a child was "gifted." However, the director of the College explained to me that no "objective" criteria would be employed to determine which children were "gifted," and that if parents believed their child was gifted, the child was accepted into the College. Given this type of admission procedure, I felt more at ease. The tuition for the College for Kids was reasonably low, and scholarships were given to families that could not afford to pay.

I taught a three-week course on storytelling and creative dramatics two summers in a row, meeting every day from nine to noon with ten to fifteen children between the ages of seven and ten. Though I had directed plays for children in Milwaukee and Berlin, this first summer was very experimental because I had never worked so intensely with children in such a compact program. I did not at first intend to produce a play with them. My basic aim was to tap the storyteller and actor within each of them, and this became easy. However, I did have a major problem to overcome both summers: the neediness of the children. It did not matter whether the children came from poor or rich families, nor did their ethnic background make a difference; they were all starved for attention, and they eagerly if not desperately wanted to display their talents. Whether they were "gifted" or not was incidental to me because I considered and consider all children gifted in some way. Here it seemed to me that parents were sending their children to this College because they realized that the schools were not giving their children enough opportunity to be creative. "Gifted" began to assume a new meaning for me, and it had more to do with a lack at school, a gap, an emptiness. In addition, the situation reminded me very much of Alice Miller's provocative book *The Gifted Child,* in which she depicts how parents and adults manipulate children in their infancy so that they feel obliged to please their parents by performing amazing feats. Certainly, some of the Milwaukee parents had placed their children in this position of "gifted child" and expected "great" things from them this summer in all their "college" courses. In contrast, I believed that the storytelling session could be used for the children to express their own needs. My goal was to give them a sense of accomplishment no matter what we did during the program, not to produce a "finished" product.

Once the program began, I used all sorts of improvisational games to dramatize the stories I told. Generally one or two parents assisted me. We also did a great deal of writing and drawing, and after the first day, I suggested certain topics about which the students could write at home if they liked. Each day thereafter, I began the session with the sharing and acting of stories and pictures brought in from home. We formed a circle, and I asked for volunteers. The children liked to show off, and their "shows" were often incredible, for they began bringing in props and developing their own characters and stories with great ease during the next three weeks. After the first two weeks I told the children that I thought their skits were remarkable, and I asked whether we might choose a few of them to perform at the end of the third week. So together we decided to conclude the program with a group of skits that they developed through improvisation, and to perform these skits for their parents and friends. There were to be no scripts, and I kept reminding the children that it was not important to memorize their "lines" perfectly and not a problem if the play was somewhat unfinished. In fact, their skits kept changing up to and through their "final" performances, which were well-received by parents and friends alike.

The following summer I had a better sense of how I wanted to structure my program. Working with my wife, who had developed stimulating compositional games for the children, I began exploring different classical fairy tales and fables through enactment and written revisions. By the middle of the second week, the children had decided that they wanted to rework *The Three Little Pigs*. I had already told them a contemporary version of this fable, in which three unemployed workers unite to fight against a crooked landlord, who takes their houses away from them because they have no money. The emphasis was on "strength through unity," and the landlord was defeated in the end. We dramatized *The Three Workers and the Landlord*, and then I asked the children whether they wanted to create their own version. We began to discuss other possibilities, and since many of them were fascinated by "break dancing" at this time, they came up with the following rough plot: A poor mother has three children who do no work around the house. She herself is employed as an aerobics teacher at the Y, but does not earn much money. Soon there is nothing left to eat, so she kicks them out of the house to find work and make something out of their lives. Since all three love break dancing, they decide to open up three break-dance studios made of straw, wood, and brick. However, they make a great deal of noise. A policeman harasses them and wants to close down their studios. But if they promise to give him money as a bribe, he will let them operate their studios. In the meantime, their mother has died, and her ghost warns them each time the policeman approaches one of their studios to shut or blow the studio down. The ghost helps the first child escape to the wooden studio, and when the policeman comes again, she helps the other two run off to the brick studio. Then the three break dancers set a trap for the policeman, and he is almost killed. However, he sees how unfair he is and makes peace with the break dancers. The mother comes back to life, and there is a final celebration with music and break dancing.

Once we had the bare outline of this story—and there were heated discussions about whether or not to kill the policeman, and whether or not the mother should come back to life—we decided who would play what role, who would work on the script, who would bring in the music, and what costumes we would need. Then we divided the story into scenes and enacted them through improvisation. I helped the students by blocking the play and setting the "stage" for them in an open room that we transformed into a theater. The blocking of the play was intended to provide a narrative structure and thus a sense of order. However, this order was not fixed, and the students learned how to alter the blocking through repeated improvisation of the scenes. Each time they performed their play, they discovered contradictions or had new ideas, so the story kept changing. These changes upset one of the girls, who had actually spent an entire afternoon and evening typing a script on a computer for everyone. As director/scriptwriter, she had wanted the rest of the children to stick to the script that they had initially developed. But she was unsuccessful, and she relented. If arguments developed, we sat down in a circle and discussed our disagreements until we reached a consensus about how to proceed. Sometimes brief quarrels developed, and the students resolved them on the spot.

Since I did not want them to become totally absorbed by a kind of "achievement-oriented goal" project, I still spent the first two hours of each day on other types of storytelling, writing, and improvisation, all of which contributed to the students' play *The Three Break Dancers*. The more we worked on the play, the more the students began sharing ideas and helping each other. For instance, one of the boys was an awkward dancer, and he admired another one of the boys, who was an exceptional dancer. Instead of making fun of the clumsy boy, the other tried to teach him certain steps and movements to improve his break dancing. The "rigid" scriptwriter who had originally refused to play a role and had been helping with the direction of the skit decided that she wanted to be in the play, so we changed the story once again and built in a role for her during the last week. Each day, as we worked on the scenes, the students gained a sense of how to make the plot move and became aware of each other, as people and as actors. They discovered their own strengths and weaknesses, asked for guidance, and helped each other. It was difficult to predict which "version" of the play would be the final version for the invited guests because the story kept changing up to the very last second. We videotaped one session to give the students a sense of how they appeared and moved, and we discussed how we might change certain facets of the play. We did not, however, make effective use of the video because we did not have enough time.

By the time the play was performed, parents and friends had also contributed to the production by providing costumes, helping the students at home, and planning the event, which ended in a party. That is, this play was a type of communal celebration that brought the parents and friends of the students together. Though our production was clearly rough and unfinished, the students conveyed a deeper sense of story to their audience through their "underlying, unwritten" script, for their efforts and gestures told the story of what they could do and hoped to do through their imagination.

In later workshops with older students, I devised (always with the help and cooperation of teachers) a way to better incorporate the video camera into the development of the play. For example, when I worked with a group of thirteen-year-olds who wanted to dramatize a local legend from their community, I introduced the camera into the project right away. A group of five students formed a camera team, and they had a twofold task: 1) to film the play in progress, that is, all the discussions, rehearsals, and research; 2) to film the final production as though they were making a film. Of course, they could not film all the discussions, but they tried to capture what they thought were the highlights of the preparations. Sometimes they used two different cameras. As a team, these students made all their own decisions. It should be pointed out, however, that the students worked with a video specialist first, who taught them how to use all the equipment: on how to hold the cameras, how to move them, how to work with perspective, and how to edit.

The other students divided themselves into actors, writers, set designers, costume makers, researchers, and directors. The assignment of roles was always done with the teacher's consultation and advice. At times there was friction, but we always sat down and discussed our choices and tried to reach a consensus. Once the researchers had gathered all the oral and written material for the production of the legend, we decided to mount two productions, one for the screen and one for the stage. Therefore, the two directors worked together. One was in charge of shooting "takes" for the film production, and after the scenes had been improvised and set. These takes were repeated, and they served as rehearsals for a play that the students performed for the school and community. The play and film took six weeks to prepare, and both were performed and shown on a weekend. Later, the film and records of the production were stored in the school library and made available to anyone who wanted to use them.

Though the final production of the legend was fairly well polished, we did not use a script, nor did we copy Hollywood or Broadway models in preparing the play. The focus was on the legend, and we used what we "found" in improvisation and in our research as the basis for the play. The camera crew recorded the preparations, and eventually they designed their own film based on the rehearsals they observed. In the end the students had three different versions of the story: the improvised rehearsals, the stage version, and the film. In the process they learned new technical and creative skills, and they gained a sense of multi-perspective narration and interdisciplinary work.

Berlin

In 1978–79 I was a visiting professor at the Pädagogische Hochschule Berlin or the Pedagogical University of Berlin, which is now part of the Free University of Berlin. Much of my later work with children in the States developed out of experiments that I conducted with German university students between the ages of twenty and thirty. During the first semester I taught two courses, one on improvisation and one on the adaptation of fairy tales for children's theater. By the time the second semester began in January of 1979, I had asked the theater department if I could develop a children's play through improvisation with a group of twenty students, and as a visiting professor, I was fortunately given what the Germans call "*Narrenfreiheit*," the freedom of fools. I took advantage of this freedom by transforming two courses into a theater project.

When I met with the students, I suggested a few fairy tales that we might explore through improvisation, and we finally settled on *Prince Fortunatus* because it enabled us to address questions of solidarity, feminism, and power in the form of a parody. Although we did some camera work to observe and criticize scenes, the entire project was geared toward the stage.

There are many versions of *Prince Fortunatus*, a tale similar to the *How Six made their Way through the World*, and to start our work, I chose to read Madame D'Aulnoy's *Belle-Belle or The Chevalier Fortuné*, which goes as follows.

Once upon a time there was a very good, mild king. He was a powerful monarch, but his neighbor, the Emperor Matapa, was more powerful still. In the last of the great wars they had waged against each other, the emperor had won a tremendous battle. After killing or taking prisoner the greater portion of the king's officers and soldiers, Matapa besieged and conquered the king's capital city, and took possession of all of its treasures. The king had just enough time to save himself and the queen, his sister, who had become a widow at a very early age. Though intelligent and beautiful, she was, to tell the truth, also proud, violent, and difficult to approach.

The emperor sent all of the king's jewels and furniture to his own palace, and he carried away an extraordinary number of soldiers, women, horses, and anything else that he found useful or pleasant. After he had ravaged the greater part of the kingdom, he returned triumphantly to his own, where he was joyously received by his wife, the empress, and his daughter.

In the meantime, the defeated king was not inclined to accept his misfortune lightly. Rallying his remaining troops around him, he gradually formed the nucleus of an army. To increase their numbers as quickly as possible, he issued a proclamation requiring all the noblemen of his kingdom to come and serve him in person, or to send a well-mounted and armed son disposed to support his ventures.

Now, there was an old nobleman, eighty years of age, who lived on the frontier of the kingdom. He was a wise and prudent man, but fortune had not been kind to him, and he found himself reduced almost to poverty after having been quite wealthy at one time. He would have endured such straits if his three beautiful daughters had not been compelled to share his fate. They were so understanding that they never grumbled at their misfortunes, and if by chance they discussed them at all with their father, they did so more to console him than to add to his disquiet. Without the least desire to seek a better life, they lived with him in their rustic setting.

When the king's proclamation reached the ears of the old man, he called his daughters to him, looked at them sorrowfully, and said, "What can we do? The king has ordered all the noblemen of his kingdom to join him in order to fight the emperor, and if they refuse, he intends to levy a heavy tax. I'm not in a position to pay the tax, and therefore, I'm in a terrible dilemma. This will either be my ruin or my death."

The next day, the eldest daughter asked permission to disguise herself as a knight and represent her father as his son. After he consented, she rode off, and along the way she met a shepherdess in need. But she did not stop to help the shepherdess, who was actually a fairy, and therefore, the fairy exposed her as a woman and compelled her to return to her father. The same thing happened to the second daughter. Finally, the third, named Belle-Belle, stopped to help the fairy shepherdess and was rewarded with a magic horse named Comrade, who had great wisdom and other extraordinary powers. She was also given a magnificent coat of arms. Then the fairy dubbed her with the name Chevalier Fortuné. Along the way Fortuné and Comrade met and recruited a powerful woodcutter named Strongback, a fast hunter named Swift, another hunter named Sharpshooter, a farmer named Hear-all, a miller named Blow-all, a drinker named Tippler, and a voracious eater named Gorger who was gobbling 60,000 loaves of bread. Each one of the seven men agreed to serve Fortuné, who promised them good cheer and a better life and began procuring fine clothes and great horses for them.

When Fortuné arrived in the city, she became the talk of the town because "he" was so handsome and had such fine servants and horses. As soon as Fortuné was introduced at court, the king and queen were impressed by the chevalier. The king felt a strange attraction, and his sister, Floride, fell in love with Fortuné. However, when Fortuné, who had fallen for the king, rebuked the advances made by the aggressive Floride, the queen took revenge on the knight by demanding that Fortuné be sent to fight a dragon that had been devastating the countryside. The king hesitated, but his sister told him that it would be to Fortuné's credit and glory if he defeated the dragon. Or course, with the help of the seven amazing servants, Fortuné did vanquish the dragon and return to the court. The queen was more in love with Fortuné than ever, and the king was also duly impressed and fond of Fortuné, who was still in love with the king. Once again she rebuffed Floride, and this time the queen compelled Floride's brother to send Fortuné to fight the Emperor Matapa for the treasures that the tyrannical Matapa had taken from the king. Once again, the seven servants worked together to defeat the Emperor by helping Swift win a footrace against the Emperor's daughter and by taking everything from the palace. When Fortuné returned to the king, she was adored by everyone, and Floride made one last effort to win the Chevalier's love. Fortuné refused her, and Floride pretended that she had been attacked and violated by Fortuné, who was then condemned to be stabbed three times in the heart with a dagger (because it was "his" heart that was guilty and allegedly responsible for the crime). On the day of the execution, however, the guards led Fortuné to a stake and tore off "his" robe to pierce "his" heart. Of course, they discovered that he was a she, and the people rejoiced. Floride took poison, while the king rewarded Fortuné's loyalty and bravery by marrying her. Moreover, her amazing servants were also given important positions in the realm, and the fairy protectress arrived to grace their wedding.

Though this fairy tale is somewhat long and complicated, it provided all sorts of opportunities for us to comment on the abuse of power by different tyrants and the use of collective power to bring about harmony. The structure of the tale was very suitable for a division into scenes.

    I.   The Poor Lord's Home
    II.   The three encounters with the fairy shepherdess and the transformation of Belle-Belle into Fortuné, whom we understood as Fortunatus
   III.   The seven encounters with the miraculous attendants
   IV.   The arrival in court and the attraction of the king and queen
    V.   Floride's attempt to seduce Fortunatus
   VI.   The fight with the dragon
  VII.   Second attempt to seduce Fortunatus
VIII.   The Meeting with Matapa and the defeat of Matapa's daughter in a footrace with the help of the seven attendants
  IX.   The third attempt by Floride to seduce Fortunatus and the condemnation of Fortunatus
   X.   The denouement—Fortunatus is revealed as a woman. Floride commits suicide. The king marries Fortunatus/Belle-Belle, and the seven attendants are rewarded.

We had several discussions about how we could cut some of the scenes, and how we could also try to add contemporary references to the political situation of the two Germanies and the role of women. Once we began improvising, the concept of our play began to take form, and we began making assignments. I took notes during the improvisations, and though I guided the direction of the play, all decisions were made collectively as the story kept shifting. Contemporary political allusions, slang, archaic language, and proverbs were carefully incorporated into the play. The students divided themselves into actors, set designers, songwriters, costume makers, and photographers. We met twice a week for three to four hours, and we often changed roles and assignments as the play developed. At one point we decided to eliminate the two sisters and the dragon-fighting scene because we felt they were superfluous. We tried to emphasize the remarkable gifts of Fortunatus as a strong and courageous woman and the exceptional talents of her seven attendants. We depicted the king as somewhat helpless without Fortunatus and the attendants, and his love and his sister's love for Fortunatus as a source of humor. Although we wanted to show the androgynous nature of Fortunatus in a positive light and focus on sexual desire, our major effort was to show how the "oppressed" could work to attain certain goals while exposing the arbitrary power of the monarchs.

We made arrangements with a church in Kreuzberg, a working-class district in Berlin that houses many foreigners and students, to perform the play during a festival weekend in June, and we worked closely with the minister of this church and the people in the community to make our project part of a local celebration. In addition, we performed the play the following week for a group of students from another university in Germany who were interested in organizing theater projects for children in their region along the same lines. After all three of the performances, we discussed the play with the audience: how we developed it, and why we made certain choices.

Unfortunately, we did not make a video of the play, although we made use of video during rehearsals. The students wrote all the songs and music for the play and met on weekends to prepare music for the rehearsals. We never wrote a script, and the lines changed during all three performances, but the actors were so in tune with one another and knew the plot so well that there was never any confusion; they all worked together as if they were one storyteller narrating experiences of "once upon a time" that became very contemporary as they acted out their roles.

My projects in Berlin and Milwaukee were not unusual. For instance, Joe Winston has been doing some very important experimentation with drama in England involving extensive interdisciplinary work. In his article "Giants, Good, and Bad: Story and Drama at the Heart of the Curriculum at Key Stage 1,"[2] he describes how he developed two six-week programs in schools using Juliet and Charles Snape's *Giant* and the traditional tale of

Jack and the Beanstalk to develop a learning curriculum designed to stimulate self-responsibility in the children. In his work with *Giant*, a story about
a mountain as female giant who decides to leave her village because the
people do not appreciate what the mountain provides them, Winston spent
six weeks using drama and storytelling to explore topics related to geogra-
phy and math (developing a map of the giant and village and grouping
animals, trees, and fields), science (discussing and depicting the giant's
natural habits and the mountain's role as a provider), environment (showing how the mountain's disappearance in the story caused waste and pollu-
tion), social studies (showing how the people in the village could work
together to bring back the mountain and prevent the destruction of
nature), and biology (investigating the importance of motherhood and
nurturing as represented by the female giant who helps the villagers take
care of their community). In general, Winston sets up significant paradigms
for effective work with storytelling and drama in schools, work that creates
a strong sense of cooperation and community among the children.

Theater groups have traditionally incorporated storytelling and improvisation techniques to develop plays, and there are hundreds of plays that
make consummate use of folk tales and folklore. However, not enough
projects in schools have used storytelling, drama, film, and video to develop
performances and foster a sense of community inside and outside the
school. There is nothing like a long-range theater and/or film project to
bring together students, teachers, parents, and people in the community. In
particular, if such a project is based on a local legend or an episode in the
regional history, it enables children to attain their own understanding of
the past and relate the past to their present situation. In developing a
theater/film project, certain basic procedures are worth keeping in mind.

1. Choice of topic—Whether the students choose a legend, historical
    event, or fairy tale, it is important that they reach a consensus, other-
    wise they will not be motivated. It is best to ask for suggestions or
    provide different alternatives, and this can be done within each
    school's curricular guidelines. If there is a special historical commemo-
    ration or celebration in the community, the students may want to link
    their work to the plans of an outside association or group.
2. Research—Once the topic is chosen, the students should form
    research groups and bring in material related to the topic. They can
    then tell stories about or share their own versions of the topic. Once

this is done—and it is possible to collect different versions of the same event, fairy tale, or legend—there should be a consensus about which story line to pursue.

3. Assignment of roles—It is not necessary to fix the storyline, and the students may want to combine two or three perspectives in developing the play. But before they begin improvising, the students should divide into groups of directors, scriptwriters, actors, camerapeople, set designers, and costume makers. Within the groups, the students can determine roles, with the storyteller/teacher providing a guiding hand to settle disputes.

4. Improvisation—The acting out of the different scenes is a narrating process, and here the students must all cooperate to develop their story. If the students have not been exposed to the theater, it is a good idea for the storyteller or teacher to start with improvisational games and with coaching on staging and filming. The improvisation aims to test different perspectives and modes of dramatic expression. If the students are going to use video, it is essential that they learn about camerawork and film editing. If they plan to use music and song, they must decide when and where they might want to introduce the music. After each improvised scene, there should be discussion and proposals to keep or change various components of the plot or characteristics of a figure.

5. Production—Once the improvisation assumes more definite contours, that is, once the broad outlines of the play are clear, the improvisation moves into the rehearsal stage. If there is to be a film version, it is best to use this rehearsal phase to shoot the film takes for editing by the film group. In the meantime, the other groups can build and create costumes. These groups participate in all discussions. While the rehearsals proceed, the liaison group, which may consist of the teacher, storyteller, and other students, makes arrangements for a production within the school and possibly outside the school. Here the publicity work calls for artists and printers.

A theater/film project demands two to three months of preparation. Of course, it is possible to do such a project in a week's time, if the storyteller and teacher work with a group of students eight hours a day and do not insist on a polished production. One of my friends does theater workshops like this for schools, some lasting two to three weeks, but they are exhausting and nerve-wracking. If storytelling is to be used effectively with creative dramatics and film, it must be a long process that enables children to explore aspects of a story and learn how technology can be used to bring out the story they *want* to tell. The students may have been strongly influenced by commercial television and films, and at first, they may imitate what they have seen and experienced. However, through improvisation and acquiring skills, they will ultimately tell their own story, whether it be history, legend, or fantasy. They will work together, pool their talents, and begin to make their own way through the world.

Storytelling

in

Context

❦ *12* ❦

On the Use and Abuse
of Storytelling

In reviewing the revival of interest in balletic and operatic performances of old-fashioned fairy tales for the *New York Times* in 1987, Bruno Bettelheim restated his optimistic view that we are drawn to fairy-tale performances and fairy tales because they give the child in us a chance to fulfill childish wishes for what is experienced as a perfect world of enchantment.[1] Most adults would probably agree with him. Don't we always talk primarily about the happy end or the utopian aspect of the tales? Don't they all end in triumph for the tormented, lovely girl like Cinderella or the little guy like Tom Thumb? Certainly today's remakes of the Grimms' tales proclaim their faith in eventual resurrection or the triumph of the underdog. Films like *The Princess Bride* or *The Neverending Story*, TV series like *Beauty and the Beast* or Jim Henson's *The Storyteller*, Broadway musicals like *Into the Woods*, video tapes like Shelly Duvall's Faerie Tale Theater, Disney films like *Beauty and the Beast* and *Aladdin*—they all focus on the resolution of conflicts, or what Bettelheim cavalierly refers to as the positive reorganization of sexual drives that enables children to overcome oedipal complexes and sibling rivalries.

Yet, to my mind, such focus on resolution and happiness only points to our tenacious capacity to avoid unpleasant realizations about childhood experiences. In contrast to Bettelheim, I suspect that our continued attraction to the tales, especially the classical Grimms' tales, is based on something specific that we repress and are afraid to talk about, something the Grimms knew about two hundred years ago but also repressed. I'm talking about child abuse, neglect, and abandonment, and how children survive all this in the tales with good will and the desire to lead a different life. We tend to ignore or repress the cruelty children experience in both the Grimms' fairy tales and their contemporary commercial remakes in light of the many happy endings that follow them.

The repression of unpleasant experiences in the way we relate to fairy tales as adults is nothing new. These tales have been with us hundreds of years, and we tend to forget that *adults* were the ones who first told them, wrote them down, and circulated them—and the ones who still do. Fairy tales, as well as other genres like the myth, fable, and legend, have always expressed an adult viewpoint on family relations and power. Though they may ultimately defend the right of children and underdogs to survive, they do so only by rationalizing the actions of the adults, who want to make certain that their children are socialized to forget the abuse they have suffered.

I do not mean to exaggerate, to argue that fairy tales completely rationalize abusive attitudes and behavior toward children. To a certain extent, they were told and written down to reveal the shame and guilt that adults have felt over the centuries or to redress wrongs. More than anything, I believe, they reveal what the psychiatrists Alice Miller[2] and James Hoyme[3] have identified as the ambivalent feelings many parents have toward their children—their desire to abandon them, and the shame they feel when they actually abuse them. Thus, it is not by chance that contemporary publishers (under pressure from parents) want to expurgate all details from fairy tales that suggest how violently young children are treated and punished. In fact, many violent acts are eliminated from mass market fairy-tale books, such as the wolf swallowing Granny and Little Red Riding Hood or Cinderella's sisters' eyes being pecked out. Some tales are simply not printed, such as *All Fur*, in which a king wants to marry his daughter, or *The Maiden without Hands*, in which a daughter is compelled to have her hands chopped off because of her father's indiscretion.

There is more that meets the eye in our "love" for fairy tales, much more than we want to accept. To this extent, the popular reception of Bettelheim's soothing interpretations of fairy tales is in keeping with the saccharine Disney film and book versions of the tales: they want to prevent us from recognizing the contradictory attitudes many parents have toward their own children. There is no doubt that most parents want to love and do love their children, but it is more difficult to admit that many have strong desires at times to abandon their children, to do away with them, or to confine them. Since all parents have difficulty admitting to such desires, we seek manifold ways to cover up these uncomfortable feelings. In part, fairy tales help parents do this: they conceal and rationalize our drives to punish our children for intruding into our lives and for creating predicaments that we really create. The happy end is but our way of acknowledging that we really love our children, those underdogs, in spite of ourselves.

If we were to examine of the corpus of the Grimms' tales in depth—and this is also the case in many other collections such as Andersen's tales and Calvino's *Italian Folk Tales*—we would find well over a hundred tales in which the main focus is on children who experience some form of abuse. Numerous tales begin with children being kidnapped, used as objects in a barter with the devil, or abandoned. Abandonment and continual persecution are central issues in *Brother and Sister*, *Hansel and Gretel*, and *Jorinda and Joringel*—who else is the stepmother/witch but the real mother of the children? (The Grimms consciously changed mother figures into stepmothers in the tales they collected, for they could not face the fact that a "true" mother could be abusive.)

The Grimms' and other fairy tales are filled with signals to children that they, not their elders, are the ones responsible if they are harmed or violated. As I have already demonstrated, the most classic version is *Little Red Riding Hood*. The poor heroine is held accountable for both her own rape and Granny's. Never, she tells everyone at the end of the tale, will *she* ever veer from the straight path. Children are not to explore nature. They are not to be adventurous. They are to be afraid of the world. But who has made the world such a dangerous place, and who does most of the violating that children are asked to feel responsible for causing?

Throughout the Grimms' tales children bear the brunt of parents' frustration and rage. In *Mother Trudy*, a disobedient girl has her curiosity repaid by a witch who turns her into a log of wood that will be burned. In *The Jupiter Tree*, a boy is murdered by his stepmother because she wants her own daughter to inherit everything from her husband. In *The Young Boy in the Grave*, an orphan boy is beaten by his master and finally driven to suicide, while the orphan girl in *The True Bride* is continually berated by her stepmother.

There is hardly a tale in the Grimms' collection that does not raise the issue of parental oppression. Yet we purposely avoid taking note of these particular tales or similar ones in such other grand collections as Andrew Lang's numerous fairy tale books of different colors. We do not reprint them as single books because their brutality is so flagrant, and in some cases they contain racism or anti-Semitism. Even with those popular tales that we do reprint in the thousands, such as *Rumpelstiltskin* and *Rapunzel*, we rarely talk about how the miller's daughter is forced by her father into a terrible situation of spinning straw into gold, or how Rapunzel is locked up by her foster mother and maltreated just as children are often locked up in closets and abused today. We refuse to discuss the trauma in the tales based on children's real experiences of maltreatment because we want to believe that such trauma did not and does not exist. We want desperately to forgive the parent in us and happily resolve what can never be completely resolved.

I suspect that, after all's been said and done, the reason we return to old-fashioned fairy tales and continue to forge new tales in the Grimm tradition is that we want to overcome the repressed trauma of childhood without dealing with its consequences in our everyday lives. In this sense, the Grimms' fairy tales that have become our classics in all sorts of forms will remain magical and mysterious. Like the Grimms themselves, we *want* to continue to be baffled and amazed by our attraction to these tales, which provide clues to crucial familial and social problems of the modern world. Unfortunately, we also want to overlook these clues of ambivalent feelings by focusing on childish enchantment and happy ends.

If storytellers in schools and communities continue to overlook and repress these clues, they will do children a huge disservice. Given the increase of violence toward children in Western society, most storytellers and teachers are concerned with minimizing the dangers threatening children, and many schools have programs to help raise children's consciousness of abuse and violence on the streets and in the homes. Yet storytellers and teachers overlook the fact that many of their fairy tales and other stories rationalize the trauma of abuse. Afraid of being too violent with their tales, they unwittingly mislead children by concealing the manner in which violence originates in familial and social relations. In America, it is easier to be funny or mysterious as a storyteller than to be a wise animator. As a comical stand-up storyteller, one can gloss over the serious nature of the humor in fairy tales and aim for a laugh of forgetfulness. As a mysterious cult figure, a storyteller can pretend to know the source of wisdom and appear as a powerful healing figure not unlike a mythic god, priest, or therapist.

In each instance, the storyteller perpetuates the rationalization of abuse through well-told narratives that forge illusions about harmony. Such storytelling is related to the entertainment business and is no better than the commercial TV programs, films, and video games that make consumers out of children.

But storytelling need not be used to serve such abuse. As I have shown, it can be used to expose social conditions, provide narrative tools for children, enhance pleasure through insight into the causes of conflict, and teach young listeners to grasp differences between people and alternatives to distressing situations. By no means am I arguing that a storyteller must act as a social critic or social worker, or that a storytelling session should be like a therapeutic session in which all the participants discover the essence of their identity. One of the dangers of storytelling today is the neo-Jungian school that takes various New Age forms in books like Robert Bly's *Iron John* and Carlissa Pinkola Estes's *Women Who Run with the Wolves*. These authors and their disciples spread their holy word and believe that fairy tales can heal all of our wounds and solve all of our problems if we learn how to read and follow their symbols. At their worst, neo-Jungians depict the world and our psyche as though they were coloring books with numbers on the parts of each picture; if we paint the right colors on the parts, our lives will become harmonious. Everything depends on the unification of the anima and animus and our recognition of the roles archetypes play in our lives. At best, qualified Jungian therapists use stories as a means for comprehending how their analysands grasp and cope with the world around them. But even here, they often designate symbols according to a dictionary of meanings that limits their understanding of the exceptional and unique ways their analysands may be trying to narrate their lives. Freudian analysts are no better, especially if they adhere to the orthodox notions of Freud as Bettelheim did for the most part in his book, *The Uses of Enchantment*. Not only are many of Freud's notions about psychic development and conflict questionable when applied to tales, but the analysis itself tends to rationalize rather than disclose them.

Storytellers cannot and should not pretend to be therapists, gurus, or social workers. They should not pretend that stories have a magic power of healing the woes of children and the community, that stories can work wonders for each troublesome situation. Storytellers must know that a tale can contribute to a healing process and can be used to address a particular situation, but it is not the role of the storyteller to be the healer, the shaman, the omniscient guru. I tend to think that the model for the story-teller should be the little child in Andersen's *The Emperor's New Clothes*. As we know, this child is the only individual among hundreds of people who boldly steps up to the naked king and tells him the truth. I see the child as wise beyond his or her years, someone who speaks what everyone else in the community knows but is afraid to articulate. The child's words expose the ridiculous nature of power and the shame of the community. They clear the picture, enable everyone to understand what is happening. The child's single sentence is a provocative and subversive story, for it liberates the bystanders to think and speak what they have been repressing. Once this little storyteller speaks, there is no longer a need for repression. The people can laugh, share this story, and pass it on as wisdom, just as Andersen did, and we shall continue to do.

The truthful exposure in storytelling has indeed its therapeutic and cathartic moment, and storytellers must be aware of that moment. But if they are going to use tales consciously to offset the abuse that children suffer in little and big ways in their daily lives, I believe they must pay more attention to exposing and sharing their lore and craft. By showing children, through the interaction, the diverse forms and strategies of narrative and story and how specific genres are used to address social situations, the story-teller empowers children and gives them the means to articulate their needs and wishes. In addition, by playing with genres and revealing the different ways one can deal with conflict and realize one's dreams, the story-teller can offer a joyous opportunity of recognition. Unless one is trained as a psychologist or therapist, it is extremely difficult to know exactly what an individual child is recognizing during the telling or enacting of a tale, and even then—even if one is a so-called psychological specialist—it is difficult to grasp the impact a story has on a child or group of children. Storytelling always takes place in a sociohistorical context, and this context shapes the reception of a tale as much as the tale or teller does. As the context changes, so does the function of the storyteller, and it must currently be viewed in light of advanced technological and communication network systems.

Despite all these changes, there is one function that the "genuine" story-teller must maintain, otherwise storytelling is an abusive way of manipulat-ing children to adjust to social designs that limit their potential for growth.

Here I am invoking Walter Benjamin's notion that the genuine storyteller shares his or her wisdom with the listeners, knows how to listen to the listeners and the environment, and exposes what he or she knows for the benefit of the community. Yet it is not simply the sharing of wisdom that is important. The genuine storyteller must feel the urge to divulge what it means to live in an age when lies often pass for truth in the mass media and the public realm. The storyteller must feel the urge to contrast social reality with a symbolic narrative that exposes contradictions. From this contrast, the storyteller gives birth to light, lightens our lives, and sheds light on the different ways in which we can become our own storytellers.

Notes and Source Material

Introduction: Storytelling in Schools

1. Gianni Rodari, *Grammatica della fantasia: Introduzione all'arte di inventare storie* (Turin: Einaudi, 1973). This book has not been translated; see below for some practical details of Rodari's activities.

2. For an excellent critique of the ideological ramifications of setting standards for cultural literacy, see Herbert Kohl's chapter "Uncommon Differences: On Political Correctness, Core Curriculum, and Democracy in Education" in his book *"I Won't Learn from You" and Other Thoughts on Creative Maladjustment* (New York: The New Press, 1994), 103–126.

3. Michael W. Apple, *Official Knowledge: Democratic Education in a Conservative Age* (New York: Routledge, 1993), 62–63.

4. See Geneviève Calame-Griaule, ed., *Le Renouveau du Conte / The Revival of Storytelling* (Paris: Centre National de la Recherche Scientifique, 1991).

5. Penelope Leach, *Children First* (New York: Knopf, 1994), 146–47.

6. See Jean Piaget, *The Development of Thought: Equilibration of Cognitive Structures*, trans. Arnold Rosin (New York: Viking, 1977) and *Judgement and Reasoning in the Child*, trans. Marjorie Warden (Towata, NJ: Littlefield, Adams, 1976) and Arthur Applebee, *The Child's Concept of Story: Ages Two to Seventeen* (Chicago: University of Chicago Press, 1978).

7. Kieran Egan, *Teaching as Storytelling* (Chicago: University of Chicago Press, 1986), 25.

8. Patsy Cooper, *When Stories Come to Schools* (New York: Teachers & Writers Collaborative, 1993), 88.

9. Edward de Bono, *Children Solve Problems* (London: Allen Lane, 1972), 12.

10. Egan, *Teaching as Storytelling*, 14.

11. Herbert Kohl, *"I Won't Learn from You" and Other Thoughts on Creative Maladjustment* (New York: The New Press, 1994), 130.

12. Bob Barton and David Booth, *Stories in the Classroom* (Portsmouth, NH: Heinemann, 1990), 66. Although their concept of community is somewhat different from mine, Barton and Booth have an excellent discussion on the importance of community in their book *Stories in the Classroom* (Portsmouth, NH: Heinemann, 1990), 31–53.

   For more information about creating community through storytelling, see Marni Schwartz's recent article, "Building a Classroom Community Through Storytelling," *Storytelling* 6 (July 1994): 14–15.

Gianni Rodari's Art of Inventing Stories

Rodari introduced many activities that teachers and storytellers can use to stimulate children's creative writing. Rodari emphasized the basics in showing children how to use and form words and sentences into remarkable stories with ease and pleasure. His activities can be incorporated into a storytelling session or employed in follow-ups by the teacher. I have adapted some of his innovative ideas and games from *Grammatica della fantasia* and used the following activities in my storytelling sessions.

I. Throwing Words About

A word thrown into a pond can produce a series of waves that lead to associations, meanings, images, and memories. Take the word *rock*.

1. Form words that begin with the letter r but are not followed by an o, such as:

   rat, rink, relish, race, rich, reap, rye.

2. Form words that begin with *ro*, such as:

   roll, robot, roman, rotten, Roman.

3. Forms words that rhyme with *rock* such as:

   sock, block, mock, clock, knock, stock.

4. Form words that are related to *rock* in meaning, such as:

   brick, marble, pebble, stone.

Write a story about a rock. What do you associate with rock? What does a rock remind you of? Rodari believes that the imagination can be used to rediscover the past and, at the same time, reacquaint ourselves with reality and represent it with new forms. All this is done by exploring one word. For instance, if we break down the word vertically and place our associations with it next to each new letter, we can conceive new phrases.

r   robot

o   obsessed

c   claims

k   knife

With each word we can form a sentence or find another association. Or we can form nonsense poems.

II. The Imaginary Binoun

Children's thoughts generally form couples, such as hard/soft or hot/cold. However, the imaginary binoun is not necessarily formed by opposites but by two unrelated nouns. The child forms the association that links them in some manner. Choose two words randomly, either by asking the children to suggest words or by taking them randomly from the dictionary or a book that the class has been reading. In this way, the words are uprooted, singled out, isolated, and estranged. For instance, let us take *bear* and *truck*:

Each one of these combinations offers us an imaginative possibility to create a story.

The bear with a truck

The truck of the bear

The bear on the truck

The bear in the truck

The truck with the bear

III. The Imaginary Hypothesis

What would happen if?
What would happen when?

Here an entire question can be asked, such as, What would happen if you were turned into a kangaroo? What would happen when the world collided with a comet?

Another possibility: Ask the children to name a verb, such as *to fly*. Then have another child form a "what if" sentence, such as, What would happen if you flew to the moon? The purpose of this exercise is to allow the child to enter reality through the back window rather than through the front door. This way is more amusing and more useful. It also shows that reality can be shaped, grasped, and conquered in different ways.

IV. The Arbitrary Prefix

Here new words are formed by adding unusual prefixes. For instance, the teacher can set up a list of prefixes in one column and nouns in another to form new words. The original word is deformed, but a new image is created and can be used as the basis for starting a story featuring this word.

mini	cow
super	skirt
semi	car
tri	bird
bi	city
inter	hair

V. Montage

Cut out headlines from a newspaper and mix them to form sentences that are absurd, sensational, or amusing. Then write a story, poem, or report using the new sentence.

VI.

Write on the board a series of questions suggested by the children such as:

> Who was it?
> Where was he?
> What did he do?
> What did he say?
> What did people say about this?
> What was the result?

As each child asks a question, she or he writes the answer on a piece of paper, folds the paper, and hands it to the teacher/storyteller. When all the responses are gathered, they are read in order, and they form an amusing or nonsensical story.

VII. Creative Errors

The storyteller begins a familiar classical fairy tale in this manner.

> Once upon a time there was a girl named Little Green Riding Hood, and she had a grandfather who liked her so much that he gave her a sports car as a present so that she could speed off to grandmother's house every Sunday.

> or

> Once upon a time there was a girl named Senderella whose stepmother liked her better than her own two daughters. The stepmother made her own daughters work in the kitchen.

The storyteller should anticipate interruptions and questions from the children, but he or she should continue making "creative errors" until the end of the tale. The children "correct" the storyteller, but at the end, there is another "new" story based on his or her errors. Once the "new" story has been told, the storyteller asks the children to take a specific tale and begin it by making some mistakes and seeing where the mistakes lead them.

Other activities in Rodari's book can be used to animate children to tell their own stories. The key to each one of his "games" is to prompt children to think more imaginatively while at the same time acquiring the basic skills to conduct their own linguistic and artistic experiments.

Chapter 1—The Initial Encounter: Little Red Riding Hood

1. For a complete historical background of *Little Red Riding Hood*, see my book, *The Trials and Tribulations of Little Red Riding Hood*, 2nd ed. (New York: Routledge, 1993).

2. Ibid., 5–6.

3. This version can be found in *Trials and Tribulations of Little Red Riding Hood*, 234–38.

4. I have collected thrity-eight versions in *Trials and Tribulations*. Another good source book is Alan Dundes's *Little Red Riding Hood: A Casebook* (Madison: University of Wisconsin Press, 1989).

   There are many unusual folk versions in French and Italian, and sometimes I use the following folk tale from Charles Joisten's *Versions Populaires Haute-Alpines des Contes de Perrault* (Gap: Ribaud Frères, 1959) instead of *The Tale of the Grandmother*.

Once there was a little girl in a village, and she was called Red Riding Hood because of the way she adorned her hair with poppy flowers.

One Saturday afternoon, her mother sent Red Riding Hood to her grandmother with a pot of honey and some cake. On her way she amused herself by listening to the song of birds and by gathering nuts and flowers.

But time passed so quickly that it soon became night, and she began to walk rapidly through the forest. There she met the wolf, and the wolf asked her,

"Where are you heading, my little girl?"

"I'm taking a pot of honey and some cake to my grandmother who lives in the first house of the next village," she answered.

So he asked her, "What path are you taking?"

"The *path of needles* to mend my dress, which has a hole in it."

The wolf left the little girl and took the *path of pins,* which was shorter. When he arrived at the grandmother's house, he tapped at the door—"Tick-tock"—and the grandmother said, "Pull the latch, turn the knob, and the door will open."

Later, when Red Riding Hood arrived, he said to her, "Well, light the fire. There's some blood on the side of the chimney, and I want you to cook it."

So Red Riding Hood lit the fire, put the pan on top, and poured the blood into it. While the blood was cooking, the wolf said to her,

"Grubby grub, grub

It's grandma's blood."

"Ah!" the little girl said. "Did you hear, Grandmother, what the pan said?"

"Oh, those are just the evil spirits in the chimney," the wolf responded.

When the blood was cooked, Red Riding Hood ate a little of it, but she did not like the taste and stopped eating. Then she went and lay down beside the wolf, believing that he was her grandmother.

"What a large head you have, Grandma!" she said.

"That's because of old age, my little one."

"What large legs you have, Grandma!"

"The better to run, my child."

"What long hair you have, Grandma!"

"That's because of old age, my child."

"What big arms you have, Grandma!"

"The better to catch you with, my child."

"What big teeth you have, Grandma!"

"The better to eat you with, my child."

But he was still digesting the Grandmother, and the little girl now knew it was the wolf.

"I want to go pee-pee, Grandma," she said.

"Make pee-pee here," the wolf responded.

"Oh, but I've also got to make cacka, Grandma."

"Make cacka here," the wolf responded.

"Oh, that will smell bad," the little girl said. "If you're afraid that I'll escape, tie a rope around me, and you can hold me."

So the wolf attached a rope to her, and the little girl went outside, where she took a small knife out of her pocket, cut the rope, and escaped.

The wolf ran after her in pursuit, but he met up with a hunter, who killed him. Then Red Riding Hood returned home to her mother and told her the story.

Chapter 2—Mixing It Up with Salad Games and Acrostics:
The Frog King and Cinderella

For background material on *The Frog King*, see Wolfgang Mieder, *Tradition and Innovation in Folk Literature* (Hanover: The University Press of New England, 1987) and Lutz Röhrich, *Wage es, den Frosch zu küssen!* (Cologne: Diederichs, 1987). For *Beauty and the Beast*, see Betsy Hearne, *Beauty and the Beast: Visions and Revisions of an Old Fairy Tale* (Chicago: University of Chicago Press, 1989) and "The Origins of the Fairy Tale" in my book *Fairy Tale as Myth / Myth as Fairy Tale* (Lexington: University of Kentucky Press, 1994). For *Cinderella*, see Alan Dundes, ed., *Cinderella: A Casebook* (Madison: University of Wisconsin Press, 1981); Neil Philip, ed., *The Cinderella Story* (London: Penguin, 1988); and Judy Sierra, ed., *Cinderella* (Phoenix: Oryx Press, 1992).

Here is another version of *The Frog King*, based on a Mexican folk tale, that I have used in my program:

The Marvelous Sea Frog

Once there were a man and woman who were very poor, so poor that they could barely keep themselves and their three sons alive. Their farm was small, and the land was dry and rocky. When the three boys were grown up, the eldest went to his father and said, "Father, I have spoken to my brothers, and we are nothing but a burden to you here. So we want to go out into the world and try our luck. Please give us your blessing."

At first, neither the father nor the mother wanted to let their sons depart. But they were so poor, so very poor, that they finally decided to let their sons leave, and wished them well.

Since the sons had heard that there were jobs in a village near the sea, they set out in the same direction, but they soon separated because the eldest wanted to arrive at the village before his two younger brothers to find the better job. He traveled for a long time, and when he reached the sea, he lay down next to a bush to rest. All of a sudden, he heard the lovely voice of a woman coming from the bush, but he could not see her because the bush was thick and covered with sharp needles.

"Why don't you come out, my lovely one?" said the young man. "With a voice like yours, I'll marry you on the spot."

"No, no," said the voice. "I can't come out. You won't like what you see."

But the eldest brother insisted and pleaded until the voice relented. All of a sudden, the bush parted, and a marvelous green frog jumped into the lap of the young man. When he looked at her, he cried out, "Uggh! I thought you were a woman, not a frog!" And he picked her up, flung her back into the bush with all his might, and disappeared.

Soon thereafter, the second brother appeared at the bush and sat down to rest. When he heard the lovely voice of the frog, he too said, "Why don't you come out, my lovely one? With a voice like yours, I'll marry you on the spot."

"No, no," said the marvelous frog. "Yesterday a young man came by, and when he heard me singing, he proposed to me. But when I came out of the bushes, he didn't like what he saw and threw me away."

"But I'm not like other men. Your voice is so enchanting. Please come out!" the second son said.

"I'm afraid," the frog responded.

"You can trust me," said the young man, and he kept pleading until the frog jumped out of the bush and onto his lap.

"Uggh! I thought you were a woman, not a frog!" And he picked her up and flung her back into the bush with all his might, and went on his way.

Well now, the youngest brother appeared the following day, and when he lay down to rest by the bush, he heard the wonderful singing like his brothers before him, and he said, "Why don't you come out of the bush, my lovely one, I'd like to get to know you."

"Certainly not!" responded the frog. "Two young men were already here, and both of them coaxed me to come out of my bush. But when I did, they threw me back with disgust."

"But I'm not like them."

"That's what you young men always say."

"Please believe me," pleaded the youngest son.

"Never ever ever," said the frog.

"I promise."

"Promises are made to be broken."

"Look, I haven't crossed my fingers, and besides, if you don't come out, I'll drown myself in the sea!"

There was a long pause, and finally, the frog hopped out of the bush onto his lap.

"What a marvelous frog!" said the young man, and he lifted her gently and put her into his pocket. Then he continued on his way.

After they had wandered about for some time, they came to the village where his brothers were now living. Since the brothers had found wives for themselves and were making a good living as fishermen, they had become very proud of themselves and liked to show off in front of the villagers. The youngest son had also married, but he had married the marvelous frog, and people thought he was a bit touched in his head.

When the three sons came together, they wrote their parents and told them that they had married, and they even sent presents. Then the wives of the two older sons wrote letters, but the marvelous green frog could not do this, and the two older brothers laughed. Soon the parents wrote back to their sons and asked all three wives to sew and embroider three beautiful long shawls.

The youngest brother became very sad and went to the marvelous frog to tell her what his parents had written.

"Don't worry," she said. "Just take me to the sea and throw me into the water."

So the young man carried the frog to the seaside and flung her into the water. Soon thereafter, she returned to land with a beautiful shawl embroidered with gold.

"Send this shawl to your parents," she said in her lovely voice.

So the sons sent the presents to their parents, and the old couple was astonished by the shawl embroidered with pure gold. Then they wrote to their sons that they would like to get to know their wives, and they asked their sons to return home with them. The young men answered that they would be delighted to visit them, but the youngest son became depressed again.

"What should I do now?" he asked himself. "My wife doesn't resemble a woman in the least. They might think I'm crazy."

And he went home and told the little frog what the brothers had decided, and she replied, "Don't worry. I'll certainly come with you."

Since the frog knew that the wives of the brothers were very jealous and vain, she washed her head with lime to make it glisten. When the two women saw the frog's skin sparkle in the sun, they decided to use the lime on their hair, too. But when they washed their heads, all their hair fell out, and they were completely bald.

That evening, the frog went to her husband and said, "I want you to throw me into the sea again. But this time, I want you to throw me as far as you can. Then you are to return home and fetch me the next morning."

The young man did this, but he was very sad about it, for he believed he would never see his little frog again. The next morning he rose very early and went to the seaside to search for the frog. However, when he arrived, he saw a marvelous princess sitting in a splendid coach. He was about to turn away, when he heard a voice cry out, "Here I am. You finally broke the spell. Now we can visit your parents."

Astonished but pleased, he jumped into the coach and sped toward his parents' home with his wife, for his brothers had already started out on their journey. When they had all arrived, their parents were very happy to see their sons with wives. Of course, the wives of the two older brothers wore kerchiefs on their heads so that the parents could not see that they were bald.

In the evening, the happy parents prepared a meal for everyone as best they could with their modest means. While they were eating, the princess pretended to put the chick peas and eggs down the front of her dress, but she was really hiding silver coins. Since the two bald-heads were envious and watched her every move, they followed her example and put real chick peas and eggs down the front of their dresses. Then, after the meal they all began dancing. The villagers came, and everyone admired the princess, who was dressed in a sparkling green dress. They called her the most beautiful woman they had ever seen and admired her graceful dancing. Each time she turned, silver coins fell to the ground, and the guests picked them up and carried them to the parents of the youngest son. When the two baldheads saw what was happening, they decided to show off their dancing as well, but each time they turned, chick peas and eggs fell to the ground. The dogs ran to lick up the chick peas and eggs, and the wives of the elder brothers fled in shame and were followed by their husbands. But the youngest son stayed in the village, and some say that he is still living there with his princess, who occasionally takes dips in the sea.

For other versions of the Native American "Cinderella" tale, see Charles G. Leland, *The Algonquin Legends of New England: Myths and Folklore of the Micmac, Passamaquoddy, and Penobscot Tribes* (Boston: Houghton Mifflin, 1884); May H. Arbuthnot, "Little Burnt-Face" in *Time for Fairy Tales* (Chicago: Scott, Foresman, 1952), 199–201; Zena Sutherland and Myra Cohn Livingston, ""Little Burnt Face" in *The Scott, Foresman Anthology of Children's Literature* (Glenview, Illinois: Scott, Foresman, 1984): 388–89. Rafe Martin, *The Rough-Face Girl* (New York: Scholastic Books, 1993).

The salad game and acrostics can be used with most any classical fairy tale. Several important collections provide fascinating variants that can be retold for different groups. Oryx Press has recently created The Oryx Multicultural Folktale Series and published very useful books such as Betsy Hearne, ed., *Beauties and Beasts* (Phoenix: Oryx Press, 1993) and Margaret Read MacDonald, ed., *Tom Thumb* (Phoenix: Oryx Press, 1993). For *Snow White*, see Carol Edwards, "The Fairy Tale 'Snow White'," in *Making Connections Across the Curriculum: Readings for Analysis*, ed. Patricia Chittenden and Malcolm Kiniry (New York: St. Martins Press, 1986), 579–646.

Chapter 3—Playing with Fortune: Rumpelstiltskin and Spinning Tales

1. Marsha Kinder, *Playing with Power in Movies, Television, and Video Games* (Berkeley: University of California Press, 1991), 38.

2. This tale can be found in my book *Breaking the Magic Spell* (1979) (reprint, New York: Routledge, 1994).

   For historical background material on spinning, see Hans Medick, "Village Spinning Bees: Sexual Culture and Free Time Among Rural Youth in Early Modern Germany" in H. Medick and D. Sabean, eds., *Interest and Emotion: Essays on the Study of Family and Kinship* (Cambridge: Cambridge University Press, 1984), 317–40. See also Jane Schneider, "Rumpelstiltskin's Bargain: Folklore and the Merchant Capitalist Intensification of Linen Manufacture in Early Modern Europe" in Annette B. Weiner and Jane Schneider, eds., *Cloth and Human Experience* (Washington, DC: Smithsonian Institute Press, 1989), 177–213.

   There is an interesting *Tom Tit Tot* version in Joseph Jacobs's *English Fairy Tales* (London: Nutt, 1890), which I sometimes adapt and tell in place of *Rumpelstiltskin*. It goes as follows.

Tom Tit Tot

Once upon a time there was a woman, and she baked five pies. And when they came out of the oven, they had not risen, and she thought they would rise if they had some fresh air. So she said to her daughter,

"Daughter," she said. "Put these here pies on the shelf in the pantry and let them sit for awhile. I'm sure they'll rise and come back. They always come back with some fresh air."

Of course, the mother meant that the crust would rise, but the daughter, who was not the brightest girl in town, thought to herself, "Well, if they always rise and come back, I might as well eat them now."

So when her mother went about her chores, the daughter set to work and ate them all, every single one down to the last crumb. Well, when supper time arrived, the mother said to her daughter, "Go and get one of those pies. They must have risen and come back by now."

The girl went and looked, but there was nothing to be seen except the empty pans in which the pies had been baked. So she returned to her mother and said, "No, they haven't risen, and they certainly haven't come back yet."

"None of them?" asked the mother.

"Nope," responded the daughter.

"Well, come again or not, I'll have one for my supper," said the mother.

"But you can't," said the girl.

"Of course I can," the woman declared. "They may not taste as good, but I certainly can. So go and fetch me one, the best of the lot."

"I can't bring you the best or the worst," the daughter answered, "because I've eaten them all. So you've got to wait until they've risen and come back again."

Well, the mother was furious, but knowing her daughter, she knew it would do no good to scold her or explain her mistake. So, she took her spinning wheel to the door to spin away her anger, and as she spun, she sang,

> My daughter has eaten five pies today, five pies today,
> My daughter has eaten five pies today, five pies today,
> And I wish someone would take her away!

Just then, the king happened to be riding down the street on a magnificent white horse, and he heard the woman singing. However, he could not hear the exact words. So he stopped and said,

"What was that pretty song you were singing, my good woman?"

The mother was ashamed to let him hear what her daughter had done, and so she sang,

> My daughter has spun five spools today, five spools today,
> My daughter has spun five spools today, five spools today,
> And I can't stop her from spinning away.

"Glory be!" said the king. "I never heard of a girl who could spin five spools in one day and wants to keep spinning all the time."

"It's the truth," said the woman. "She works too hard to please me, and she just loves what she does."

"Look here," said the king, "I want a wife who's not afraid of work, and I've got a mind to marry your daughter, but before I do, let's settle our bargain. Eleven months out of the year, your daughter will have all she likes to eat, and all the gowns she likes to wear, and all the company she likes to keep, but the last month of each year, she'll have to spin five spools every day, and if she doesn't, I'll have her killed. What do you think?"

"Done," said the woman, for she thought how grand it would be to have her daughter married to a king. As for the five spools, the mother thought her daughter would find a way to get out of doing the work, as she always did, and anyway, the king would probably forget all about it.

So the king and the spinner's daughter were married. And for eleven months the girl had all she liked to eat, and all the gowns she liked to wear, and all the company she liked to keep. But when the eleven months were almost over, she began to think about the spools and wonder if he had remembered. But he never said a word about them, and she thought he had forgotten.

However, on the last day of the eleventh month, he took her to a room she had never seen before. There was nothing in it but a spinning wheel and a stool. And he said, "Now, my dear, tomorrow you'll be shut in here with some food and some flax. If you don't spin five spools by night, it will be off with your head. But since I know how much you love to work, I'm sure you have nothing to fear."

And away he went about his business, but she was terrified because she had always been lazy and did not know the first thing about spinning. What was she to do the next day when it was impossible to reach her mother? Besides, nobody could spin five spools in one day. She went to her room and sat down on a stool, and my how she did cry!

All of a sudden, however, she heard a knock down low on the floor, and she noticed a latch door that led to an underground passage. So she got up and opened it, and what did she see but a small little creature, covered with charcoal and wiggling a long tail. It looked like it was half elf and half beast, and she jumped back in fright.

"What are you crying for?" it said.

"What's that to you?" she replied.

"Never you mind," it said. "Just tell me what you're crying for."

"That won't do me any good if I do," she declared.

"You don't know that," the creature responded, and it twirled its tail around.

"Well," she said, "it won't do any harm if I tell, and maybe you really can do some good." She promptly told the ghastly creature about the pies, the spools, and everything.

"I'll tell you what I'll do," said the little creature. "I'll come to your window every morning and take the flax and bring it back to you fully spun at night."

"But what's your pay?" she asked.

The creature looked out of the corner of its eyes and said, "I'll give you three chances every night to guess my name, and if you haven't guessed it before the month is up, you shall be mine."

Well, since she thought for sure that she'd be able to guess the creature's name in a month's time, she said, "All right, I agree."

"It's a done deal!" the creature cried as he sprang in the air out of joy, wagged his tail, and disappeared.

Well, the next day, the king took his wife into the room, and there was the flax and enough food for a day.

"If this flax isn't spun by tonight, off goes your head, my dear!" he warned, and then he went out and locked the door. But no sooner had he gone than there was a knocking against the window. The young queen opened it, and sure enough, there was the little old creature sitting on the ledge.

"Where's the flax?" he asked.

"Here it is," she said, and she gave it to him.

Well, when evening arrived, there was a knock at the window. She got up and opened it, and there was the little old thing with five spools of flax.

"Here they are, as promised!" he boasted, and as he gave them to her, he asked, "Now, what's my name?"

"Is it Bill?" she said.

"Nooo, that isn't it," he responded, and he twirled his tail.

"Is it Ned?"

"Nooo," that isn't it," he responded, and he twirled his tail again.

"Is it Mark?"

"Nooo siree," he responded and he twirled his tail and flew away.

Well, later, when her husband came in, there were five spools ready for him.

"I see that I won't have to kill you tonight, my dear," he said. "You'll have your food and flax in the morning." And away he went.

Well, every day the flax and the food were brought, and every day the ghastly creature came in the morning and evening. And during the day, the girl sat and tried to think of names to say to the creature when it came at night. But she never hit on the right one. And as the end of the month approached, the imp began to look more and more malicious and twirled its tail faster each time she guessed and failed.

Finally, on the day before the last, the creature came at night with five spools and said, "Haven't you guessed my name yet? What's wrong with you?'

"Is it Nicodemus?" she asked.

"Not on your life."

"Is it Sammle?"

"Not at all."

"Perhaps it's Methusalem?"

"Forget it!" He looked at her with eyes like coals of fire and said, "Woman, there's only tomorrow night, and then you'll be mine!"

And away he flew.

Well, she felt terrible and desperate and was about to break into tears, when she heard the king coming along the hall. He unlocked the door, and as he entered, he said, "Well, my dear, I see you've spun another five spools, and since I'm sure you'll do five more by tomorrow night, I won't have to kill you. So let's have supper here tonight."

Then two servants brought in the supper, and the the king and queen sat down to eat. Just as the king was about to take a sip of wine, he stopped and began to laugh.

"What is it?" she asked.

"Well, he said, "I was out hunting today, and I reached a place in the wood that I'd never seen before. And there was an old charcoal pit, where I heard a kind of humming. So I got off my horse and quietly approached the pit. Well, when I looked down, I saw the funniest and dirtiest creature you ever set eyes on. And guess what it was doing? It had a spinning wheel and was spinning faster than even a machine could spin and twirling its tail even faster. And as the creature spun, it sang a ditty:

Nimmy nimmy not
My name's Tom Tit Tot!
Nimmy nimmy not
My name's Tom Tit Tot!

Well, when the girl heard this, she felt as if she could have jumped out of her skin for joy, but she did not reveal a thing to her husband. Nor did she say one word except to smile.

The next day the little thing looked especially malicious when it came for the flax. Then, when night arrived, the girl heard the knocking on the windowpane. As she opened the window, the ghastly thing hopped onto the ledge and threw the five spools onto the floor. It was grinning from ear to ear, and its tail swirled and twirled.

"What's my name?" it asked.

"Is it Solomon?" she replied, pretending to be afraid.

"Not it's not," said the creature, and it moved into the room.

"Well, is it Zebedee?" she guessed again.

"Not at all!" said the imp, and it laughed and twirled its tail so fast that you could hardly see it. "Now, you better take your time, woman. Next guess, and you're mine!

The creature stretched out its filthy hands, and she looked straight into the thing's eyes and said,

"Nimmy nimmy not
Your name's Tom
Tit
Tot!"

Well, when the creature heard her answer, it uttered an awful shriek and flew away into the dark. From that time on, the young queen had her peace and never saw the creature again. Moreover, her husband decided they had enough flax to last them a lifetime and never asked her to spin again.

For background material on *Tom Tit Tot*, see Edward Clodd, *Tom Tit Tot: An Essay in Savage Philosophy* (London: Duckworth, 1898) and Howard Wright Marshall, "'Tom Tit Tot': A Comparative Essay in Aarne-Thompson 500— The Name of the Helper," *Folklore* 84 (1973), 51–57.

Chapter 4—In Celebration of Peace: Soldiers, Strong Men, and Knights

For source material, aside from the two books I mention in this chapter, see Ed Brody, et al., *Weaving Words, Spinning Hope* (Philadelphia: New Society Publishers, 1991) and Margaret Read MacDonald's *Peace Tales* (Hamden, CT: 1992). Also important is Ann Durrell and Marylin Sachs, eds., *The Big Book of Peace* (New York: Dutton, 1990).

For a provocative and fascinating revision of the legend of the Knights of the Round Table, see Michael Morpurgo's *Arthur, High King of Britain* (San Diego: Harcourt Brace, 1995).

Chapter 5—The Wisdom of the Beasts: Animal Tales and Fables

1. See Karen Kennery and Herbert Kohl, *Fables: A Curriculum* (New York: Teachers and Writers Collaborative, 1968) and Herbert Kohl, *Reading, How To* (New York: Dutton, 1973), 83–88.

2. See Marsha Kinder, *Playing with Power in Movies, Television, and Video Games* (Berkeley: University of California Press, 1991), 73. Kinder convincingly argues:

> Our consumer culture has developed a new form of totemism in which we alleviate anxiety and gain an illusory sense of empowerment by bestowing our conception of human individuality onto animals—by giving homes to them (rather than to orphans or the homeless, who themselves are frequently treated as an animal species devoid of individuality); by letting them substitute for missing members of the dysfunctional family; by interpellating them as icons of uniqueness with unusual names like Heathcliff, Garfield, and Orson; and by transforming them into voracious consumers for whom we are always buying new products and with whom we thereby increasingly identify.

For background material on cats, see Dorothy Margaret Stuart, *A Book of Cats: Legendary, Literary and Historical* (London: Methuen, 1959); Katharine Briggs, *Nine Lives: The Folklore of Cats* (New York: Pantheon, 1980); and Frank de Caro, *The Folktale Cat*, illus. Kitty Harvill (Little Rock: August House, 1992).

Chapter 6—Paying the Piper, or How Legends Lead People On

For background material on *The Pied Piper*, see Wolfgang Mieder, "The Pied Piper of Hamelin: Origin, History, and Survival of the Legend" in *Tradition and Innovation in Folk Literature*, (Hanover: University Press of New England, 1987), 45–83, and Elke Liebs, *Kindheit und Tod: Der Rattenfänger-Mythos als Beitrag zu einer Kulturgeschichte der Kinder* (Munich: Fink, 1986).

For the Browning version and other adaptations, see Robert Browning, *The Pied Piper of Hamelin*, illus. Frances Brundage (New York: Saalfield, 1926); Sara and Stephen Corrin, *The Pied Piper*, illus. Errol Le Cain (San Diego: Harcourt Brace Jovanovich, 1989); Donna Diamond, *The Pied Piper of Hamelin* (New York: Holiday House, 1981); and Thomas Head Raddall, *The*

Pied Piper of Dipper Creek and Other Tales (Toronto: McClelland & Stewart, 1943).

Here is another interesting and useful version of *The Pied Piper*, taken from Joseph Jacobs's *More English Fairy Tales* (London: David Nutt, 1894). It was first recorded by Abraham Elder in *Tales and Legends of the Isle of Wight* (London: 1839), then adapted by David Nutt. It is interesting to see how both Elder and Nutt revised the legend to make it appear as if this event actually happened on the Island of Wight.

The Pied Piper

Newtown, or Franchville, as 'twas called of old, is a sleepy little town, as you all may know, upon the Solent shore. Sleepy as it is now, it was once noisy enough, and what made the noise was—rats. The place was so infested with them as to be scarce worth living in. There wasn't a barn or a cornick, a storeroom or a cupboard, but they ate their way into it. Not a cheese but they gnawed it hollow, not a sugar puncheon but they cleared it out. Why, the very mead and beer in the barrels was not safe from them. They'd gnaw a hole in the top of the tun, and down would go one master rat's tail, and when he brought it up, all the friends and cousins would crowd round, and each would have a suck at the tail.

Had they stopped here, it might have been borne. But the squieking and shrieking, the hurrying and scurrying, so that you could neither hear yourself speak nor get a wink of good honest sleep the livelong night! Not to mention, Mamma must needs sit up and keep watch and ward over baby's cradle, or there'd have been a big ugly rat running across the poor little fellow's face, and doing who knows what mischief.

Why didn't the good people of the town have cats? Well, they did, and there was a fair stand-up fight, but in the end the rats were too many, and the pussies were regularly driven from the field. Poison, I hear you say? Why, they poisoned so many that it fairly bred a plague. Ratcatchers! Why, there wasn't a ratcatcher from John o' Groats' House to the Hand's End that hadn't tried his luck. But do what they might, cats or poison, terrier or traps, there seemed to be more rats than ever, and every day a fresh rat was cocking his tail or pricking his whiskers.

The Mayor and the town council were at their wits' end. As they were sitting one day in the town hall racking their poor brains, and bewailing their hard fate, who should run in but the town beadle. "Please your Honour," says he, "here is a very queer fellow come to town. I don't know what rightly to make of him." "Show him in," said the Mayor, and in he stept. A queer fellow, truly. For there was no color of the rainbow but you might find it in some corner of his dress, and he was tall and thin, and had keen piercing eyes.

"I'm called the Pied Piper," he began. "And pray what might you be willing to pay me if I rid you of every single rat in Franchville?"

Well, much as they feared rats, they feared parting with their money more, and fain would they have higgled and haggled. But the Piper was not a man to stand nonsense, and the upshot was that fifty pounds were promised him (and that meant a lot of money in those old days) as soon as not a rat was left to squeak or scurry in Franchville.

Out of the hall stept the Piper, and as he stept he laid his pipe to his lips and a shrill, keen tune sounded through street and house. And as each note pierced the air you might have seen a strange sight. For out of every hole the rats came tumbling. There were none too old and none too young, none too big and none too little to crowd at the Piper's heels and, with eager feet and upturned noses, patter after him as he paced the streets. Nor was the Piper unmindful of the little toddling ones, for every fifty yards he'd stop and give an extra flourish on his pipe just to give them time to keep up with the older and stronger of the band.

Up Silver Street the Piper went, and down Gold Street, and at the end of Gold Street was the harbor and the broad Solent beyond. And as he paced along, slowly and gravely, the townsfolk flocked to door and window, and many a blessing they called down upon his head.

As for getting near him, there were too many rats. And now that he was at the water's edge he stepped into a boat, and not a rat, as she shoved off into deep water piping shrilly all the while, but followed him, plushing, paddling, wagging their tails with delight. On and on he played until the tide went down, and each master rat sank deeper and deeper into the slimy ooze of the harbor, until every mother's son of them was dead and smothered.

The tide rose again, and the Piper stepped onshore, but never a rat followed. You may fancy that the townfolk had been throwing up their cats and hurrahing and stopping up rat-holes and setting the church bells a-ringing. But when the Piper stepped ashore and not so much as a single squeak was to be heard, the Mayor and the Council, and the town-folk generally, began to hum and to ha and to shake their heads.

For the town money chest had been sadly emptied of late, and where was the fifty pounds to come from? Such an easy job, too! Why, the Mayor himself could have done that if only he had thought of it.

So he hummed and ha'ed and said at last, "Come, my good man you see what poor folk we are; how can we manage to pay you fifty pounds? Will you not take twenty? When all is said and done 'twill be good pay for the trouble you've taken."

"Fifty pounds was what I bargained for," said the Piper shortly, "and if I were you I'd pay it quickly. For I can pipe many kinds of tunes, as folk sometimes find to their cost."

"Would you threaten us, you strolling vagabond?" shrieked the Mayor, and at the same time he winked at the Council. "The rats are all dead and drowned," muttered he, "so you may do your worst, my good man," and with that he turned short upon his heel.

"Very well," said the Piper, and he smiled a quiet smile. With that he laid his pipe to his lips afresh, but now there came forth no shrill notes, as it were, of scraping and growing, and squeaking and scurrying; the tune was joyous and resonant, full of happy laughter and merry play. And as he paced down the streets the elders mocked, but from school-room and playroom, from nursery and workshop, not a child but ran out with eager glee and shouts, following gaily at the Piper's call. Dancing, laughing, joining hands and tripping feet, the bright throng moved along up Gold Street and down Silver Street, and beyond Silver Street lay the cool green forest full of old oaks and wide-spreading beeches. In and out among the oak trees you might catch glimpses of the Piper's many-colored coat. You might hear the laughter of the children break and fade and die away as deeper and deeper into the lone green wood the stranger went and the children followed.

All the while, the elders watched and waited. They mocked no longer now. And watch and wait as they might, never did they set their eyes again upon the Piper in his parti-colored coat. Never were their hearts gladdened by the song and dance of the children issuing forth from amongst the ancient oaks of the forest.

For good background material and American legends, see B.A. Botkin, ed., *A Treasury of American Folklore* (New York: Crown, 1944) and Tristram Potter Coffin and Hennig Cohen, eds., *Folklore from the Working Folk of America* (New York: Anchor/Doubleday, 1974).

Chapter 7—Mythmaking

1. Mircea Eliade, *Myth and Reality*, trans. Willard R. Task (New York: Harper & Row, 1963), 195.

   For some good collections of myths for children, see Olivia E. Coolidge, *Greek Myths*, illus. Edouard Sandoz (New York: Houghton Mifflin, 1949); Morris Schreiber, *Stories of Gods and Heroes: Famous Myths and Legends of the World* (New York: Grosset and Dunlap, 1960); Alice I. Hazeltine, ed., *Hero Tales from Many Lands* (New York: Abingdon, 1961); Eric and Tessa Hadley, *Legends of Earth, Air, Fire, and Water* (New York: Cambridge University Press, 1985); and Anne Rockwell, *The Robber Baby: Stories from the Greek Myths* (New York: Greenwillow, 1994).

   One of the best sourcebooks for myths is Edith Hamilton, *Mythology* (Boston: Little Brown, 1940).

Chapter 8—Tall Tales

For books about Cocaigne and Schlaraffenland, see Elfriede Marie Ackermann, *Das Schlaraffenland in German Literature and Folksong* (Chicago: University of Chicago Press, 1944) and Dieter Richter, *Schlaraffenland: Geschichte einer populären Phantasie* (Cologne: Diederichs, 1984).

There are some excellent tall tales in B.A. Botkin's, *Treasury of American Folklore* (see notes to ch. 6) and *A Treasury of New England Folklore* (New York: Crown, 1947), and in Adrien Stoutenburg, *American Tall Tales*, illus. Richard M. Powers (New York: Viking, 1966).

Chapter 9—Somewhere over the Rainbow: Utopia and Wishing Tales

1. Oscar Wilde, *The Soul of Man under Socialism*, ed. Robert Ross (London: Humphreys, 1912), 43.

   There is an excellent version of "The Little Old Woman Who Lived in a Vinegar Bottle" in Margaret Read MacDonald's *The Storyteller's Start-Up Book* (Little Rock, AR: August House, 1993), 117–24. See also Rumer Godden's *Old Woman Who Lived in a Vinegar Bottle* (New York: Viking Press, 1970).

Chapter 10—Strange Encounters with Science Fiction

To my knowledge, not much work has been done with science fiction and storytelling in classrooms. Numerous anthologies can be used to introduce science fiction, and it might be interesting to experiment first with the fairy tales written by science fiction writers in Lester Del Rey and Risa Kessler, eds., *Once Upon a Time: A Treasury of Modern Fairy Tales*, (New York: Ballantine, 1991). One of the best sources for science fiction tales is David Hartwell's comprehensive anthology *The World Treasury of Science Fiction* (Boston: Little, Brown and Company, 1991).

Chapter 11—New Perspectives through Creative Dramatics and Video

1. Kinder, *Playing with Power*.

2. Joe Winston, "Giants, Good and Bad: Story and Drama at the Heart of the Curriculum at Key Stage 1," *Education* 3 (March 1994), 44–54.

   Aside from the books on drama that I have already noted, Robert Breen's *Chamber Theatre* (Englewood Cliffs: Prentice Hall, 1978) should be cited, and mention should also be made of Paul Sills's work with story theater during the 1960s and 1970s, analyzed in the journal *Yale Theatre*. In addition, two other very useful books by Viola Spolin are worth noting: *Theater Games for the Classroom: A Teacher's Handbook* (Evanston: Northwestern University Press, 1986) and *Theater Games for Rehearsal: A Director's Handbook* (Evanston: Northwestern University Press, 1985).

Chapter 12—On the Use and Abuse of Storytelling

1. Bruno Bettelheim, "A Return to the Land of Fairies," *New York Times*, July 2, 1987, sec. 2.

2. See Alice Miller, *The Drama of the Gifted Child*, trans. Ruth Ward (New York: Basic Books, 1981) and *For Your Own Good: Hidden Cruelty in Child-Rearing and the Roots of Violence* (New York: Basic Books, 1983).

3. See James B. Hoyme, "The 'Abandoning Impulse' in Human Parents," *The Lion and the Unicorn* 12 (December 1988): 32–46.

Bibliography

I have divided the bibliography into three parts: 1) Anthologies of Folk and Fairy Tales, Fables, Legends, and Myths; 2) Tales by Individual Authors; 3) Reference Works. By no means are these lists complete or intended to designate some type of "definitive catalogue of the best tales, fables, legends, and myths for storytelling." Most of the tales and reference works that I have listed are texts that have been useful to me in my work. In particular, I recommend that storytellers, teachers, and other interested readers adapt the tales to suit their interests. Since it is often difficult to find a good bibliography of tales and references for storytelling, I have tried to provide the most recent books on the topic and to include books that contain additional references.

I. Anthologies of Folk and Fairy Tales, Fables, Legends, and Myths

Aesop. *Fables of Aesop*. Trans. S.A. Handford. Harmondsworth: Penguin, 1954.

Asbjornsen, Peter Christen and Jørgen Moe. *Norwegian Folk Tales*. New York: Viking, 1960.

Abrahams, Roger D., ed. *Afro-American Folktales*. New York: Pantheon, 1985.

Afanasiev, Aleksandr Nikolaevich. *Russian Fairy Tales*. 1855–1864. Trans. Norbert Guterman. Reprint, New York: Pantheon, 1945.

Andersen, Hans Christian. *The Complete Fairy Tales and Stories*. Trans. Erik Christian Haugaard. New York: Doubleday, 1974.

Arbuthnot, May H, ed. *Time for Fairy Tales*. Chicago: Scott-Foresman, 1952.

Barchers, Suzanne I., ed. *Wise Women: Folk and Fairy Tales from Around the World*. Littleton, Colorado: Libraries Unlimited, 1990.

Basile, Giambattista. *The Pentamerone of Giambattista Basile*. 2 vols. Trans. from the Italian of Bendetto Croce by N. M. Penzer. 2 vols. London: John Lane the Bodley Head, 1932.

Berry, Jack, trans. *West African Folk Tales*. Ed. Richard Spears. Evanston: Northwestern University Press, 1991.

Bierhorst, John, ed. *The Red Swan: Myths and Tales of the American Indians*. New York: Farrar, Straus, and Giroux, 1976.

Botkin, B.A., ed. *A Treasury of American Folklore*. New York: Crown, 1944.

———, ed. *A Treasury of New England Folklore: Stories, Ballads and Traditions of the Yankee People*. New York: Crown, 1947.

Briggs, Katharine M. and Ruth L. Tongue, eds. *Folktales of England*. Chicago: University of Chicago Press, 1965.

———, ed. *Nine Lives: The Folklore of Cats*. New York: Pantheon, 1980.

Brody, Ed, Jay Goldspinner, Katie Green, Rona Leventhal and John Porcino, eds. *Spinning Tales, Weaving Hope: Stories of Peace, Justice and the Environment*. Philadelphia: New Society Publishers, 1992.

Bruchac, Joseph. *Native American Stories*. Golden, Colorado: Fulcrum, 1991.

Burg, Marie, *Tales from Czechoslovakia*. London: University of London Press, 1965.

Bushnaq, Inea, ed. *Arab Folktales*. New York: Pantheon Books, 1986.

Calvino, Italo, ed. *Italian Folktales*. Trans. George Martin. New York: Harcourt Brace Jovanovich, 1980.

Caro, Frank de, ed. *The Folktale Cat*. Illus. Kitty Harvill. Little Rock, AR: August House, 1992.

Carter, Angela, ed. *Sleeping Beauty and Other Favourite Fairy Tales*. New York: Schocken, 1984.

———, ed. *The Old Wives' Fairy Tale Book*. New York: Pantheon, 1990.

Chase, Richard, ed. *The Jack Tales*. Boston: Houghton Mifflin, 1943.

———, ed. *Grandfather Tales*. Boston: Houghton Mifflin, 1948.

———, ed. *American Folk Tales and Songs*. New York: New American Library, 1956.

Chinen, Allan B. *In the Ever After: Fairy Tales and the Second Half of Life*. Wilmette, Illinois: Chiron, 1989.

———. *Once Upon a Midlife: Classic Stories and Mythic Tales to Illuminate the Middle Years*. New York: Putnam, 1992.

Christianesen, Reidar Th., ed. *Folktales of Norway*. Chicago: University of Chicago Press, 1964.

Clarkson, Attelia and Gilbert B. Cross, eds. *World Folktales: A Scribner Resource Collection.* New York: Charles Scribner's Sons, 1980.

Coffin, Tristram Potter and Hennig Cohen, eds. *Folklore from the Working Folk of America.* New York: Anchor/Doubleday, 1974.

Colum, Padraic, ed. *Legends of Hawaii.* New Haven: Yale University Press, 1937.

Crane, Thomas Frederick, *Italian Popular Tales.* Boston: Houghton Mifflin, 1889.

Crossley-Holland, Kevin, ed. *The Norse Myths.* New York: Pantheon, 1980.

————, ed. *British Folktales.* London: Orchard Books, 1987.

Degh, Linda, ed. *Folktales of Hungary.* Chicago: University of Chicago Press, 1965.

Del Rey, Lester and Risa Kessler, eds. *Once Upon a Time: A Treasury of Modern Fairy Tales.* Illus. Michael Pangrazio. New York: Ballantine, 1991.

Eberhard, Wolfram, ed. *Folktales of China.* University of Chicago Press, 1965.

El-Shamy, Hasan M., ed. *Folktales of Egypt.* Chicago: University of Chicago Press, 1979.

Erdoes, Richard and Alfonso Ortiz, eds. *American Indian Myths and Legends.* New York: Pantheon, 1984.

Field, Rachel, ed. *American Folk and Fairy Tales.* New York: Charles Scribner's Sons: 1929.

Fitzgerald, Burdette S. *World Tales for Creative Dramatics and Storytelling.* Englewood Cliffs, New Jersey: Prentice-Hall, 1962.

Fontaine, Jean de la. *The Complete Fables of Jean de la Fontaine.* Trans. Norman B. Spector. Evanston: Northwestern, 1988.

Glassie, Henry, ed. *Irish Folk Tales.* New York: Pantheon, 1985.

Grimm, Jacob and Wilhelm. *The German Legends of the Brothers Grimm.* 2 vols. Trans. and ed. Donald Ward. Philadelphia: Institute for the Study of Human Issues, 1981.

————. *The Complete Fairy Tales of the Brothers Grimm.* Trans. and ed. Jack Zipes. New York: Bantam, 1987.

Grundtvig, Svend. *Danish Fairy Tales.* Trans. and ed. Gustav Hein. New York: Crowell, 1914.

Hadley, Eric and Tessa. *Legends of Earth, Air, Fire, and Water.* Illus. Bryna Waldman. New York: Cambridge University Press, 1985.

Harris, Joel Chandler. *The Complete Uncle Remus.* Ed. Richard Chase. Boston: Houghton Mifflin, 1955.

Hart, Carole, Letty Cottin Pogrebin, Mary Rodgers and Marlo Thomas, eds. *Free To Be . . . You and Me.* New York: McGraw-Hill, 1974.

Hartwell, David, G., ed. *Masterpieces of Fantasy and Enchantment.* New York: St. Martin's Press, 1988.

————, ed. *The World Treasury of Science Fiction.* Boston: Little, Brown and Company, 1989.

Jacobs, Joseph, ed. *English Fairy Tales*. London: David Nutt, 1892.

————, ed. *More English Folk and Fairy Tales*. London: G. P. Putnam's Sons, 1894.

————, ed. *Celtic Fairy Tales*. London: David Nutt, 1892.

————, ed. *Indian Fairy Tales*. London: David Nutt, 1892.

Jagendorf, Moritz, ed. *New England Bean-Pot: American Folk Stories to Read and to Tell*. Intro. B. A. Botkin. New York: Vanguard Press, 1948.

————. *Upstate Downstate. Folk Stories of the Middle Atlantic States*. Intro. Henry Shoemaker. New York: Vanguard Press, 1949.

Jones, Gwyn. *Scandinavian Legends and Folk-tales*. Illus. Joan Kiddell-Monroe. Oxford: Oxford University Press, 1956.

Judd, Mary Catherine. *Classic Myths*. Chicago: Rand-McNally, 1901.

Hearne, Betsy, ed. *Beauties and Beasts*. Illus. Joanne Caroselli. Phoenix: Oryx Press, 1993.

Komroff, Manuel, ed. *The Great Fables of All Nations*. Illus. Louise Thoron. New York: Dial, 1928.

Kennerly, Karen, ed. *Hesitant Wolf and Scrupulous Fox: Fables Selected from World Literature*. New York: Random House, 1973.

Leland, Charles G. *The Algonquin Legends of New England: Myths and Folklore of the Micmac, Passamaquoddy, and Penobscot Tribes*. Boston: Houghton Mifflin, 1884.

Lurie, Alison, ed. *Clever Gretchen and Other Forgotten Folktales*. New York: Crowell, 1980.

————, ed. *The Oxford Book of Modern Fairy Tales*. Oxford: Oxford University Press, 1993.

MacDonald, Magaret Read, ed. *Peace Tales: World Folktales to Talk About*. Hamden, CT: Linnet Books, 1992.

————, ed. *Tom Thumb*. Illus. Joanne Caroselli. Phoenix: Oryx Press, 1993.

MacKaye, Percy. *Tall Tales of the Kentucky Mountains*. New York: Doran, 1926.

Massignon, Genevieve, ed. *Folktales of France*. Chicago: University of Chicago Press, 1968.

McKinley, Robin, ed. *Imaginary Lands*. New York: Greenwillow, 1986.

Megas, Georgios A., ed. *Folktales of Greece*. Chicago: University of Chicago Press, 1970.

Mieder, Wolfgang, ed. *Disenchantments: An Anthology of Modern Fairy Tale Poetry*. Hanover: University Press of New England, 1985.

Minard, Rosemary, ed. *Womenfolk and Fairy Tales*. Boston: Houghton Mifflin, 1975.

Noy, Dov, ed. *Folktales of Israel*. Chicago; University of Chicago Press, 1963.

O'Faolain, Eileen. *Irish Sagas and Folk-Tales*. Illus. Joan Kiddell-Monroe. New York: Henry Z. Walck, 1954.

O'Sullivan, Sean, ed. *Folktales of Ireland*. Chicago: University of Chicago Press, 1966.

Paredes, Americo, ed. *Folktales of Mexico*. Chicago: University of Chicago Press, 1970.

Pellowski, Anne. *The Story Vine: A Sourcebook of Unusual and Easy-to-Tell Stories from Around the World*. New York: Macmillan, 1984.

Phaedrus. *The Fables of Phaedrus*. Austin: University of Texas, 1992.

Phelps, Ethel Johnston, ed. *Tatterhood and Other Tales*. Old Westbury, NY: Feminist Press, 1978.

———. *The Maid of the North. Feminist Folk Tales from around the World*. New York: Holt, Rinehart & Winston, 1981.

Philip, Neil, ed. *The Cinderella Story*. London: Penguin, 1988.

Pino-Saavedra, Yolanda, ed. *Folktales of Chile*. Chicago: University of Chicago Press, 1968.

Pogrebin, Letty, ed. *Stories for Free Children*. New York: McGraw-Hill, 1982.

Ramanujan, A.K., ed. *Folktales from India*. New York: Pantheon, 1991.

Randolf, Vance, ed. *The Devil's Pretty Daughter and Other Ozark Folk Tales*. New York: Columbia University Press, 1955.

Ranke, Kurt, ed. *Folktales of Germany*. Chicago: University of Chicago Press, 1966.

Roberts, Moss, ed. *Chinese Fairy Tales and Fantasies*. New York: Pantheon, 1979.

Schimmel, Nancy, ed. *Just Enough to Make a Story*. Berkeley: Sisters' Choice Press, 1992.

Schreiber, Morris. *Stories of Gods and Heroes: Famous Myths and Legends of the World*. New York: Grosset and Dunlap, 1960.

Seki, Keigo, ed. *Folktales of Japan*. Chicago: University of Chicago Press, 1963.

Sierra, Judy, ed. *Cinderella*. Phoenix: Oryx Press, 1992.

Straparola, Gianfranco. *The Facetious Nights*. Trans. William G. Waters. Illus. E. R. Hughes. London: Lawrence and Bullen, 1894.

Sutherland, Zena and Myra Cohn Livingston. *The Scott, Foresman Anthology of Children's Literature*. Glenview: Illinois: Scott-Foresman, 1984.

Thompson, Stith, ed. *Tales of the North American Indians*. Bloomington: Indiana University Press, 1966.

———. *One Hundred Favorite Folktales*. Illus. Franz Altschuler. Bloomington: Indiana University Press, 1968.

Tong, Diane, ed. *Gypsy Folktales*. New York: Harcourt Brace Jovanovich, 1989.

Tyler, Royall, ed. *Japanese Fairy Tales*. New York: Pantheon, 1987.

Uchida, Yoshiko. *The Dancing Kettle and Other Japanese Folk Tales*. Illus. Richard C. Jones. New York: Harcourt, Brace, and World, 1949.

Weinreich, Beatrice, ed. *Yiddish Folk Tales*. Trans. Leonard Wolf. New York: Pantheon, 1989.

Williams-Ellis, Amabel. *More British Fairy Tales*. London: Blackie, 1960.

Williamson, Duncan. *Fireside Tales of the Traveller Children*. Edinburgh: Canongate, 1983.

————. *The Broonie, Silkies and Fairies*. Edinburgh: Canongate, 1985.

Wolkstein, Diane. *The Magic Orange Tree and Other Haitian Folktales*. New York: Schocken, 1980.

Wyatt, Isabel. *The Golden Stag and Other Folk Tales from India*. Illus. Anne Marie Jauss. New York: David McKay, 1962.

Yolen, Jane, ed. *Favorite Folktales from Around the World*. New York: Pantheon, 1986.

Young, Richard Alan and Judy Dockrey, eds. *African-American Folktales for Young Readers*. Little Rock, AR: August House, 1993.

Zeitlin, Steven J., Amy J. Kotkin, and Holly Cutting Baker, eds. A *Celebration of American Family Folklore: Tales and Traditions from the Smithsonian Collection*. New York: Pantheon, 1982.

Zipes, Jack, ed. *The Outspoken Princess and the Gentle Knight: A Treasury of Modern Fairy Tales*. New York: Bantam, 1994.

————, ed. *Don't Bet on the Prince: Contemporary Feminist Fairy Tales in North America and England*. New York: Routledge, 1986.

————. *The Trials and Tribulations of Little Red Riding Hood: Versions of the Tale in Sociocultural Context*. 2nd ed. New York: Routledge, 1993.

II. Tales by Individual Authors

Ade, George. *Ade's Fables*. New York: Doubleday, 1914.

————. *Fables in Slang and More Fables in Slang*. New York: Dover, 1960.

Alexander, Lloyd. *The Foundling and Other Tales*. New York: Dutton, 1973.

————. *The Town Cats and Other Tales*. New York: Dutton, 1977.

Appiah, Peggy. *Tales of an Ashanti Father*. Illus. Mora Dickson. Boston: Beacon, 1967.

Babbitt, Natalie. *The Devil's Storybook*. New York: Farrar, Strauss, 1974.

Barber, Antonia. *The Enchanter's Daughter*. London: Jonathan Cape, 1987.

Browning, Robert. *The Pied Piper of Hamelin*. Illus. Frances Brundage. New York: Saalfield, 1926.

Calmenson, Stephanie. *The Principal's New Clothes*. Illus. Denise Brunkus. New York: Scholastic, 1989.

Coolidge, Olivia E. *Greek Myths*. Illus. Edouard Sandoz. New York: Houghton Mifflin, 1949.

Coombs, Patricia. *Molly Mullet*. New York: Lothrop, Lee & Shepard, 1975.

Carrick, Donald. *Harald and the Giant Knight*. New York: Clarion Books, 1982.

Carter, Angela. *The Donkey Prince*. New York: Simon & Schuster, 1970.

———. *The Bloody Chamber*. New York: Harper & Row, 1979.

Cole, Babette. *Princess Smarty Pants*. New York: G. P. Putnam's Sons, 1986.

———. *Prince Cinders*. New York: G.P. Putnam's Sons, 1987.

Coville, Bruce. *Sarah and the Dragon*. New York: Lipincott, 1984.

Corbalis, Judy. *The Wrestling Princess and Other Stories*. London: André Deutsch, 1986.

Corrin, Sara and Stephen. *The Pied Piper of Hamelin*. San Diego: Harcourt Brace Jovanovich, 1989.

Curtin, Jeremiah. *Myths and Folk Tales of Ireland*. New York: Dover, 1975. Reprint of *Myths and Folk-Lore of Ireland*. Boston: Little Brown, 1890.

———. *Fairy Tales of Eastern Europe*. New York: Robert McBride, 1931.

Dahl, Roald. *Revolting Rhymes*. London: Jonathan Cape, 1982.

Diamond, Donna. *The Pied Piper of Hamelin*. New York: Holiday House, 1981.

Dunstan, Mike. *Of Fisherman, Felons, Farmers, Fools ... and Resourceful Sisters*. Torquay, UK: Audley Park Secondary School, 1992.

Gardner, John. *Dragon, Dragon and Other Timeless Tales*. New York: Knopf, 1975.

———. *Gudgkin the Thistle Girl and Other Tales*. New York: Knopf, 1976.

Godden, Rumer. *The Old Woman Who Lived in a Vinegar Bottle*. Illus. Mairi Hedderwick. New York: Viking, 1970.

Hazeltine, Alice I. *Hero Tales from Many Lands*. Illus. Gordon Laite. New York: Abingdon, 1961.

Hughes, Ted. *How the Whale Became and Other Stories*. London: Faber, 1985.

Kennedy, Richard. *Collected Stories*. New York: Harper & Row, 1987.

Kipling, Rudyard. *The Jungle Book*. London: Macmillan, 1884.

Kramer, Rita. "Rumpelstiltskin: His Story." *South Dakota Review* 25 (Summer 1987): 78–81.

Lee, Tanith. *Princess Hynchatti and Some Other Surprises*. London: 1972.

———. *Red as Blood or Tales from the Sisters Grimmer*. New York: Daw, 1983.

Lobel, Anita. *The Straw Maid*. New York: Greenwillow Books, 1983.

Macmillan, Cyrus. *Canadian Wonder Tales*. London: John Lane, 1920.

Mahy, Margaret. *The Changeover*. New York: Scholastic, 1974.

Martin, Rafe. *The Hungry Tigress: Buddhist Legends and Jataka Tales*. Berkeley: Parallax Press, 1990.

———. *The Rough-Face Girl*. New York: Scholastic, 1993.

Mayer, Mercer. *Herbert the Timid Dragon*. New York: Golden Press, 1980.

McKinley, Robin. *The Door in the Hedge*. New York: William Morrow, 1981.

Morpungo, Michael. *Arthur, High King of Britain*. San Diego: Harcourt Brace, 1975.

Munsch, Robert. *The Paper Bag Princess*. Illus. M. Marchenko. Toronto: Annick Press, 1980.

Myers, Bernice. *Sideny Rella and the Glass Sneaker*. New York: Macmillan, 1985.

Paterson, Katherine. *The Crane Wife*. Illus. Suekichi Akaba. New York: Morrow, 1981.

Raddall, Thomas Head. *The Pied Piper of Dipper Creek and Other Tales*. Toronto: McClelland & Stewart, 1943.

Redgrove, Peter. *The One Who Set Out to Study Fear*. London: Bloomsbury, 1979.

Rockwell, Anne. *The Robber Baby: Stories from the Greek Myths*. New York: Greenwillow, 1994.

Schickel, Richard. *The Gentle Knight*. New York: 1962.

Shapiro, Irwin. *Heroes in American Folklore*. Illus. Donald McKay and James Daugherty. New York: Julian Messner, 1965.

Shorto, Russell. *Cinderella and Cinderella's Stepsister*. Illus. T. Lewis. New York: Carol Publishing Group, 1990.

Sendak, Jack. *The King of the Hermits and Other Stories*. New York: Harper, 1966.

Snape, Juliet and Charles, *Giant*. London: Walker Books, 1989.

Storr, Catherine. *Clever Polly and the Stupid Wolf*. London: Faber and Faber, 1955.

Stoutenberg, Adrien. *American Tall Tales*. Illus. Richard M. Powers. New York: Viking, 1966.

Rosen, Michael. *Quick, Let's Get Out of Here*. Harmondsworth: Puffin, 1985.

Rushdie, Salman. *Haroun and the Sea of Stories*. New York: Viking, 1990.

Shannon, Monica. *California Fairy Tales*. Illus. E.C. Millard. New York: Stephen Daye, 1926.

Scieszka, Jon and Steve Johnson. *The Frog Prince Continued*. New York: Viking, 1991.

Skurzynski, Gloria. *What Happened in Hamelin*. New York: Four Winds Press, 1979.

Tolstoy, Leo. *Fables and Fairy Tales*. Trans. A. Dunn. New York: New American Library, 1962.

Turin, Adela, Francesca Cantarelli, and Wella Bosnia. *The Five Wives of Silverbeard*. London: Writers and Readers Publishing Cooperative, 1977.

Turin, Adela and Sylvie Selig. *Of Cannons and Caterpillars*. London: Writers and Readers Publishing Cooperative, 1977.

Viorst, Judith. *If I were in Charge of the World*. New York: Athenaeum, 1982.

Waddell, Martin. *The Tough Princess*. Illus. Patrick Benson. New York: Philomel Books, 1986.

Walker, Wendy. *The Sea-Rabbit Or, The Artist of Life*. Los Angeles: Sun & Moon Press, 1988.

Williams, Jay. *The Practical Princess and Other Liberating Tales*. New York: Parents Magazine Press, 1978.

Yep, Laurence. *The Rainbow People*. New York: Harper Collins, 1989.

Yolen, Jane. *Tales of Wonder*. New York: Schocken, 1983.

————. *Dragonfield and Other Stories*. New York: Ace Books, 1985.

Young, Maud. *Celtic Wonder Tales*. Dublin: Maunsel, 1910.

Zaum, Marjorie. *Catlore*. New York: Atheneum, 1985.

III. Reference Works

Ackermann, Elfriede Marie. *Das Schlaraffenland in German Literature and Folksong*. (Chicago: University of Chicago Press, 1944).

Alpar-Ashton, Kathleen. *Histoires et Legendes du Chat*. Paris: Sand, 1992.

Apple, Michael W. *Official Knowledge: Democratic Education in a Conservative Age*. New York: Routledge, 1993.

Applebee, Arthur. *The Child's Concept of Story: Ages Two to Seventeen*. Chicago: University of Chicago Press, 1978.

Barchers, Suzanne. "Beyond Disney: Reading and Writing Traditional and Alternative Fairy Tales." *The Lion and the Unicorn* 12 (December 1988): 135–50.

Barton, Bob, and David Booth. *Writers, Critics and Children*. New York: Agathon Press, 1976.

————. *Stories in the Classroom: Storytelling, Reading Aloud and Roleplaying with Children*. Portsmouth, NH: Heinemann, 1990.

Bauman, Richard. *Story, Performance, and Event: Contextual Studies of Oral Narrative*. Cambridge: Cambridge University Press, 1986.

Bellamy, John G. *Robin Hood: An Historical Inquiry*. Bloomington: Indiana University Press, 1984.

Benjamin, Walter. *Illuminations*. Trans. Harry Zohn. New York: Harcourt, Brace and World, 1968.

Berger, John. *Ways of Seeing*. Harmondsworth: Penguin, 1972.

Bettelheim, Bruno. *The Uses of Enchantment: The Meaning and Importance of Fairy Tales*. New York: Knopf, 1976.

————. "A Return to the Land of the Fairies." *New York Times*, July 12, 1987, Sec. 2 : 1, 33.

Blatt, Glora T., Ed. *Once Upon a Folktale: Capturing the Folktale Process with Children*. Portsmouth, NH: Heinemann, 1990.

Blount, Magaret. *Animal Land: The Creatures of Children's Fiction*. New York: Avon, 1974.

Bly, Robert. *Iron John: A Book About Men*. Reading, MA: Addison-Wesley, 1990.

Bottigheimer, Ruth B., ed. *Fairy Tales and Society: Illusion, Allusion, and Paradigm*. Philadelphia: University of Pennsylvania Press, 1986.

Breen, Robert. *Chamber Theatre*. Englewood Cliffs: Prentice-Hall, 1978.

Breneman, Lucille N. and Bren. *Once Upon a Time: A Storytelling Handbook*. Chicago: Nelson-Hall, 1983.

Calame-Griaule, Geneviève. *Le Renouveau du Conte [The Revival of Storytelling]*. Paris: Centre National de la Recherche Scientifique, 1991.

Chambers, Aidan, *Introducing Books to Children*. London: Heinemann, 1983.

Chittenden, Patricia and Malcolm Kiniry, eds. *Making Connections Across the Curriculum: Readings for Analysis*. New York: St. Martin's Press, 1986.

Clodd, Edward. *Tim Tit Tot: An Essay of Savage Philosophy*. London: Duckworth, 1898.

Coles, Robert. *The Call of Stories*. Boston: Houghton Mifflin, 1989.

Cooper, Pamela J. and Rives Collins. *Look What Happened to Frog: Storytelling in Education*. Scottsdale, AZ: Gorsuch Scarisbrick, 1992.

Cooper, Patsy. *When Stories Come to School: Telling, Writing, and Performing Stories in the Early Childhood Classroom*. New York: Teachers and Writers Collaborative, 1993.

Coles, Robert. *The Call of Stories*. Boston: Houghton Mifflin, 1989.

Davies, Bronwyn. *Frogs and Snails and Feminist Tales: Preschool and Gender*. Sydney: Allen and Unwin, 1989.

De Bono, Edward. *Children Solve Problems*. London: Allen Lane, 1972.

Degh, Linda. *American Folklore and the Mass Media*. Bloomington: Indiana University Press, 1994.

Dorson, Richard, ed. *America in Legend: Folklore from the Colonial Period to the Present*. New York: Pantheon, 1973.

Dundes, Alan, ed. *Cinderella. A Casebook*. Madison: University of Wisconsin Press, 1983.

———, ed. *Little Red Riding Hood: A Casebook*. Madison: University of Wisconsin Press, 1989.

Durrell, Ann and Marylin Sachs, ed. *The Big Book of Peace*. New York: Dutton, 1990.

Egan, Kieran. *Teaching as Storytelling: An Alternative Approach to Teaching and Curriculum in the Elementary School*. Chicago: University of Chicago Press, 1986.

Eliade, Mircea. *Myth and Reality*. Trans. Willard R. Task. New York: Harper & Row, 1963.

Estés, Ph.D., Clarissa Pinkola. *Women Who Run with the Wolves: Myths and Stories of the Wild Woman Archetype*. New York: Ballantine, 1993.

Fox, Carol. *At the Very Edge of the Forest: The Influence of Literature on Storytelling by Children*. London: Cassel, 1993.

Fox, Geoff and Michael Benton. *Teaching Literature from Nine to Fourteen*. Oxford: Oxford University Press, 1985.

Garvie, Edie. *Story as Vehicle: Teaching English to Young People.* Clevedon: Multilingual Matters, 1990.

Gilligan, Carol. *In a Different Voice: Psychological Theory and Women's Development.* Cambridge: Harvard University Press, 1982.

Goforth, Frances and Carolyn Spillman. *Using Folk Literature in the Classroom.* Phoenix: Oryx Press, 1994.

Graves, Robert. *The White Goddess: A Historical Grammar of Poetic Myth.* New York: Farrar, Straus & Giroux, 1948.

Heath, Shirley Brice. *Ways with Words: Language, Life and Work in Communities and Classrooms.* Cambridge: Cambridge University Press, 1983.

Hearne, Betsy. *Beauty and the Beast: Visions and Revisions of an Old Tale.* Chicago: University of Chicago Press, 1989.

Horkheimer, Max and Theodor Adorno. *Dialectic of Enlightenment.* Trans. John Cumming. New York: Seabury, 1969.

Hoyme, James B. "The 'Abandoning Impulse' in Human Parents." *The Lion and the Unicorn* 12 (December 1988): 32–46.

Kennery, Karen and Herbert Kohl. *Fables: A Curriculum.* New York: Teachers and Writers Collaborative, 1968.

Kinder, Marsha. *Playing with Power in Movies, Television, and Video Games: From Muppet Babies to Teenage Mutant Ninja Turtles.* Berkeley: University of California Press, 1991.

Kohl, Herbert. *Reading, How To.* New York: Dutton, 1973.

————. *Making Theater: Developing Plays with Young People.* New York: Teachers and Writers Collaborative, 1988.

————. *"I Won't Learn from You" and Other Thoughts on Creative Maladjustment.* New York: The New Press, 1994.

Kozol, Jonathan. *Savage Inequalities.* New York: HarperCollins, 1991.

Leach, Penelope. *Children First.* New York: Knopf, 1994.

Lewinsohn, Richard. *Animals, Men, and Myths.* New York: Harper & Brothers, 1954.

Liebs, Elke. *Kindheit und Tod: Der Rattenfänger-Mythos als Beitrag zu einer Kulturgeschichte der Kinder.* Munich: Fink, 1986.

Livo, Norma J. and Sandra A. Rietz. *Storytelling: Process and Practice.* Littleton, CO: Libraries Unlimited Inc., 1986.

MacDonald, Margaret Read. *The Storyteller's Start-Up Book: Finding, Learning, Performing and Using Folktales.* Little Rock, AR: August House, 1993.

Marshall, Howard Wright. "'Tom Tit Tot': A Comparative Essay in Aarne-Thompson 500—The Name of the Helper." *Folklore* 84 (1973): 51–57.

Mason, Harriet and Larry Watson. *Every One a Storyteller: Integrating Storytelling into the Curriculum.* Portland, Oregon: Lariat Productions, 1991.

McRae, John. *Using Drama in the Classroom.* Oxford: Pergamon, 1985.

Medick, Hans. "Village Spinning Bees: Sexual Culture and Free Time among Rural Youth in Early Modern Germany." In H. Medick and D. Sabean, eds. *Interest and Emotion: Essays on the Study of Family and Kinship*. Cambridge: Cambridge University Press, 1984. 317–40.

Mieder, Wolfgang. *Tradition and Innovation in Folk Literature*. Hanover: University Press of New England, 1987.

———. *Proverbs Are Never Out of Season: Popular Wisdom in the Modern Age*. Oxford: Oxford University Press, 1993.

Miller, Alice. *The Drama of the Gifted Child*. Trans. Ruth Ward. New York: Basic Books, 1981.

———. *For Your Own Good: Hidden Cruelty in Child-Rearing and the Roots of Violence*. New York: Basic Books, 1983.

Pellowski, Anne. *The World of Storytelling: A Practical Guide to the Origins, Development, and Applications of Storytelling*. Rev. ed., New York: Wilson, 1990.

Piaget, Jean. *The Psychology of Intelligence* (1947) Trans. Malcolm Piercy and D.E. Berlyne. Towata, New Jersey: Littlefield, Adams, 1981.

———. *Judgment and Reasoning in the Child*. Trans. Marjorie Warden. Towata, NJ: Littlefield, Adams, 1976.

———. *The Development of Thought: Equilibration of Cognitive Structures*. Trans. Arnold Rosin. New York: Viking, 1977.

Propp, Vladimir. *Morphology of the Folktale*. Eds. Louis Wagner and Alan Dundes. Trans. Laurence Scott. 2nd rev. ed. Austin: University of Texas Press, 1968.

———. *Theory and History of Folklore*. Ed. Anatoly Liberman. Trans. Adriadna Y. Martin and Richard P. Martin. Minneapolis: University of Minnesota Press, 1984.

Richter, Dieter. *Schlaraffenland. Geschichte einer populären Phantasie*. Cologne: Eugen Diederichs, 1984.

Rodari, Gianni. *Grammatica della fantasia: Introduzione all'arte di inventare storie*. Turin: Einaudi, 1973.

Röhrich, Lutz. *Wage es, den Frosch zu küssen: Das Grimmsche Märchen Nummer Eins in seinen Wandlungen*. Cologne: Diederichs, 1987.

Rosen, Betty. *And None of It Was Nonsense: The Power of Storytelling in School*. Portsmouth, NH: Heinemann, 1988.

Rosen, Harold. *Stories and Meanings*. Sheffield: National Association for the Teaching of English, 1985.

———. *Shapers and Polishers: Teachers as Storytellers*. London: Harper Collins, 1993.

———. *Troublesome Boy*. London: English and Media Centre, 1993.

Sax, Boria. *The Frog King: On Legends, Fables, Fairy Tales and Anecdotes of Animals*. New York: Pace University Press, 1990.

Schneider, Jane. "Rumpelstiltskin's Bargain: Folklore and the Merchant Capitalist

Intensification of Linen Manufacture in Early Modern Europe." In Annette B. Weiner and Jane Schneider, eds. *Cloth and Human Experience*. Washington D.C.: Smithsonian Institute Press, 1989. 177–213.

Schwartz, Marni. "Building a Classroom Community through Storytelling." *Storytelling* 6 (July 1994):14–15.

Schwartz, Marni, Ann Trousdale, and Sue Woestehoff, eds. *Give a Listen: Stories of Storytelling in School*. Urbana: National Council of Teachers of English, 1994.

Shenkman, Richard. *Legends, Lies, and Cherished Myths of American History*. New York: William Morrow, 1988.

Sierram Judy and Robert Kaminski. *Twice Upon a Time: Stories to Tell, Retell, Act Out, and Write About*. New York: Wilson, 1989.

Simons, Elizabeth Radin. *Student Worlds, Student Words: Teaching Writing Through Folklore*. Portsmouth, NH: Heinemann, 1990.

Spolin, Viola. *Improvisation for the Theater: A Handbook of Teaching and Directing Techniques*. Evanston: Northwestern University Press, 1963.

———. *Theater Games for the Classroom: A Teacher's Handbook*. Evanston: Northwestern University Press, 1986.

———. *Theater Games for Rehearsal: A Director's Handbook*. Evanston: Northwestern University Press, 1985.

Stuart, Dorothy Margaret. *A Book of Cats: Legendary, Literary and Historical*. London: Methuen, 1959.

Taggart, James M. *Enchanted Maidens: Gender Relations in Spanish Folktales of Courtship and Marriage*. Princeton: Princeton University Press, 1990.

Tatar, Maria. *Off with their Heads! Fairy Tales and the Culture of Childhood*. Princeton: Princeton University Press, 1992.

Taylor, Archer. *Selected Writings on Proverbs*. Ed. Wolfgang Mieder. Helsinki: Academia Scientarum Fennica, 1975.

Thompson, Stith. *The Folktale*. New York: Dryden, 1946.

Tucker, Nicolas. *The Child and the Book*. Cambridge: Cambridge University Press, 1981.

Turner, Patricia A. *I Heard It Through the Grapevine: Rumor in African American Culture*. Berkeley: University of California Press, 1993.

Vygotsky, L. S. *Mind in Society: The Development of Higher Psychological Processes*. Ed. Michael Cole, Vera John-Steiner, Sykvia Scribner, and Ellen Souberman. Cambridge: Harvard University Press, 1978.

Weigle, Marta. *Spiders and Spinsters: Women and Mythology*. Alburquerque: University of New Mexico Press, 1982.

Wilde, Oscar. *The Soul of Man under Socialism*. Ed. Robert Ross. London: Humphreys, 1912.

Winston, Joe. "Giants, Good and Bad: Story and Drama at the Heart of the Curriculum at Key Stage 1." *Education* 3 March 1994: 44–54.

Zipes, Jack. *Breaking the Magic Spell: Radical Theories of Folk and Fairy Tales*. New York: Routledge, 1979.

————. *Fairy Tales and the Art of Subversion: The Classical Genre for Children and the Process of Civilization*. New York: Routledge, 1983.

————.*The Brothers Grimm: From Enchanted Forests to the Modern World*. New York: Routledge, 1988.

————. *Fairy Tale as Myth/Myth as Fairy Tale*. Lexington: The University Press of Kentucky, 1994.

Index